# The Architecture Portfolio Guidebook

*The Architecture Portfolio Guidebook* shows you how to make portfolios for both academic and professional needs to provide reviewers exactly what they are looking for. In school, architecture curricula nurture the knowledge and skills to develop design work to varying levels of presentation. In the profession, those skills are further developed and applied in the creation of the built environment. In both contexts, a portfolio is a core component for admission and advancement.

This book provides key strategies to:

- develop an understanding of the unique needs of professional and academic organizations;
- identify applicants' key differentiators;
- highlight how applicants present themselves in their portfolios to address institutional needs;
- create successful reinforcing documentation;
- communicate using portfolios.

Rather than proposing generic solutions, this book details the successful practices for portfolio creation by addressing portfolio creation academically and professionally. Supporting insights and examples from leading academics and architects from around the world reinforce the themes presented in this guidebook. An ideal read for students and professionals of architecture, landscape architecture, interior design, and urban design, looking to advance their studies and careers.

**Vincent Hui** holds several degrees including a Master of Architecture (Waterloo) and Master of Business Administration (Schulich at York). As a faculty member in Ryerson's Department of Architectural

Science, he teaches a variety of courses, from design studios to advanced architectural computing and digital fabrication. He has been awarded several teaching distinctions across different universities, including the 2015 Ontario Confederation of University Faculty Associations' Teaching Award and, most recently, Ryerson University's 2018 President's Award for Teaching Excellence. He has cultivated an extensive record of publications and research on design pedagogy, advanced simulation and rapid prototyping, and technological convergence in design praxis. A proponent of increasing connections to industry and the greater community, he has developed the Architectural Science Co-op program, as well as multiple programs for aspiring young designers. He currently serves as a co-director of Ryerson University's Design Fabrication Zone, where he has mentored several award-winning projects and innovative startups.

# The Architecture Portfolio Guidebook

## The Essentials You Need to Succeed

*Vincent Hui*

First published 2020
by Routledge
52 Vanderbilt Avenue, New York, NY 10017

and by Routledge
2 Park Square, Milton Park, Abingdon, Oxon, OX14 4RN

*Routledge is an imprint of the Taylor & Francis Group, an informa business*

© 2020 Taylor & Francis

The right of Vincent Hui to be identified as author of this work has
been asserted by him in accordance with sections 77 and 78 of the
Copyright, Designs and Patents Act 1988.

All rights reserved. No part of this book may be reprinted or reproduced or utilised
in any form or by any electronic, mechanical, or other means, now known or
hereafter invented, including photocopying and recording, or in any information
storage or retrieval system, without permission in writing from the publishers.

*Trademark notice*: Product or corporate names may be trademarks or registered
trademarks, and are used only for identification and explanation without
intent to infringe.

*Library of Congress Cataloging-in-Publication Data*
Names: Hui, Vincent, author.
Title: The architecture portfolio guidebook : the essentials
you need to succeed / Vincent Hui.
Description: New York : Routledge, 2020. |
Includes bibliographical references and index. |
Identifiers: LCCN 2019029805 (print) | LCCN 2019029806 (ebook) |
ISBN 9780415787031 (hardback) | ISBN 9780415787048 (paperback) |
ISBN 9781315226439 (ebook)
Subjects: LCSH: Architecture portfolios–Design.
Classification: LCC NA1996 .H85 2020 (print) |
LCC NA1996 (ebook) | DDC 720.22–dc23
LC record available at https://lccn.loc.gov/2019029805
LC ebook record available at https://lccn.loc.gov/2019029806

ISBN: 9780415787031 (hbk)
ISBN: 9780415787048 (pbk)
ISBN: 9781315226439 (ebk)

Typeset in Minion Pro and Avenir
by Newgen Publishing UK

# Contents

ix     Acknowledgments

xi     Preface

xiii    External Perspective Introductions

## CHAPTER **1.0**

### WHAT ARE YOU TRYING TO DO?

7     **1.1** Messaging, Media, and Methods

10    **1.2** The Two Major Types of Portfolios

12    **1.3** Showcasing Skill, Creativity, and Passion

14    **1.4** Gathering, Archiving, Curating, and Editing

20    **1.5** Planning, Scheduling, and Managing

## CHAPTER **2.0**

### IDENTIFYING YOUR KEY DIFFERENTIATORS

35    **2.1** The Economics of Portfolio Design: Unique Value Proposition, Assets, and Commodities

42    **2.2** Understanding Your Competition

CONTENTS

45 **2.3** Creativity and Critical Thinking

49 **2.4** Technical Skills

52 **2.5** Experience

57 **2.6** Accomplishments

61 **2.7** Passion

# CHAPTER **3.0**

## WHAT TO PRESENT IN A PORTFOLIO

73 **3.1** Aligning Yourself with the Audience

80 **3.2** The Balance: Design and Technical Skills

85 **3.3** The Three Things *Not* to Show: Ignorance, Laziness, and Pride

# CHAPTER **4.0**

## HOW TO PRESENT YOURSELF IN A PORTFOLIO

101 **4.1** Layout and Imagery

117 **4.2** Text

125 **4.3** Interactive Media

CONTENTS

**CHAPTER 5.0**

## PORTFOLIO PREPARATION: TARGETING AN AUDIENCE

135 **5.1** Pacing

140 **5.2** Passing the 30-Second Flip Test: Impression, Expression, and Retention

149 **5.3** Feedback and Refinement

**CHAPTER 6.0**

## THE PORTFOLIO AS A SUCCESSFUL REINFORCING DOCUMENT

163 **6.1** Letters: Cover Letter and Letter of Intent

169 **6.2** Résumé/CV: Outline of Your Potential

178 **6.3** Transcripts: External Assessment

182 **6.4** Letters of Recommendation: Validation

**CHAPTER 7.0**

## COMMUNICATION USING YOUR PORTFOLIO

193 **7.1** Online: Websites and Social Media

200 **7.2** Complementary Materials

204 **7.3** Interview: The Tipping Point

209 **7.4** Following Up

CONTENTS

213 Epilogue

217 Appendix

242 *List of Illustrations*

256 *About the Author*

257 *Index*

# Acknowledgments

This book would not be possible were it not for the support of friends and family who, in their own way, whether they were aware of it or not, contributed to my development.

I wish to thank my wife, Donna, for always believing I was capable of better things even when I did not. Her dedication and sacrifice for our family is boundless. My children Ella, Delia, and Joshua all have taught me to be a better person and I know that it cascades into my teaching career. I would never have embarked upon this path had it not been for the incredible teachers I have had throughout my life. From Roger, Louise, and Robert at SMCS to Terri, Mike, and Thomas in university, there have been so many educators who have influenced my teaching and character.

Were it not for the students, staff, and colleagues at Ryerson University's Department of Architectural Science, I would never have had the supportive environment to not only write this book but also engage in extracurricular work with groups such as [R]ed[U]x Lab. None of my research work, especially in this book, would have ever been possible without every invaluable member of my research team, I am especially grateful to my editorial assistant, Tatiana, for her indispensable organizational oversight.

The greatest motivation behind this book has always been the students I have taught, continue to teach, and will be blessed to teach in the future. I hope this book helps them all in some way during their architectural pursuits.

[R]ed[U]x Lab Members: Abhishek Wagle | Adrian Chiu | Agnes Yuen | Ailsa Craigen | Alex Fown | Andrew Barat | Ariel Cooke | Aris Peci | Arnel Espanol | Benjamin Bomben | Brandon Bortoluzzi | Brant York | Cathy Truong | Ciara Martins | Dadin Duldul | Daniel Sobieraj | Deena Jamokha | Diana Sobaszek | Diana Koncan | Dylon Feyen | Elizabeth Chong | Eranga De Zoysa | Erik Aquino | Farah Elmajdoub | Filip Tisler | Florence Chu | Florencio IV Tameta | Garbo Zhu | Gary Luk | Glearda Sokoli | Gloria Zhu | Gregor Tratnik | Gregorio Jimenez | Haya Alnibari | Henry Mai | Irina Solop | Ishan Patel | Ivan Efremov | James Munroe | Jason Brijraj | Jason Glionna | Jason Ramelson | Jasper Leung | Jessica Hoang Chen | Jessica Walker | Jeff Jang | Joana

## ACKNOWLEDGMENTS

Benin | John Benner | John Zhang | Jonathan Kim | Jonathan Santaguida | Jordan So | Karen Fang | Katherine Swainson | Keegan Toscano | Kenan Elsasser | Kevin Pu | Kristen Sarmiento | Kristen Smith | Krystyna Ng | Liam Hall | Liam Van Steekelenburg | Lily Jeon | Lisa Batoulava | Lisa Chien | Louise Shin | Marissa Liu | Martina Cepic | Marwa Al-Saqqar | Matthew A. Suriano | Matthew Breton-Honeyman | Matthew Koniuszewski | Matthew Lau | Michael Evola | Michael Stock | Michael Suriano | Mike Fik | Michael Hankus | Michelle Ashurov | Monika Mitic | Nan Xiao | Naveed Kahn | Nathaniel Mendiola | Nineveh Rashidzadeh | Nivin Nabeel | Noeline Tharshan | Pamela Lin | Pierre-Alexandre Le Lay | Rachel Law | Razmig Titizian | Rémi Carreiro | Rita Ruotao Wang | Robin Nong | Robyn Thomson | Sahil Saroy | Sarah Ives | Sarah Lipsit | Sam Ghantous | Sang-Kyu Joo | Shawn Zivontsis | Shengyu Cai | Shengnan Gao | Shivathmikha Suresh Kumar | Stephanie Tung | Stephanie Wu | Stephen Jones | Stuart Vaz | Tatiana Estrina | Teresa Mytkowski | Tess Macpherson | Tiffany Zhang | Tiffany Cheung | Tim Fu | Tess Macpherson | Thomas Gomez Ospina | Thy Vo | Timothy Lai | Tricia Arabian | Valerie Gershman | Valerie Poon | Vivian Kinuthia | Yekaterina Korotayeva | Zeenah Mohammed Ali.

# Preface

This book is a guide on strategies one should adopt in developing one's architecture portfolio for academic and professional applications. Distilled from decades of experience in both realms and reinforced with feedback from a range of perspectives, these strategies serve as the framework for individual designers to adopt and adapt into their own portfolio of work as they embark upon their architectural aspirations. The strategies presented in the book highlight both the overt and nuanced differences between academic and professional portfolio creation. A single document does not address these two contexts. Each chapter provides insights on each phase of assembling a portfolio for different purposes, supplemented with insights from employers and faculty from around the world. This book provides the strategies to create not simply a single portfolio targeted at one employer or school, but instead empowers readers to create portfolios for future endeavors to a diversity of audiences with ease.

In an age where graduate degrees are increasingly mandated for professional licensure and work experience is the currency for employment, the portfolio has become a seminal component to progress in architectural praxis. While architectural curricula touch upon a vast range of topics critical to an architect's knowledge base, from studio and semiotics to structures and software, there is a surprising dearth of formalized support and guidance on producing such an instrumental and influential document in an architect's arsenal. Discussion on the tools of production or informal workshops may be available, however the creation of a portfolio is rarely inculcated in architectural pedagogy. While portfolios are personal documents facilitating an individual's architectural aspirations, they need not be generated in a vacuum.

This book is not solely about imagery, layout, résumés, or interviews; there are other resources for those components of a successful application. Instead it focuses upon the key differentiator between architectural pursuits and other disciplines – an applicant's portfolio. There is no definitive template for a good portfolio. They are as unique, diverse, and personalized as their authors and audiences. You are reading this book because you want to get into a select architecture program or secure a particular position in the architecture industry. The reasons *why* are fairly clear. While this book can provide direction on *what* work to include, *how* it may be presented, *where* it should be placed, and *when* it should be showcased in a portfolio, the insights are tempered by *who* the audience for the application is. While there are countless dimensions to consider when assembling a portfolio, this book addresses the essential components necessary to assess alignment between a portfolio author and their audience.

# External Perspective Introductions

While this book outlines a series of production strategies in generating a portfolio, it is imperative to present a range of opinions for authors to create as robust a document as possible. Drawn from academia and industry, the following distinguished guest contributors offer a diversity of opinions ranging from multinational leaders in the architecture, engineering, and construction (AEC) industry to bespoke boutique firms. Like any guest critic panel, they are a cross-section of authorities engaged with architecture portfolios. Although they may differ in opinion on some issues based upon their backgrounds and experiences, these insights offer validation and direction for catering a portfolio for different purposes and audiences.

**ALISON BROOKS**

Alison Brooks, Principal and Creative Director of Alison Brooks Architects, is one of the leading architects of her generation. Born in Ontario, Canada, she moved to London after graduating with a BES and BArch from the University of Waterloo. Her work has attracted international acclaim for its conceptual rigor, sculptural quality, and ingenious detailing, exemplified by the spectacular new Cohen Quadrangle for Exeter College, Oxford. In 2017 Alison was appointed as a Royal Designer for Industry by the Royal Society for the encouragement of Arts, Manufactures, and Commerce (RSA) and selected as Mayor's Design Advocate for London. She was honored with the 2017 AJ 100 Contribution to the Profession Award, giving the keynote speech to the UK's 100 largest practices.

Named in 2012 by Debrett's as one of 'Britain's 500 Most Influential', Alison Brooks is the only British architect to have won all three of the UK's most prestigious awards for architecture: the RIBA Stirling Prize, Manser Medal, and Stephen Lawrence Prize. She was awarded 2013 Woman Architect of the Year by the *Architect's Journal* in recognition of her work in housing, regeneration, and education.

In 2016, she received an Honorary Doctorate of Engineering from the University of Waterloo, Canada. Alison was appointed as the John T. Dunlop Design Critic in Architecture at Harvard Graduate School of Design, taught

a Master's in Collective Housing at ETSAM, Universidad Politécnica of Madrid, and is currently External Examiner at the Architectural Association where she taught a Diploma Unit from 2008 to 2010.

**BRANKO KOLAREVIC**

Branko Kolarevic is Dean of the Hillier College of Architecture and Design at the New Jersey Institute of Technology. He has taught architecture at several universities in North America and Asia and has lectured worldwide on the use of digital technologies in design and production. He has authored, edited or co-edited several books, including *Mass Customization and Design Democratization* (with José Pinto Duarte), *Building Dynamics: Exploring Architecture of Change* (with Vera Parlac), *Manufacturing Material Effects* (with Kevin Klinger), *Performative Architecture* (with Ali Malkawi), and *Architecture in the Digital Age*. He has served in leadership roles as president of the Association for Computer Aided Design in Architecture (ACADIA), Canadian Architectural Certification Board, and Association of Collegiate Schools of Architecture. He is a recipient of the ACADIA Award for Innovative Research in 2007 and the ACADIA Society Award of Excellence in 2015. He holds Doctoral and Master's degrees in design from Harvard University and a diploma engineer in architecture degree from the University of Belgrade.

EXTERNAL PERSPECTIVE INTRODUCTIONS

**GRANT SUZUKI**

Grant Suzuki is an architect and a partner at Shigeru Ban Architects. Upon completion of his studies in architecture in Canada, Grant interned as an architectural designer at Hardy Holzman Pfeiffer Associates. With more than 20 years of experience working with Shigeru Ban Architects, Grant has ascended from associate and director to partner, overseeing hiring and mentoring of employees and interns within the Tokyo office. Grant's extensive portfolio of work spans the globe including the United States of America, Qatar, Russia, China, and Australia, meriting distinctions such as the 26th Annual Fukushima Architectural Culture Award for Dormitory H and the Architectural Design Prize of the Architectural Institute of Japan in 2009 for the Nicolas G. Hayek Center.

**NOVA TAYONA**

Nova Tayona is a Canadian architect, born on the east coast in Halifax, NS, and now lives and practices in Toronto, Ontario. She is licensed in Ontario and Nova Scotia, with projects in both provinces. After completing degrees in English (BA, St. Mary's), and architecture (BEDS, MArch, Dalhousie University), Nova worked for eight years gaining invaluable experience at one of Canada's leading architecture practices, Ian Macdonald Architect (IMA). She has also worked at design offices in London and Amsterdam, cities where she developed an appreciation for old, established architecture existing alongside the fantastical and new. Nova's written work on architecture and the city has appeared in *Azure*, *Canadian Architect*, and *Halifax Magazine*, and she is collaborating with Ian MacDonald and Terrance Galvin on a monograph about the work of IMA, to be published by TUNS Press. Nova has taught design studios at the Daniels Faculty of Architecture, Landscape, and Design at the University of Toronto, at the University of Waterloo and at Dalhousie University (with Brian MacKay Lyons and Richard Kroeker). She has also served as a visiting critic at Dalhousie University, Ryerson University and the University of Waterloo.

EXTERNAL PERSPECTIVE INTRODUCTIONS

**OMID NAKHAEI**

Omid Nakhaei is an associate principal in Arup Architecture team and has more than 15 years of professional experience. Through his involvement in design and delivery of several metro and rail projects in all stage of the design process, Omid has gained holistic knowledge of public transport, including civil works, transportation systems, and station planning and enhancement. He has key skills in leadership, design management, delivery, and procurement of rail projects in both public and private sectors. During the past decade, by working on international projects in the Middle East and Europe, Omid has acquired a unique skill set combining analytical and design thinking to identify opportunities in large infrastructure projects.

**POOYA BAKTASH**

Pooya Baktash co-founded PARTISANS in 2012. An award-winning architectural studio specializing in the integration of design and vision, technology and craftsmanship, invention and activation, PARTISANS has established itself as an experimental design practice, always on the lookout for new and innovative ideas.

As part of the studio, Pooya has been deeply involved in and has led numerous projects to completion. Some of the projects he worked on include the public realm and infrastructure design for Sidewalk Toronto, revitalization of Union Station, and the Hearn – Luminato Festival, among others. His works have won numerous national and international awards and have found their place in various prestigious publications. Pooya also leads research and development at PARTISANS, lending his expertise to original concepts and unconventional ideas. He believes a radical shift in the role and nature of architecture is needed in the current scenario of society building to bring about a positive overall change. A lot of his designs and ideas are reflective of this philosophy.

Pooya obtained his Bachelor in Architecture from the University of Azad in Tehran, Iran, and later got his Master's degree at the University of Waterloo, Toronto. Before co-founding PARTISANS, he worked at renowned architecture firm EBA, recipient of the Aga Khan Award.

Currently, he can be found lecturing at the University of Toronto when not shuffling between interesting ideas and projects at the PARTISANS Studio.

EXTERNAL PERSPECTIVE INTRODUCTIONS

**RANDALL DEUTSCH**

Randall Deutsch AIA, LEED AP has been the Associate Director for Graduate Studies and Clinical Associate Professor at the University of Illinois Urbana-Champaign, teaching and conducting research in design, professional practice, building technology, and digital technology. Randy is an international keynote speaker, workshop leader, and design technology authority. An architect responsible for the design of more than 100 large, complex sustainable projects, Randy has been an Exec Ed program leader at Harvard Graduate School of Design. He has written for DesignIntelligence, has been a speaker at Design Futures Council events, has been featured in ARCHITECT Magazine and Architectural Record, and is the author of four books: *Superusers: Design Technology Specialists and the Future of Practice* (2019); *Convergence: The Redesign of Design* (2017) on the nature of the ongoing convergence of technology and work processes in the profession and industry; *Data Driven Design and Construction: Strategies for Capturing, Analyzing and Applying Building Data* (2015) on the innovative individuals and firms who are leveraging data to advance their practices; and *BIM and Integrated Design: Strategies for Architectural Practice* (2011) tracking the social and organizational impacts of the new technologies and collaborative work processes, among other publications.

# CHAPTER 1.0
## WHAT ARE YOU TRYING TO DO?

**1.1** Messaging, Media, and Methods — 7

**1.2** The Two Major Types of Portfolios — 10

**1.3** Showcasing Skill, Creativity, and Passion — 12

**1.4** Gathering, Archiving, Curating, and Editing — 14

**1.5** Planning, Scheduling, and Managing — 20

# CHAPTER 1

# External Perspectives

## HOW MANY PORTFOLIOS DO YOU TYPICALLY RECEIVE?

**GS:** The Tokyo office gets quite a few, I'm getting ten a day.

**AB:** Probably about ten or 20 a day.

**NT:** We get something every day – at least one or two a day.

**ON:** In our architecture office – around five to ten each month but they usually go to our HR first.

**PB:** On average 15–20 a week, from across the world. It depends on the season – towards the end of classes, we get a lot. Sometimes five or six a day.

**RD:** When I had my firm, easily well over 100 each year, depending on the market. But I would say at school, in my administrative role, I look at well over 100 portfolios, often in the hundreds.

## HOW LONG WOULD YOU TYPICALLY SPEND REVIEWING A PORTFOLIO?

**GS:** Quite honestly, a few minutes each. I read through the résumé and then just flip through the pages. We also request that a letter is written as to why you would like to join us. That should not be something sent to every office, as that is just a copy-and-paste thing. That's a large determining factor as to how well one knows our office and what their reasons are for joining.

**NT:** A cursory glance if we are not hiring, since it is always good to keep strong applicants in mind and filed away for future searches. If

CHAPTER 1.0 | WHAT ARE YOU TRYING TO DO?

it's not too long and it's on an easy format – plus or minus ten minutes depending on the level of experience.

**ON**: Five minutes each.

**BK:** On average ten to 15 minutes on the strong ones, I quickly skim through the portfolio, then the statement of interest. If I'm put off by something like the quality of the work is poor or if the statement of interest is poorly written, then there is no point in looking at the rest.

**RD:** For graduate admissions, if the student is a slam dunk, their GPA is exceptional, their letters are off the charts, and in their essay they have some sense of direction, then the portfolio then becomes icing on the cake, more out of curiosity, but it's not a deal-breaker. So I will only spend about ten minutes looking at that portfolio. For several other students who might be shoulder to shoulder in terms of getting into the program, the portfolio then does become a deal-breaker and the deciding factor and I can spend upwards of 20–30 minutes on that portfolio, scrutinizing and having a dialog with it, asking myself whether certain things are there that lead me to think that this person would succeed if they came to our program.

**PB:** I spend five or ten seconds on a portfolio.

## IS THERE AN IDEAL PAGE LENGTH FOR A PORTFOLIO?

**AB:** Probably about 20 pages is about right to give enough breadth to projects. Obviously the key is for people to distill the information that they have in their portfolio into the key drawings and diagrams that actually communicate the quality of their work in a relatively concise way with very beautiful graphics.

**BK:** Ten pages. The shorter the better. I'm not interested in everything you did, but show me your best. So brevity has value in my world.

**NT:** Twenty pages but it also depends on the page and image size.

**JS:** We ask people to upload something up to 3MB. We limit page count that way.

**RD:** I think it's more important to show that you're agile, have good judgment and are decisive, so keep your portfolio 20 to 25 pages long enough to tell your story without making it look like you've already have a full career behind you.

**PB:** Not really – it depends on the projects, but you really need to be selective. You don't go with a 200-page document. I think more than 30 pages is too many unless someone has years of experience.

## WHAT ADVICE WOULD YOU HAVE FOR STUDENTS IN ARCHITECTURE AS THEY CREATE THEIR PORTFOLIOS?

**BK:** You want to include things that would show you at your best. If your background is in the arts, you would illustrate the projects that you've done as part of your development as an artist. If you come from engineering, present the things that you created like the assemblies that you made, the projects that you worked on, etc. If you come from other fields, let's say, biology or geography, demonstrate some creative abilities through drawings diagrams that are not necessarily related to architecture. You know there could be a beautiful drawing of an organism. You simply want to see evidence of somebody diving deep into a certain subject and then using visual means of expressing material related to the themes studied subject to diagramming drawing, or sketching.

**AB:** I think one of the key things is not to have too many drawings especially if they are very small and you can't understand them. Lots of postage stamp-sized information is just not a very good approach

**PB:** Be honest and find out what audiences are actually looking for specifically the type of job they're looking to fill. Some people are good at documentation, some well-versed in visualization, and some good in design. Go through your work, pick those projects that you actually want to emphasize because a lot of firms, especially my firm we're not just hiring bodies, we're hiring talent and looking for a specific talent sometimes. Look at what you are good at and just focus on highlighting that. And clarity – it has to be very clear. Sometimes a nice image can just capture you and you think "Oh that's interesting" and you spend more time on the portfolio. It's just like how any good movie has a good trailer – it's short and gets us interested.

**NT**: Merge the skills that you are good at. There are ways to combine those things that make the portfolio more personal and unique; I find the portfolios that stand out are the ones that aren't totally cut and dry like the ones you normally see. For example, I have seen hand-bound booklets with different paper type – vellum, watercolor, etc. – that speaks to the attention to detail / level of craft someone has.

**RD**: The very first thing to ask is "Does the portfolio tell a story?" The order in which the work is presented tells a story. Is that deliberate and purposeful or is it just chronological? *Don't bury the lede.* There's nothing more heart-wrenching than looking through a mediocre portfolio only to discover the best work in the last three pages. I have never found the table of contents to be useful; it gets in the way of getting to the goods. I look for the strongest image. It doesn't necessarily have to be tied to a project. I want to see that upfront to help me make my way into the portfolio. I'm looking for what the student is capable of. Don't make it hard to find an answer to that question. I'm looking for consistency, such as a font that carries through from project to project.

**ON**: I think the most important advice would be that they need to be honest with their portfolio. They should show their capability in a short and concise manner so that it becomes appealing to any potential interviewer or hiring manager in a way that also speaks to the architectural quality of an individual. I see a portfolio as an architectural project. Applicants need to understand that you may need to tweak your portfolio, for example when you are sending it to Arup

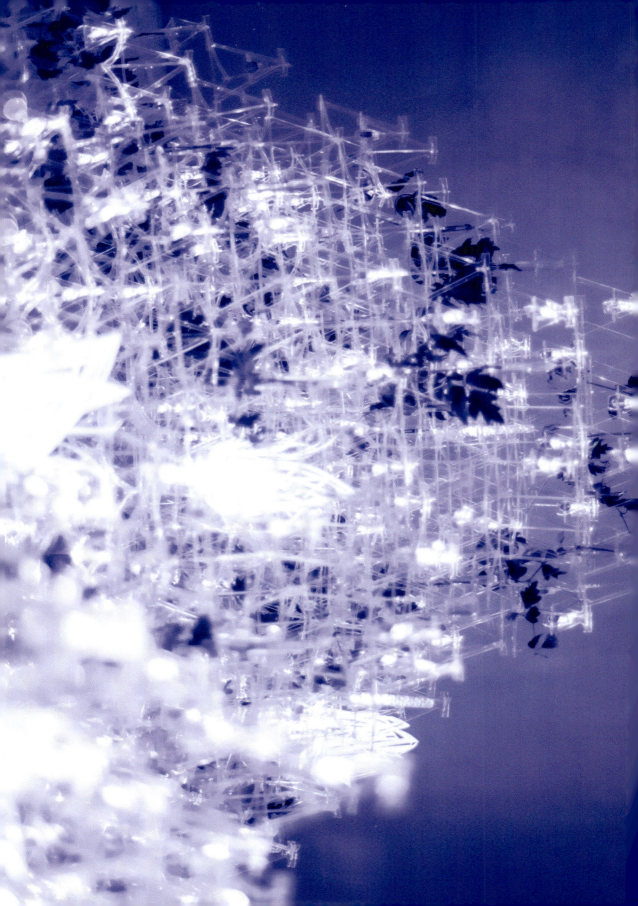

**CHAPTER 1.0**

# What Are You Trying to Do?

## 1.1 MESSAGING, MEDIA, AND METHODS

The portfolio is the seminal document that both quantifiably and qualitatively validates an individual's candidacy for a position, whether it is as a promising student, a suitable employee, or a suitable service provider. For architecture students and professionals, it serves as proof and precedent. Where other disciplines rely on a combination of the honesty of résumés, validation of interviews, and corroboration of referees, the portfolio evidences the range of traits, skills, and experience one has as exhibited in past works. Those in architectural praxis are increasingly expected to not only have an exceptional design background but also the acumen with the tools of architectural production in a range of contexts. Unfortunately, within such a context, this has resulted in contemporary portfolios that are generic and bloated with untargeted works rather than succinct documents aligned to the needs of specific audiences.

Proper messaging is vital to the success of a portfolio. Unlike other application documents, a portfolio in architecture is both a vessel for, and an embodiment of, your creative and technical experience. The medium serves as the messaging. While this book outlines general guidelines and strategies for successful application in academic and professional contexts, it does not profess to be a manual of creative style or formatting; that is as unique and potent as a portfolio's author. Beyond the curation of media presented in a portfolio, the document is a design exercise in its own right. From layout and pacing to the minutiae of typography and line weights, every single component in

**1.0**
*Chlorophytum* by [R]ed[U]x Lab.

Source: [R]ed[U]x Lab, *Chlorophytum*, 2014, Digital Image, 4912 x 7360, Toronto, Canada.

a portfolio is understood as a design exercise in user experience. This holds true in hardcopy and digital formats.

One of the critical flaws in portfolio creation is misalignment. Get into the audience's mindset. If developing a professional portfolio, read the job description and understand what skills, experience, and backgrounds are needed. Draw upon basic research on a firm's portfolio of work to find ways to align with their design philosophy, workflows, and values. Understanding what they are looking for in a prime candidate affords you the ability to have those dimensions resonate in your portfolio. The same holds true for portfolios for academic application. Different programs uniquely position themselves on their curricular priorities. From foci on advanced fabrication and computational design to adaptive reuse and urbanism, there are a range of foundations that architecture programs prioritize. By understanding the core values of the different programs, a clearer case for your candidacy with that institution may be presented.

One of the most important guidelines that is surprisingly often neglected in developing a portfolio is to not only know the audience but also to understand their demands. In doing so, the objective of an author of a portfolio is to articulate how they can fulfill these demands as showcased in the projects in the document. The messaging at its core is simple: a portfolio is a curated exhibit of work highlighting the author's alignment with their audience's needs. Anything outside of this is extraneous and potentially compromises a portfolio's success. To dump a chronology of studio work at best would demonstrate some level of design maturation but does not highlight any precision in research or investigative potential. Similarly, a compilation of working drawings would inadequately articulate an applicant's potential within an architecture firm outside of serving as a draftsperson. In both cases, a lack of messaging focused on aligning audience demands with the potential in portfolio projects diminishes the overall success of the application. If the messaging in the academic context were to highlight an alignment between an applicant pursuing an architecture thesis on sustainable design, then the corresponding portfolio should emphasize overtures to sustainability in multiple projects they have undertaken. Likewise, a professional portfolio where an applicant is targeting an innovative digital design firm should deliberately showcase a range of technical acumen and design capacity with digital tools in their portfolio of work.

Where alignment is a necessity in messaging, the medium is more flexible. The ubiquity of digital workflows and publishing affords designers great diversity in both the types of projects and the ways they may be presented. Such robustness mandates that permutations of a student's portfolio should be made to cater to specific requirements; casting a wide net with a single portfolio is inappropriate and a waste of resources. By doing so, audiences are unable to understand candidates' alignment to outlined criteria and authors invest energy in a document that poorly represents their suitability.

Hardcopy portfolios have long been the conventional documents required for many applications including academic admissions and employment interviews. While most of the content and its organization are generated digitally, hardcopy portfolios afford audiences the ability to quickly pore through materials, flip back to relevant content, and closely examine pages of interest. The degree of success via this method of conveyance is not simply determined by the content, but also the quality of the physical output. From the size of the printed pages and legibility of line work through to the color fidelity and type of binding, there are a host of factors at play that authors must anticipate and negotiate. This is also quite a potentially heavy financial undertaking. Test prints or better paper stock are often unaccounted for when authors budget the volume of printing required for distributing to multiple stakeholder groups.

While not a complete anachronism, hardcopy portfolios are becoming less commonplace in favor of rapidly cost-effective, customizable, accessible, and multimedia-saturated digital portfolios. Most of the aforementioned factors in transposing a digital document to a hardcopy portfolio are not relevant on account of the resolution and screen navigation capacity in viewing digital content. Desktop publishing software for both websites and electronic

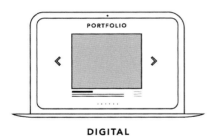

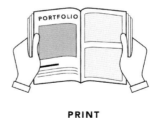

1.1.1
Comparison of digital and print formatting of portfolios.

documents are increasingly powerful with minimal learning curves and empower authors to generate multiple portfolios with great specificity or channels for users to quickly access desired content. That digital portfolios allow authors to integrate a range of multimedia content ranging from videos and interactive 3D models through to mixed reality material adds layers of engagement and depth of elaboration unprecedented in portfolio design. While standards and conventions on multimedia content in digital portfolios may still be developing, it is clear that digital portfolios have a strength in not only conveying more insights on a particular design project, but also presents an author's digital acumen, which is increasingly becoming the currency in contemporary architectural praxis.

## 1.2 THE TWO MAJOR TYPES OF PORTFOLIOS

If you are reading this book, you are interested in creating a portfolio to either enter an academic institution or apply for a professional placement. They are not the same document. It may be a worthwhile endeavor to attempt to produce an all-in-one solution, but the reality is that different agencies with distinct agendas require different portfolios highlighting an author's relevant work and experience. Where an academic portfolio may emphasize design and theoretical explorations in a specific topic in the interest of demonstrating suitability to a particular graduate program, a professional portfolio would showcase relevant technical skills or work experience with specific typologies that reinforces the alignment between the author and a design firm.

Professional portfolios are the currency of securing employment in two key ways: a) for an individual to secure a position within a firm, and b) for the firm to secure projects from a client. In both cases, they are documents that essentially market the alignment and suitability of an applicant to a target audience. With the former, it is a matter of highlighting skills and experience with an employer's needs, whereas with the latter it is a demonstration of alignment between a practice's experience and expertise in fulfilling a client's needs and scope of work. Showcasing past projects that reinforce messaging is once again key. Whether highlighting individual past academic design projects and awards or in profiling a firm's notable built work, accomplishments and credentials of project teams, firm-generated portfolios emphasize an agency's ability to execute tasks and projects.

While a greater focus in the media has been on guides for portfolios catered to professional advancement, there is a dearth of supporting material for academic portfolios to secure placements in architecture and design programs. From admissions to under-graduate degrees to entry into graduate studies, portfolios have increasingly become a core component in academic applications to architecture programs. Given the rapid commodification of graduate degrees and the growing necessity to hold one as a component to architectural licensure, more students are challenged with produ-cing an academic portfolio to enter graduate schools. This has also created a difficulty in differentiation when creating professional and academic portfolios. This often presents a challenge where authors do not know if academic projects have any place in a portfolio to secure a professional placement. Worse still, what does an author showcase in a professional portfolio when they have never worked in the industry? Alternatively, if someone has been working in industry and wishes to return to graduate school, does their work demon-strate any theoretical underpinnings or investigation required in graduate studies?

Potential portfolio projects should not be categorically relegated to either an academic or professional work. If anything, you should be familiar with, first, the key messaging intended for conveyance, and, second, the different ways projects may be leveraged in reinfor-cing that message. For example, an academic studio project calling for the design of a church would inherently demonstrate not only an awareness of religious sensitivities, phenomenological aspirations, and adherence to regulatory and structural parameters, but also showcase a host of technical skills in the generation and representa-tion of the design. A strong acumen with digital tools in the work-flow is inherent to the project. As such, the church project has facets that would be extremely relevant to both professional and aca-demic audiences. Projects should not be understood only as falling in one category or the other. So long as authors are aware of what their projects are able to showcase to specific audiences, they should have confidence in having a robust stable of work to present in their portfolios.

1.2.1
Religious project showcasing both technical skills and the representation of concept. *Church of Transition* by Timothy Lai.

Source: Timothy Lai, *Church of Transition*, 2016, Digital Drawing, 6250 × 3258, Toronto, Canada.

## 1.3 SHOWCASING SKILL, CREATIVITY, AND PASSION

Unless there are prescribed requirements outlined by a particular audience, the portfolio is completely at the discretion of its author. It is the one opportunity where they can present anything that shows their alignment with the audience, however they wish. This expansive freedom may also be overwhelming. Given the variety and volume of work an author has likely compiled, they will be hard-pressed to present everything in a strong portfolio. Although the projects and organization are at the author's discretion, one lens to determine what is included and how it is presented would be to ensure each project, or better yet each page, showcases a combination of technical skill, creativity, and passion.

Technical skill is a broad term referring to one's aptitude with the production of architectural design. In current practice this can refer to everything including strengths in software (digital visualization, Building Information Modeling [BIM], and digital fabrication – see Figure 1.3.1), more traditional architectural media (hand-rendering, physical modeling, and sketching – see Figure 1.3.2), and knowledge bases (including detailing, construction, and structures). Creativity often is a nebulous term that encompasses everything from design through to innovative concepts. Creativity is only conveyed through technical skill and, in turn, technical skills only have value in a portfolio when reinforcing a strong design. This balanced symbiosis is necessary when considering what goes into a portfolio and how it is presented. You should make a point of ensuring that at least two technical skills are showcased on any given page in support of a strong design. For example, a strong conceptual design presented with

CHAPTER 1.0 | WHAT ARE YOU TRYING TO DO?

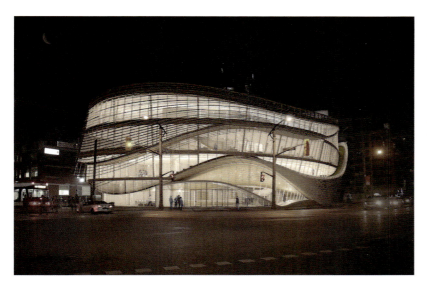

**1.3.1**
Image generated using digital software. *Curating Complexity* by Antonio Cunha.

Source: Antonio Cunha, *Curating Complexity*, 2016, Digital Image, 3000 x 2000, Toronto, Canada.

**1.3.2**
Physical model created using traditional architectural media. *Condenser Distillery* by Jessica Gu.

Source: Jessica Gu, *Condenser Distillery*, 2017, Physical Model, 4899 x 3214 , Toronto, Canada.

engaging imagery via a computer-generated render supported with basic detailing or structural depth provides a convincing package that fulfills technical and creative potential.

To limit the work in a portfolio to a demonstration of skill confines your perceived role to that of a technician – simply capable of executing documentation of either other people's inspired projects or one's own lackluster work. While there may be a greater propensity for technical skill in certain instances, such as gaining employment, it must be kept in mind that if the portfolio serves as a marketing tool, an author is using it to sell their qualifications on technical merit alone, essentially divesting their value as a designer. To only highlight

THE ARCHITECTURE PORTFOLIO GUIDEBOOK

creative concepts without any precision or adherence and responsibility to execution or context may be conducive to present yourself as a strong designer but undermines articulation of your awareness and acumen with the tools of architectural production.

The third dimension that is critical to the portfolio beyond the technical skill and creative capacity is passion. Whether referred to in architectural praxis as tenacity, grit, determination, or intensity, *passion* is likely the most difficult component to convey in a portfolio. While every project in a portfolio has the potential to demonstrate technical knowledge and design innovation, they do not all showcase a genuine motivational force behind them. In many instances portfolio works exhibit telltale signs of a mandatory school project or assigned task on a professional contract. Lackluster effort, shallow generic presentation, and little elaboration are hallmarks of work that is simply used to pad a portfolio. An author's focus in a portfolio becomes an audience's perceived reality. Their passion in their projects is often pronounced by the depth and elaboration in a portfolio. Just as there is no template layout for the ideal portfolio, there is no preset number of images or pages one has to allow for any project. In many cases, a higher level of elaboration, whether in detail or developmental work, often emphasizes additional investigation, if not genuine interest, in a project. Employers and educators alike value passion in employees and students respectively. There is no value in employing or admitting candidates who neither care nor are willing to go beyond the baseline requirement. If there is no interest affiliating with certain projects, do not include them in the portfolio. If there are projects that need updates and edits to demonstrate care about your work, then the extra effort must be invested.

### 1.4 GATHERING, ARCHIVING, CURATING, AND EDITING

If the first real step in creating a portfolio is developing a sensitivity to an audience's needs, then the next step is assessing what you have in your collection of projects that supports and validates your ability to fulfill those needs. Over your career you will continuously add new work to your portfolio; with time and experience you will be able to identify which projects cater to different types of demands outlined by your audience. Better yet, with experience, cultivate the ability to honestly assess the strengths and weaknesses in your work and curate it to best showcase your potential.

As a preface to the accumulation and archiving of portfolio content, it is imperative to take the time to actively engage one critical step in your workflow: proper nomenclature. Naming files for future reference and operations will save everyone a great deal of time and reduce frustration. Understandably, during a late deadline pressures may be high, but the extra few seconds of thought and proper naming will prove to be indispensable when returning to projects when assembling a portfolio. Stories abound of students and young architects stressfully poring through their directories for hours looking for a working file in their directories or desperately asking past instructors and IT staff for archival material only to discover that it was simply named "FINALFINAL-UseThis" somewhere on an external drive (see Figure 1.4.1). Don't be that person. Properly name, locate, save, and back up all project content. It is highly recommended to save content in at least two local, physical forms of media and one remote repository. Data is the currency of contemporary practice and to lose it is inexcusable.

**1.4.1**
Comparison of poor and proper digital archiving techniques.

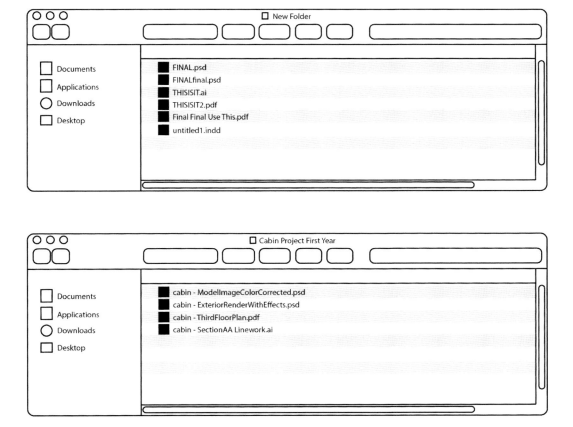

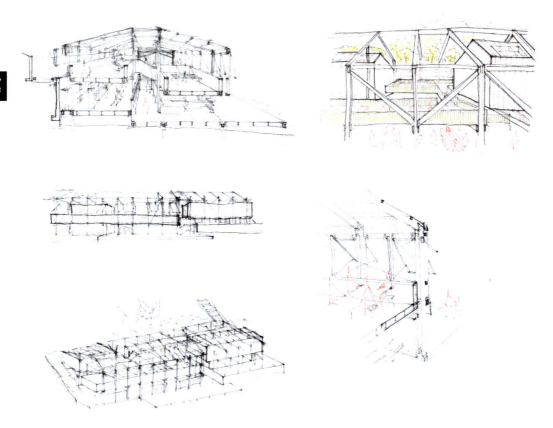

**1.4.2**
The various iterations of a design process using sketches. *Non-Motorized Water Sports Centre* by Timothy Lai.

Source: Timothy Lai, *Non-Motorized Water Sports Centre*, 2018, Hand Sketches, 3315 x 2648, Toronto, Canada.

Gathering work is not simply reserved as an activity done in the aftermath of a project. Accumulating work should also be done in a comprehensive manner for future reference. With the methods of digital archiving and documentation (whether it is saving working model files or taking digital photos or video), the near limitless capacity for storage, and increasingly secure and accessible methods (including automated cloud archives), there should never be an excuse for missing documentation of not only final production material but also developmental phases of a project. Interim models, initial concept sketches, and even preliminary iterations are worth retaining for future purposes; regret is just as debilitating as embarrassment when assembling a portfolio, so keep as much content as possible. It is also to your advantage to keep notes from reviews or feedback from clients and employers about work in a project directory to ensure recollection of inputs critical in the evolution of a project (see Figure 1.4.2). This is a step often neglected by students and practitioners alike. Despite having worked on a project for long hours over weeks or months, people often have difficulty recalling some of the context that gave rise to design decisions once a project is complete. Retention of developmental work as well as critical feedback is important as future portfolio applications may mandate a showcase of these dimensions. Some academic portfolios request a limited number of projects where authors are required to demonstrate the evolution of their work, while some firms wish to receive validation that applicants have carried through a design with feedback from clients, contractors, and regulatory bodies. To have the content available is one less cause for stress.

Archiving the work is an additional step beyond gathering it. As you create subsequent portfolios for different roles and audiences, the ability to revisit projects and have a range of content easily navigable at your disposal will be indispensable in presenting design depth. The last thing anyone wants is to have to rely upon a scant handful of images for any project. Retention of not only final presentation imagery, but working files affords authors the ability to edit existing material, generate new content, or even reformat it for different media. In professional offices, project files from correspondence and design models through to tender sets and commissioning documents are filed in a boilerplate project directory structure. This is not only to ensure materials are kept in an organized framework, but also provides invaluable access for future reference. While this is a conventional method in the profession, similar infrastructures are adopted by students in architecture schools. To provide greater ease of access in future archival work, students should get into the practice of at the very least into dated folders in categories including: Developmental Work (subdivided into directories such as sketches, models, and digital files), Insights (subdivided into directories such as crits, written reviews, and precedents), and Presentation Work (which may be broken into desk reviews, interim crits, and final presentation). Such an archival infrastructure allows students to keep track of their work without too much drilldown oversight or heavy administration. You know what works best for you; for some, this investment of organizational energy may be excessive as they will never resort to revisiting work, whereas most people realize the benefit of such a system in facilitating a healthy archive of projects.

Curating content is an ongoing component of assembling and maintaining a portfolio. Each different version of a portfolio catered

**1.4.3**
The various iterations of a design process using sketch models. *Physical Model Iterations* by Andrew Lee.

Source: Andrew Lee, *Physical Model Iterations*, 2016, Physical Models, 3883 x 2838, Toronto, Canada.

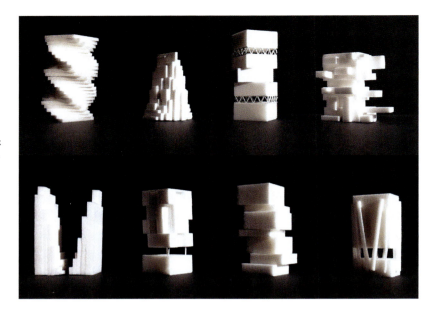

to a specific institution, firm, or client requires a high level of editorial oversight both in terms of content and in its manner of presentation. Projects that may be relevant in an academic portfolio, such as a charrette painting, might not have very much weight in a strong professional portfolio. While it may contribute to presenting strengths in specific media or techniques, it may not directly cater to the fulfillment of an employer's needs such as experience with certain typologies or software. As a portfolio will be different for each application, authors must be selective of what is presented and how. For some portfolios, it might be shifting the sequence of projects, so that there is a prioritization of flagship pieces that showcase features assessors deem useful. For others, more aggressive curatorial intervention may need to be exercised and certain projects may need to be replaced altogether with alternatives that are more appropriate. For instance, a prospective architecture intern might feel that there is a propensity of residential work in her portfolio and instead opt to replace one of the works with an improved performance hall if applying for a position with a firm that specializes in library design. In all cases, when gathering and archiving content, it is imperative to present work that aligns to audiences' needs. This curation of content ensures each portfolio is as unique as each of the different audiences one applies to.

Over time, a portfolio of work will evolve with its author, but it is important to note that editing content will ensure it maintains current and focused. The ability to append projects is invaluable as it provides authors an opportunity to showcase currency without creating entirely new projects. At the most basic level, editing content to ensure it is properly displayed or correct is necessary to give any project real value. It is unfortunate when portfolios have project imagery that is illegible and poorly presented; it is unforgivable to see errors in portfolios that should have been fixed. For example, many students in architecture school simply transpose their final studio projects into their portfolios and neither consider the dramatic format change (from an A0 sheet to a letter-sized booklet) nor the need to incorporate remedies to project errors (such as a lack of egress stairs or an inconsistency between orthographic drawings). Legibility of material in transposing architectural work is no small feat and necessitates time to adjust, which includes ensuring labels and typographic content are reassessed. Similarly, having an egregious error go unresolved in a portfolio not only demonstrates poor design or technical skill, but also reflects poorly on an author as it highlights their inability to be self-critical and proactive in fixing the mistake. Neither academics nor professionals see value in these types of traits.

Beyond the baseline of legibility and proper execution, editing content is a standard practice undertaken to ensure portfolios present authors in the most appropriate light possible. It is not uncommon for authors to revisit work completed in their early undergraduate career to showcase a greater knowledge base or highlight a skill that would improve their success of their portfolios. For example, a student looking to apply for a graduate architecture program with a focus on sustainable design may revisit a small building design from their undergraduate career and adjust the design for more passive daylighting strategies and then run it through simulations to demonstrate a sensitivity to the integration of technical acumen to her design work. Other scenarios for editing content may include translating design work into new media. For example, a job applicant may revisit an old project from her academic work and translate it into an appropriate software package that a prospective employer uses in their workflow. In both cases, revisiting and editing content not

THE ARCHITECTURE PORTFOLIO GUIDEBOOK

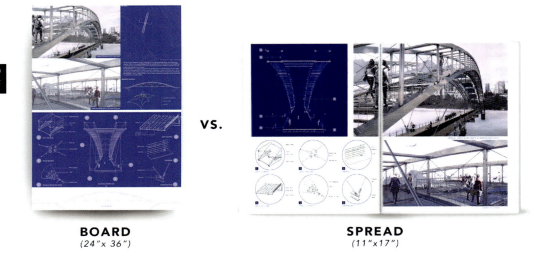

**BOARD**
(24"x 36")

**VS.**

**SPREAD**
(11"x17")

**1.4.4**
Transposing a project directly into a portfolio vs. reformatting. *Weaving Waves* by Shengyu Cai and Ruotao Wang.

Source: Shengyu Cai et al., *Weaving Waves*, 2018, Digital Image, 7686 x 3987, Toronto, Canada.

only demonstrate a synthesis of technical and design acumen, but also reinforces an alignment with the targeted audience, whether an admissions committee or a hiring manager.

## 1.5 PLANNING, SCHEDULING, AND MANAGING

Reading this text may be overwhelming as it presents a host of measures to undertake in developing a portfolio; that is not this book's intention. By understanding the key steps not only while assembling a portfolio, but having an insight on precautionary and proactive steps before doing so, as well as how to maintain an infrastructure to ease the process of making a portfolio, will be key to developing future portfolios that will inevitably emerge throughout your career. Planning out a portfolio goes beyond amassing work in an engaging presentation; it also necessitates a clear awareness of who the audiences would be and what they are looking for. A lack of awareness of this fundamental step ensures authors will create generic portfolios with little specificity in addressing different groups' needs. Do the homework. Whether looking for firms to work at for several months as an intern or seeking entry into a graduate program, it makes sense to invest a few hours to conduct basic research on what prospective employers and academic institutions would like to see in successful applicants. A few hours of research may prevent months of disappointment. Research during the basic planning phase will also allow for both streamlining and expanding options.

On the one hand, an individual may realize through research that certain graduate programs may have great reputations but have little alignment or resources to support the potential thesis research they may wish to undertake in graduate studies. This would allow them to reduce the number of portfolios they would have to create as it saves them making an application to something they would rather not undertake. On the other hand, research during the planning phase might uncover other institutions that may be far more appropriate for their interests and development. In investigating a popular architecture firm, they may discover some contemporaries that share characteristics that resonate even more with them (such as location, types of projects, or even office culture) and follow up with an additional portfolio for an application with these new firms.

When planning out a portfolio application, it is also useful to know rough timeframes and deadlines that are in effect. For some architecture firms, they may need a couple of months in lead time from soliciting applicants before a candidate would actually begin working in their office. At the same time, most post-secondary architecture programs have fixed deadlines throughout the year for application to start in either the next term or academic year. With that in mind, scheduling and pacing a portfolio of work is important in actually getting the document completed to your liking and submitted on time to the different audiences. While it gets faster with time and more experience, assembling a portfolio still takes quite a great deal of energy and effort.

Set realistic goals when planning out a portfolio. First and foremost, ensure that there is an appropriate time to get work done. Be honest with yourself. To assume you can assemble a portfolio from scratch over the course of an all-nighter, is simply lying to yourself. Make a schedule for a few hours each day over the course of a couple of weeks to not only get a draft portfolio assembled but to also have someone review the document and to implement any appropriate changes. This allows architects and students to juggle their already busy schedule of working in an architecture firm or working on studio projects in school while realistically toiling away at a portfolio. You know you best. If you take a great deal of time arduously assembling a strong layout of your projects, then set a realistic goal of a certain number of pages each day. If, after assessing your work and potential audiences, you need to essentially revisit and redo projects, then ascribe a specific number of days to redo the work before even venturing into assembling the portfolio. Knowing your own productivity and the expectations for a portfolio should be a good starting point for developing your portfolio

In scheduling assembling a portfolio, professionals and students alike often neglect to share their work with others for feedback as well as discount the time required for production and output. Ironically, despite a curriculum and a profession that mandates a high level of incorporating and responding to critical feedback, many people do not feel that level of iterative design should exist in developing a portfolio. There is little value in creating a portfolio that will be assessed by other people when the only arbiter is yourself. Having a classmate, professor, or coworker go through a draft portfolio is a useful exercise in not only assessing if the portfolio messaging is successful, but also provides an opportunity to refine it. These types of reviews also provide another set of eyes to check for typographic errors, legibility of line work and labels, and layout gaffes often missed when assembling the document.

Upon receiving feedback, the remaining steps are to make the appropriate revisions to the document and issue it for the intended audience. The closer the draft circulated for review is to the document an audience would receive, the greater the feedback on account of the fidelity of the medium. It makes little sense to review a document intended to be printed in color on 11" × 17" tabloid pages on a reduced black and white, 8" × 11" letter-sized page in the interest of saving time or money. Likewise, the value of a printout for review markup for a portfolio meant to be distributed and visualized electronically is very limited. Aside from resolution and interface issues, multimedia content does not translate into a hardcopy format. It is also important to schedule appropriate time for submission of the content. For electronic circulation, this is often simply a matter of taking the appropriate time and precautions to ensure the correct documents are distributed to the correct employers or institutions. For hardcopy portfolios, authors must be mindful of printing turnover times, availabilities of printing facilities, and binding options that occasionally are not accounted for. While 90% of the output is generated in the final 10% of the time in architectural praxis, you must account for production time.

Unfortunately two components of a portfolio that are often put aside until the final phase of production are also often the most instrumental in establishing a first impression – the portfolio cover and its binding. The investment and allocation of time for these publishing components might not appear to pay dividends if done well – however, if poorly considered or planned, the fallout can essentially invalidate a portfolio.

If your portfolio serves as a condensed overview of the evolution of your entire design career in a matter of multiple layouts, its cover has an even more challenging task of concentrating this design ethos in a way that balances graphic appeal with design restraint. Like a good book cover or movie poster, a strong portfolio cover accomplishes three critical tasks: a) it fulfills mandatory components, b) it positively attracts attention, and c) it references ideas elaborated upon in the work.

Although the imagery for a cover is at the discretion of a portfolio author, often the most fundamental components of a portfolio cover go missing, most notably the name of the author, portfolio type, and timeframe. The last thing an author would want is for a prospective employer to be floored by a portfolio's contents only to be left searching for who the candidate actually is. Put your name on your portfolio cover. A résumé or letter of intent may have been submitted with an admissions or employer package but these documents may be separated from a portfolio in the assessment process. It is also useful to indicate whether a portfolio is a curation of academically focused work or if the content is directed at prospective employment. Similarly, articulating the timeframe is also useful in defining the period of portfolio output. A cover that explicitly indicates both these components prepares an audience's expectations. For example, "Michael Elmitt: Selected Undergraduate Works 2024–2028" and "Michael Elmitt: MArch Design Portfolio 2028" speak to an academic audience whereas "Michael Elmitt: Selected Professional Projects 2028" or "Michael Elmitt Design Portfolio 2024–Present" prepares an audience for a prospective employment opportunity.

The most subjective component of a cover is how it can grab an audience's attention. Although it is tempting to maintain a clarity and consistency between academic and professional portfolios, it may be worthwhile to cater the cover imagery to best attract the attention of targeted audiences. For example, if applying for employment to a design firm that focuses upon advanced computational design and digital fabrication, a cover (including potential wraparound to the back) may use imagery generated from appropriate software or a discrete detail from a complex CNC-milled project that might resonate with such an employer's interests. Alternatively an academic portfolio focused upon pursuing thesis work in smart materials may integrate thermochromic pigment on the cover and jacket such that handprint impressions are temporarily left on the spine and cover when handled by admissions adjudicators. Although there is a range of ways to attract attention, the important elements to keep in mind are to ensure that there is an awareness of what an audience may deem as interesting and, more importantly, that it is received in the most positive way possible. None of the aforementioned examples would be necessarily worthwhile as an approach to a cover if one were apply to an architecture firm specializing in large-scale multiunit residential work. Although the cover concepts would be interesting and garner attention, they would not be the most beneficial to an applicant.

A strong cover uses imagery that connects to consistent themes or ideas found in a portfolio. For some applicants, simply translating an image of a powerful section drawing or a physical model from a portfolio project is all that is needed. Another level of potency in cover design is to minimize imagery, if not eliminate it altogether. Rather than allude to particular imagery from a single project, an author may adopt graphic austerity as a method of conveying mandatory content while also drawing attention to it with typography or a personalized logo. Authors confident in their graphic design or typesetting sensibilities may find that the combination of an austere backdrop and minimal text is an effective method of attracting the attention of audiences.

At the other end of the spectrum, authors may opt to use a single graphic for a cover. To be clear, to use a single graphic requires either an incredibly potent portfolio project or more stylized imagery that does not draw attention to a single project but is eye-catching nonetheless. Another image-based strategy would be the use of exclusive imagery to demonstrate a consistency across all projects in a portfolio by placing a grid of imagery from each project. Aligning cover imagery with both audience interests and an author's strengths is a subtle method of reinforcing design strength and aptitude. To be clear, one does not have to explicitly use imagery from the portfolio on the cover. For example, a candidate applying for a potential internship with that firm specializing in multiunit residential projects may create an abstraction of a grid for the cover that hints at the rhythm of systems and programming in similar works found in the applicant's portfolio. Although the image is not found in any specific portfolio project, the creation of something altogether new for the cover appropriately references content from the portfolio that would attract the attention of a specific prospective employer.

While going beyond the three aforementioned criteria may be worth undertaking to showcase their key differentiators, or attempts at "thinking outside of the box," authors should be sensitive to audience expectations and requirements. For example, covers that are not simply graphic and instead have ornate elements such as laser cut apertures or vacuum-formed shells may demonstrate fabrication prowess, but if it is susceptible to damage in transit or falls apart when picked up, it only demonstrates an inability to design for actual use. Similarly, authors should be warned about creating overly complex custom covers such as bespoke folding mechanisms or clunky, 3D printed sleeves that only frustrate audiences as piles of portfolios remain to be assessed. Worse still, covers with sharp edges or convoluted mechanisms not only run the risk of breaking, but also of injuring reviewers. Tetanus shots and splinters do not help an applicant's prospects! Covers are as much about projecting an author's design sensibilities and identity – to brand oneself as reliant upon gimmicks or impractical through a cover is difficult to recover from.

Beyond the cover and content of the portfolio, the actual mechanism keeping all the pages together is also an active design decision that consciously messages to an audience an awareness of presentation and legibility. It goes without say that three-hole punched sheets in a binder is only marginally a step above simply stapling the top corner of a portfolio; however, there are other options that authors may consider.

The first set of binding options require fasteners that often serve as a visual distractions. These would include comb binding (where a spine of teeth keep pages together in a row of slots), coil binding (where a filament spirals along a series of holes along the spine), twin loop wire binding (a fixed variation on the comb binding with a thin wire), and Velo binding (where two narrow slats of plastic

*Parametric graphics hint to student's interests*

*Abstract representation of physical model*

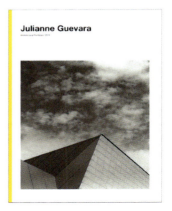
*Architectural photography*

*Hints at contents with a render*

*Personal graphics add personality to the cover*

*Simple, abstract visuals*

**1.5.1**
Sample Portfolio Covers: Portfolio Cover by Sam Ghantous; Portfolio Cover by Ruslan Ivanytskyy; Portfolio Cover by Julianne Guevara; Portfolio Cover by Leon Lai; Portfolio Cover by Lena Ma; Portfolio Cover by John Benner.

Source: Sam Ghantous, Portfolio Cover, 2012, Digital Image, 7454 x 15108, Toronto, Canada. Ruslan Ivanytskyy, Portfolio Cover, 2015, Digital Image, 7454 x 15108, Toronto, Canada. Julianne Guevara, Portfolio Cover, 2016, Digital Image, 7454 x 15108, Toronto, Canada. Leon Lai, Portfolio Cover, 2018, Digital Image, 7454 x 15108, Toronto, Canada. Lena Ma, Portfolio Cover, 2019, Digital Image, 7454 x 15108, Toronto, Canada. John Benner, Portfolio Cover, 2016, Digital Image, 7454 x 15108, Toronto, Canada.

clamp both the front and back of the document by the spine). While all of these have various benefits (as noted in Figure 1.5.2), the physical element binding the pages is difficult to integrate as a design component into a portfolio (specifically the cover), and the ease and affordability of a binding method should not compromise the holistic presentation.

A convenient option for binding a modest booklet portfolio would be saddle-stitching, which consists of stapling or sewing pages

CHAPTER 1.0 | WHAT ARE YOU TRYING TO DO?

Simple, clean, specific

Hints at contents with a render

Line work image hints at student's style

Graphic and bold

Collage of student's own work

Images of projects inside

**1.5.1.1**
Portfolio Cover by Rachel Law; Portfolio Cover by Fontane Ma; Portfolio Cover by Ernest Wong; Portfolio Cover by Tatiana Estrina; Portfolio Cover by Shengyu Cai; Portfolio Cover by Ariel Cooke.

Source: Rachel Law, Portfolio Cover, 2019, Digital Image, 7127 x 15167, Toronto, Canada. Fontane Ma, Portfolio Cover, 2018, Digital Image, 7127 x 15167, Toronto, Canada. Ernest Wong, Portfolio Cover, 2016, Digital Image, 7127 x 15167, Toronto, Canada. Tatiana Estrina, Portfolio Cover, 2019, Digital Image, 7127 x 15167, Toronto, Canada. Shengyu Cai, Portfolio Cover, 2017, Digital Image, 7127 x 15167, Toronto, Canada. Ariel Cooke, Portfolio Cover, 2019, Digital Image, 7127 x 15167, Philadelphia, USA.

together through a crease in the portfolio spine. The subtle location of the mechanical connection in the document does not distract from any design of the cover, however the key disadvantages to saddle-stitching are the limited number of pages and the lack of a spine. It may seem convenient to use staples and saddle-stitch documents with office or school staplers but unless the proper tools are available, it is not worth ruining expensive, color pages in the pursuit of quick production.

THE ARCHITECTURE PORTFOLIO GUIDEBOOK

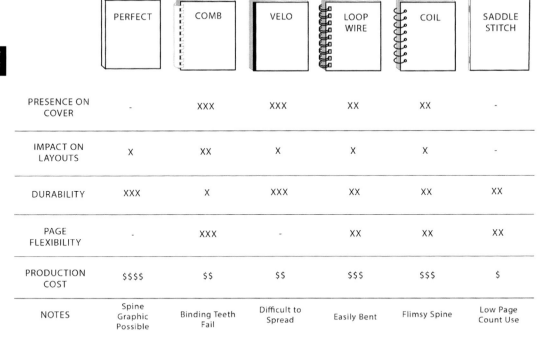

| | PERFECT | COMB | VELO | LOOP WIRE | COIL | SADDLE STITCH |
|---|---|---|---|---|---|---|
| PRESENCE ON COVER | - | XXX | XXX | XX | XX | - |
| IMPACT ON LAYOUTS | X | XX | X | X | X | - |
| DURABILITY | XXX | X | XXX | XX | XX | XX |
| PAGE FLEXIBILITY | - | XXX | - | XX | XX | XX |
| PRODUCTION COST | $$$$ | $$ | $$ | $$$ | $$$ | $ |
| NOTES | Spine Graphic Possible | Binding Teeth Fail | Difficult to Spread | Easily Bent | Flimsy Spine | Low Page Count Use |

**1.5.2**
Binding Types and Benefits.

Perfect binding is the standard for professional publications. The portfolio content is the focus of the presentation package as opposed to the fastening mechanisms. Perfect binding essentially takes multiple saddle-stitched documents and binds them all together with an adhesive spine. The ability to run graphics from the front to back cover over a spine without drawing attention to the method of connection ensures the portfolio audience is focused upon the appropriate content.

# CHAPTER 2.0
## IDENTIFYING YOUR KEY DIFFERENTIATORS

**2.1** The Economics of Portfolio Design: Unique Value Proposition, Assets, and Commodities      35

**2.2** Understanding Your Competition      42

**2.3** Creativity and Critical Thinking      45

**2.4** Technical Skills      49

**2.5** Experience      52

**2.6** Accomplishments      57

**2.7** Passion      61

THE ARCHITECTURE PORTFOLIO GUIDE BOOK

## CHAPTER 2.0

# External Perspectives

**PORTFOLIOS SERVE TO SHOWCASE APPLICANTS' A) DESIGN STRENGTHS, B) TECHNICAL SKILLS, AND C) PASSION FOR ARCHITECTURE. IS ONE COMPONENT PRIORITIZED OVER ANOTHER?**

**AB:** I think most portfolios do demonstrate passion. Except for the ones that have 200 postage stamp illustrations – that would generally be a sign that they are not passionate about their work. Everybody's trying to showcase everything to the best of their abilities. I think the most important of those three is design strength, which includes the design of the portfolio itself and the design of the cover letter.

**ON:** In order of importance, it would be passion, creativity, then technical skill. I would look to passion first – architecture is a passionate medium. If you don't have passion for it, you're going to get tired very easily. The lower you go along the list, the easier it is to learn.

**GS:** Passion, technical skill, and then design. Design skill is quite broad, because a lot of it is subjective work and so it's difficult to judge. On the technical side, I'm speaking to a level of understanding of the project that they've done. Whether that design is this or that, a preference or a style, it is technical competence that stands out. That's why I put technical in front of design. When you list the three, the passion, what they're interested in, and what they wanted to put in their portfolio to draw the interest of the office, I do think that that is important.

**BK:** Creativity is number one and I would put technical ability as a relatively distant second. Then the passion/grit would really come last in that equation because you really want to attract talented individuals who have an eye for composition, balance, etc. If you get a Bachelor's degree it's like you have already demonstrated grit – you demonstrated that you can work hard and you know what it takes to

CHAPTER 2.0 | IDENTIFYING YOUR KEY DIFFERENTIATORS

succeed. If you get good grades across the spectrum it means that you can not only succeed in what you're really interested in, but you can also do the subjects – and do them well – that are not really the crux of your interest.

**RD:** If it's to get into a graduate program, I'd say that it's design skill, technical strength, then passion.

**PB:** Passion and their personality. We can teach people skills and software. It's more about personality – how they are collaborative, how are they passionate and want to get work done, and how they want to learn. Many graduates barely know anything about construction. They know parametric modeling but they don't know how it can become something in reality. Also, passion impacts client management – how to work with people and expectations – we need to have people learn it fast. So to us, personality is more important than any parametric or BIM software package.

## WHAT TECHNICAL KNOWLEDGE SHOULD STRONG APPLICANTS HAVE?

**PB**: How things come together in reality. At the age of 22, I was put in charge as a construction manager so I learned architecture through construction rather than just memorizing details. What I'm seeing recently is that grads and students don't learn anything about construction. They're just memorizing details. And half of the details they put in their portfolios are copy-and-pasted from a magazine. If you ask a student what something in a detail is, they don't even know. You know what's a typical question I ask in an interview? "What's the size of a two by four?" And 70% of people cannot even answer that.

**BK:** The visual is crucial because our modes of communication are mostly graphical. I'm not talking about pie charts and stuff like that. I'm really talking about diagrams that illustrate some relational information that is pertinent to their subject. Something that exhibits this relationship between the eye and the hand, how I interpret what I see, and how I translate that into an artifact, be that a drawing, a painting, or a sculpture.

THE ARCHITECTURE PORTFOLIO GUIDE BOOK

**AB**: I really like seeing working drawings with everything on them that shows that this person knows about cross-referencing, dimensioning, and how to label. There's an art to working drawings, as well as a technique. It's also about passive knowledge – construction or detail drawings – and so I really like seeing one to five details. You have to care about your working drawings to realize high-quality architecture.

**NT**: They should have a really good technical knowledge of detailing, structure, and systems coordination and integration. I think they should also have IT technical knowledge from a software point of view. Solid construction and technical skills are great, and are what stand out to me, since a lot of students don't tend to have that kind of experience coming right out of school unless they grew up around a job-site through a family business or house renovations.

## AS ARCHITECTURE FIRMS INCREASINGLY INCORPORATE A BREADTH OF TECHNICAL SKILLS FOR IDEATION, VISUALIZATION, SIMULATION, AND FABRICATION, WHAT ADVICE WOULD YOU OFFER THOSE ENTERING THE INDUSTRY?

**AB:** Obviously graphic representation. In the past ten years, there's been a move away from photorealistic computer-generated images, which were hyperreal, to producing images that have an atmosphere and that capture moments in the architecture rather than focusing on the building as the object. Examples are illustrations that communicate those moments of experience and try to delve deeper into what qualities can be conveyed through the illustration. An interesting development in architectural representation, these show that rather than executing a processes to deliver a piece of architecture, the employee or student is thinking about what it would be like to be in that space. I think the conveyance of spatial quality, atmosphere, light, and a kind of intimacy means they are really engaging with the work in an intimate way.

I think if you are interested in being a designer, to being a part of the design process and testing ideas, you have to be expert at 3D

CHAPTER 2.0 | IDENTIFYING YOUR KEY DIFFERENTIATORS

modeling. Everything is modeled in 3D and you have to be fast and also be adept at many softwares and rendering programs. If you're a 3D thinker, you'll want to model it in 3D and it can be quite a handicap if you think in 2D in architecture. You need to be able to use the tools that you have as a professional to be able to manipulate and experiment in 3D.

**GS:** Every office seems to be looking for whether you can do 3D modeling and rendering. We expect that to be something that is done as a starting task because they would be assisting on other projects and a lot of their work would be doing presentation materials. Model building is an essential skill. I would also hope their general building construction knowledge would be baseline, anything as simple as how you draw foundation.

**RD:** I want to make sure that everyone who creates a portfolio makes everything in it deliberate and purposeful. If they want to design and be a designer, they should show design using representative technology relating to project content. If they want to be a project architect or a manager, they should emphasize technology, the process and the workflow. If they don't know what direction they want to take with their career at that point, especially in school, that's absolutely fine. They need to communicate that they are flexible and not just focused on design.

**CHAPTER 2.0**

# Identifying Your Key Differentiators

## 2.1 THE ECONOMICS OF PORTFOLIO DESIGN: UNIQUE VALUE PROPOSITION, ASSETS, AND COMMODITIES

At the risk of transforming this into a business manual, it is worthwhile for portfolio authors to understand the economics of portfolio design. Looking at the work of colleagues, classmates, and even comparable candidates around the world online, one will come across many portfolios that are relatively better and worse. Look to superiors: they are also the competition. The existential crisis that often arises when assembling a portfolio is realizing that despite excellent grades in studios, extracurricular accomplishments, or great performance within an architecture firm, there will always be people that are better designers, higher achievers, and superior practitioners. While this may debilitate an author assembling a portfolio, it should be seen as an opportunity to assess their unique value proposition – what they specifically offer to fulfill their audience's needs, essentially participating in their value creation.

An initial assessment of skills and design work might lull you into a sense of confidence. You might have great parametric modeling skills, comprehensive knowledge of contemporary BIM workflows, and an impressive array of digital fabrication skills, all exemplified in strong design projects. Unfortunately these are all found with your competitors as well. These common skills that are shared among all of your competition are commodities, skills that are uniform across the board, regardless of where or who they are found in. The same could be said of experience with projects. Any given architecture student or emerging practitioner will likely have worked on a small

**2.0**
*Photokerytitis* by [R]ed[U]x Lab.

Source: [R]ed[U]x Lab, *Photokerytitis*, 2016, Digital Image, 2550 x 3300, Toronto, Canada.

2.1.1
A modest design-build project. *Camp Winston* by [R]ed[U]x Lab.

Source: Arash Ghafoori, *Camp Winston Pavillion*, 2019, Digital Image, 5184 x 3456, Kilworthy, Canada.

building with a focus on construction and tectonics, a more comprehensive project at an intermediate scale and level of complexity, a project that engages larger context parameters, and potentially some modest design-build project (see Figure 2.1.1). This is not necessarily an indictment of contemporary architectural studio education, nor is it a critique of what constitutes a portfolio. It is simply a statement of fact: your background, from your skills through your projects, is the same as that of your competition. There is a risk that your skills, work, and experience are commodities in the contemporary marketplace. Your portfolio should set you apart by emphasizing your assets in forming your unique value proposition.

The key in developing a clear unique value proposition is to fill out a basic positioning statement about yourself to any given audience. A positioning statement typically is organized as shown in Figure 2.1.2.

The portfolio subsequently would serve to reinforce this statement, specifically in showcasing and validating the evidence for differentiation. When framing a positioning statement, it is important to be clear about the audience's needs, which is why it is critical to investigate and research the group a portfolio would be submitted to. The frame of reference is the summation of criteria you are applying for, it is not simply the position. Applying for a position is not simply fulfilling a role such as "design intern" or "graduate architecture student"; academic and professional audiences have clear criteria that determine a specific frame of reference. For academic institutions there may be a specific umbrella of research topics or methodologies

> To [Target Company/Institution],
>
> I am an excellent **[Frame of Reference]** that delivers **[Benefit/Differentiator]** better than other applicants because **[Evidence X, Y, and Z]**.

**2.1.2**
Positioning statement that helps an applicant frame their portfolio and application materials.

that they would expect applicants to align with. For application to employers, it would be worthwhile to understand a firm's specific portfolio of work, workflow, and trajectory in order to address explicit needs. The benefit/differentiator is essentially what you believe you are among the best at offering. You will not be the absolute authority on a topic, but the differentiator is ultimately what positively sets you apart from your competition. For example, within an academic setting this might be a unique research focus in digital fabrication evidenced not only in excellent studio design work, but which has been nurtured in award-winning design competitions, personal creative projects, and even extracurricular design-build projects. Within a professional context, a differentiator may be a candidate's expertise with a certain typological range such as educational facilities. Beyond showcasing a series of past educational institutional projects, the portfolio would benefit by highlighting innovative or unconventional design features that were implemented, thereby demonstrating great expertise within that segment. Table 2.1.1 shows a few samples of differentiators within both academic and professional contexts.

In assembling a positioning statement, the fundamental goal is to create a core message about *your* unique ability to fulfill your audience's needs. Without an awareness of the audience's needs and their frame of reference, or your own articulation of differentiation with supportive evidence, you run the risk of creating a generic inventory of your work that requires a greater investment of effort in discovering your suitability. When institutions and firms receive a deluge of portfolios, precision and potency of messaging are necessary.

**Table 2.1.1**
Differentiators that allow applicants to stand out.

| Sample Academic Differentiator | Sample Evidence |
| --- | --- |
| Adaptive reuse designer focused upon religious spaces | Award-winning studio projects demonstrating strength in both of adaptive reuse contexts and religious typologies |
| Evidence-based designer for medical facilities | Studio project followed by additional research collaboration with faculty member that goes beyond conventional scope |
| Socially responsive designer | Ethnographic and community engagement culminating in a design-build project for local charities |
| **Sample Professional Differentiator** | |
| Experience LEED-certified designer of multiunit residential work | Thorough presentation of sustainability strategies implemented in notable residential design projects |
| Innovative architectural designer with expertise in digital fabrication tools | Documented process of digital design from conception through to fabrication over multiple projects and technologies |
| Designer with extensive experience in athletic facilities in China | Multiple design projects in China highlighting sensitivity to cultural and contextual nuances in architectural design |

While the positioning statement is a critical component to understanding your own unique value proposition to a firm, it is important to be mindful of the essential skills and experiences that your competition also has. Take a moment to assess your assets – those valuable skills, distinctions, activities, and experiences that

**2.1.3**
An extracurricular design build in a portfolio could allow you to stand out within a group of other applicants. *Nest* by [R]ed[U]x Lab.

Source: [R]ed[U]x Lab, *Nest*, 2018, Digital Image, 4407 x 2938, Toronto, Canada.

**2.1.4**
Design build project for a local food charity. *Night Market Cart 2014* by [R]ed[U]x Lab.

Source: [R]ed[U]x Lab, *Night Market Cart 2014*, 2014, Digital Image, 1300 x 731, Toronto, Canada.

2.1.5
Implementing cultural design elements onto a project. *Yu Village* by Fontane Ma.

Source: Fontane Ma, *Yu Village*, 2016, Digital Image, 3400 x 2246, Toronto, Canada.

serve to fulfill conventional job descriptions or academic applications. You may even wish to set a chart to better track and self-assess your architectural value to your various audiences. If you realize that some of the assets that you have neither receive distinction or follow-through beyond specific projects, then they are commodities – they are essential but they are generic and commonplace. To have knowledge in digital fabrication such as 3D printing is a commodity as everyone from elementary school students through to manufacturers use it. Only through distinctions, experiences, and notable activities do such skills become assets to an individual's portfolio. Note in Table 2.1.2 that without any supplemental support, a listed skill or asset is a commodity.

In creating a quick chart, you can assess which of your skills or assets are commonplace commodities, as well as what may provide an opportunity to explore as key assets that may be framed in the portfolio to support your unique positioning statement. For example, everyone will articulate familiarity with digital modeling and visualization; it is a commodity. If you wish to reinforce your uniqueness and superior acumen, you must find ways to validate it, whether through digital design awards, thesis research, extracurricular

# CHAPTER 2.0 | IDENTIFYING YOUR KEY DIFFERENTIATORS

| SKILLS | DISTINCTIONS | ACTIVITIES | EXPERIENCES |
|---|---|---|---|
| • Modeling & Visualization<br>• BIM<br>• Digital Fabrication | • Top studio award<br>• Honorable mention for design competition | • Design-build work utilizing advanced software skill<br>• Extracurricular student society representative | • Worked at a small architecture firm for over three years<br>• Coordination with fabrication firm on complex millwork |
| • Manual Drafting | • Illustration awards | • Provides extracurricular workshops on stylizing drawings | • Notable work in studio projects |
| • Photography | • Photographic work published by third party | • Active photography online presence with large following<br>• Leads student photography workshops | • Contract hire by architecture firms to document work |
| • Detailing | • Highest performance in technical detailing courses | • Teaching assistant for technical courses | • Consistently well-detailed studio work<br>• Work experience with firm on innovative cladding system |

design work, or even visualization components to projects done for professional firms.

Commodity skills are the foundation of what you and your competition have to offer firms and institutions. These skills, accomplishments, and experiences are similar across all applicants in the field. Providing greater distinction in a portfolio by evidencing distinction, activity, and applied experience elevates commodities into potential assets in an application. The apex of these differentiating assets is their synthesis in a unique value proposition encapsulated in a positioning statement. This statement directly emphasizes to your

**Table 2.1.2**
A table that allows one to determine their commonplace commodities.

**2.1.6**
The photo looks photorealistic and it is a commodity, but it does not speak to an architectural design. *Half Moon House* by Fontane Ma.

Source: Fontane Ma, *Half Moon House*, 2016, Digital Image, 5000 x 3468, Toronto, Canada.

audience your unique fulfillment of their discrete requirements. The portfolio serves as a purposeful document that showcases one's past works in reinforcing and validating their unique value proposition.

## 2.2 UNDERSTANDING YOUR COMPETITION

While the initial development of a portfolio strategy and positioning statement relies upon researching your audience and assessing your unique value proposition, you must also be aware of your competitors, where are they positioning themselves, and what are they offering. This allows you to refine what your competitive advantages may be, how you may go beyond commodity offerings, and how to refine your communications to optimize your portfolio. You cannot stop what your competition is doing; however, you can learn from them in distinguishing yourself.

Within most architectural circles it is very tempting and convenient to look to coworkers' and classmates' work and gain a relative sense of accomplishment. Unfortunately, this myopic perspective undermines your ability to create a strong portfolio. Not only does it inherently limit expectations of your own capacity based upon comparisons, but it also limits your potential to apply for opportunities not taken by colleagues. For example, looking at colleagues' portfolios might define a certain level of expectations on skills and experience, but remember that their portfolios allowed them to get into the firm that you are currently working in. Although it may instill a sense of self-confidence, setting a benchmark based upon coworkers' work only ensures you are catering your portfolio to getting a similar position with similar duties, and likely in a similar context (such as size and reputation of a firm or even geographic location). In an increasingly globalized and connected world, your competition is drawn from across the world with varying skills that may exceed your own.

Poring through portfolios posted online is a good way of appraising the competitive landscape. The accessibility of online portfolios provides audiences with a sense of the levels of visual communication, design excellence, and accomplishments from around the world. Online portfolios also often provide insights on level of performance and author's background, including approximate level in university or years working in the industry since graduation. This information is helpful as it sets reasonable comparison parameters – it would be quite absurd to have recent graduates applying for firms thinking that they have to have the same portfolio of work as a practitioner with 20 years of experience. Another useful component of online portfolios is that often authors indicate where they have worked or studied in the past. While these candidates might not directly be competing with you, it may be useful to look to portfolios of candidates who have succeeded in securing positions with schools or firms that you may be interested in. Assessing common traits, skill expectations, or backgrounds would allow you to refine your own portfolio to align with the success of precedents.

At a more localized level, sharing portfolios for feedback is not an uncommon exercise. While in professional contexts this is occasionally offered to some younger staff, peer review of portfolio work is quite common within architecture schools between upper and lower year students or even members of industry. From portfolio roundtables to the 30-Second Flip Test (see Chapter 5.2), these types of events are indispensable outlets to validate the strength of your own portfolio as well as get a glimpse of what colleagues are producing. One of the key benefits of localized exposure to colleagues' portfolios is that it allows you to assess how to distinguish your work in categories your competition excels at relative to the larger marketplace. For example, if you were a second-year student from a highly technical architectural design program that mandated a comprehensiveness in all their studio work, your high level of design resolution might be diluted given that the local competition demonstrates similar levels of production. While this quality of work is exceptional for second-year

2.2.1
Photograph of a portfolio review in session.

students relative to other programs that may dwell more on the theoretical design at that stage of education, the localized comparison would be used to find ways to differentiate your work from your peers. Ideally, your portfolio of work should excel relative to global competitors but in a localized scenario where your colleagues also excel at design resolution, your work must distinguish itself from them. This could be via a range of options including going to a higher level of design resolution beyond that of your peers, or alternatively presenting the work with an additional conceptual framework to highlight the strong design drive behind the project.

In both cases, assessing the competitive landscape is an important exercise in understanding one's competition and what can be done to refine one's own work. Assessments for professional and academic portfolios may vary among institutions and contexts; however, there are five important categories of content displayed in all portfolios that one must keep in mind when comparing portfolios: creativity and critical thinking, technical skills, experience, accomplishments, and passion. While they are not always explicitly presented in a portfolio, they are criteria that are in demand by academics and professionals alike in architectural praxis. Understanding the competition in these terms and relative to one's own portfolio of work will highlight points of individual distinction as well as improvement to the document.

## 2.3 CREATIVITY AND CRITICAL THINKING

While further elaboration upon showcasing design work in a portfolio will be discussed (see Chapter 3), one of the most important characteristics in an architecture portfolio is the creativity and critical thinking required in designing a project. In order to distinguish yourself, a project should demonstrate a clear adherence to a self-imposed design objective. This will be unique to your work. Anyone creating an architecture portfolio should have the confidence in presenting their design work as a unique proposal that demonstrates their creativity and critical thinking – the essential components separating architecture from simply construction.

Far too often creativity is understood as merely an exercise in aesthetics alone. A design objective is not the project brief nor the building program. There should be an architectural intent behind the objective and it should be something that manifests itself in multiple instances in the project. For example, if designing a small residence, there is little creativity or critical thinking in simply designing a detached house even if thoroughly detailed and rendered with a consistent aesthetic veneer. A stronger design proposal would perhaps focus on having as minimal an impact on the environment it finds itself situated in. The creativity would be everything from the passive strategies in allowing light to flood the public spaces, siting to use local vegetation canopies for passive shading, and even critically looking at the prospects of water usage. Where others might have simply drawn from hypothetical plumbing infrastructure, a strong portfolio would showcase the student's critical thinking in her integration of rainwater collection and solar water heating for the residence. The adherence to the core design idea as executed by the creativity and critical thinking in assembling the project would distinguish the work from that of her peers.

Even in portfolio work from professional contexts, where design is a collaborative effort, it is important that authors are able to articulate at the very least the design intention and how it manifests itself in the project. Better yet, if there were components of the project that were under the oversight of the author, a focus on those elements in

**2.3.1**
Sun study variations based on differentiating facades. *Curating Complexity* by AnA:Ctonio Cunha.

Source: Antonio Cunha, *Curating Complexity*, 2016, Digital Image, 4724 x 1205, Toronto, Canada.

the portfolio would be very useful. For example, an author might include the design of a library in his portfolio which was driven by a focus on using light in all the major activities undertaken in the facility. Although he might not have developed that concept for the project, he may have been assigned to the design of a public gathering area whereupon he could have showcased his adherence to the overarching design concept supported by critical thinking in having light reflect off surfaces and shadows animate the spaces throughout the day. Supported with excellent visuals that emphasize this creativity and adherence to the design scheme, this work in the portfolio would distinguish her work as more than simply servicing project tasks.

A common problem with students in distinguishing themselves at a creative level is an inability to focus on the core idea and consistently carry it through in a design. As a result, many projects read quite hollow despite the photorealistic imagery of bombastic forms that are ubiquitous in contemporary portfolios. Academic administrators and employers are able to see beyond the seductive imagery and infographic diagramming – they have either been teaching students how to do it or have been paying employees to do it for years.

Creativity pertains to the visuals and design consistency through a project, so it is important for designers to ensure their work is presented appropriately and grounded in some architectural framework. While some design projects may be driven by a fascination with a monumental form, true creativity is the ability to not only share a consistency through multiple levels and adhere to core design intentions, but also ensure it is feasible on some level. Creativity without a degree of implementation is simply imagination. In some projects, imagination may be the focus (such as a theoretical exploration or design thought experiment), but in strong portfolios, such projects are in

CHAPTER 2.0 | IDENTIFYING YOUR KEY DIFFERENTIATORS

the minority whereas truly creative works actively engage constraints and provide reasonable resolution (see Figure 2.3.2). For example, a project that has an incredibly seductive form may seem to pose structural challenges. Creativity would lie in the author's ability to implement some level of structural insight in how she would propose to hold up the interesting form.

One of the greatest creative works a design student embarks upon is a thesis project. It exhibits a designer's thoughtful investment of critical thinking in creative and robust output beyond simply aesthetics. In general, unless in an academic application, research and thesis work is best presented in a consolidated series of spreads that concisely demonstrate a clear investigation and outcome. Especially for those coming right out of their graduate studies, a challenge is to remove oneself from one of two pitfalls, either running the risk of pedantically presenting excessive material or, conversely, showcasing marginal amounts of content that do not make sense to someone unfamiliar with the research work. To potential employers, the value of thesis work at the most fundamental level is its ability to articulate the level of resolution on a project when given a significant amount of time and individual investigation. Depending on the nature of the thesis, it may complement topics, typologies, and projects that exist within a firm's portfolio of work.

2.3.2
A sample of an architectonic exploration.
*A-Voidance* by Rachel Law.

Source: Rachel Law, *A-Voidance*, 2016, Digital Image, 1920 x 1080, Toronto, Canada.

As a thesis permits designers to research various facets that impact architectural praxis, ostensibly the work should be the best example of a designer's work and should be highlighted in a portfolio as such. When applying for a job, authors should consider the potential alignments between the thesis research work and a prospective employer and job description. An architecture thesis or research work focused upon a typology (such as the evolving nature of libraries or residential communities for mass immigration) or technique (such as robotics in architectural prototyping or artificial intelligence in wayfinding) that may resonate with the work or workflows within a potential employer should be highlighted appropriately in a portfolio.

Thesis and research work have a great deal of impact in the academic world as they go beyond asserting a knowledge base and demonstrate a clarity on positioning, research capacity, rigorous synthesis, and application to architectural discourse. The ability to concisely articulate a well-researched position and architectural design integration is invaluable to architectural academic success. Doing so reinforces an author's individual potential for future academic achievement in an architectural program. This also reflects the capacity for an author to undertake research or teaching responsibilities that likely would also be considered by admissions committees. For example, a student who completed an undergraduate capstone studio project on tall wood-framed buildings may find it useful to highlight her knowledge on the topic for potential research or teaching assistant roles with other faculty in the institution (especially given the relative lack of its widespread adoption and standardization by the AEC industry) when applying to graduate architecture programs. In both professional

2.3.3
A well-developed and researched timber construction project. *Timber Competition* by Julianne Guevara, Jimmy Hung, Ernest Wong.

Source: Ernest Wong et al., *Timber Competition*, 2019, Digital Image, 5363 x 2015, Toronto, Canada.

and academic contexts, such an overt connection reinforces both an author's quality of work and level of expertise, which are essential to professional and academic success.

Creativity is not the ability to propose innovative forms that break parameters, it is the ability to form innovative proposals within these parameters. To analyze, understand, and propose appropriate and creative solutions are key to critical thinking in architectural discourse. As many authors do not emphasize this in their portfolio projects, it is important to use this as a core differentiation factor in curating a portfolio. Whether in industry or academia, critical thinking is essential in daily duties and must be vigilantly showcased in each portfolio project.

## 2.4 TECHNICAL SKILLS

Technical skills are vital to display in portfolios in order to convey a level of competence in bringing design ideas to a level of feasibility. Institutions and employers alike need to have skilled personnel capable of not only design innovation, but also producing, communicating, detailing, and constructing designs. While technical acumen varies from region to region and certainly with levels of experience, it is important for authors to research enough to know how to differentiate themselves from other applicants. Successful portfolios cannot rely on a conventional display of technical skills – doing so diminishes them to commodities.

For many authors, technical skills predominantly reside in the acumen with tools in communicating and developing design work, from digital modeling and visualization through to freehand sketching and physical model making (see Figure 2.4.1). These skills on their

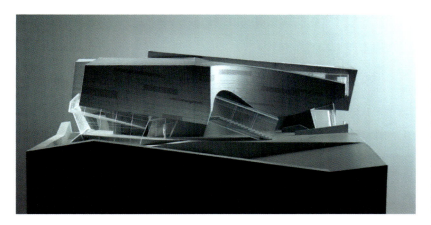

2.4.1
A physical model epitomizing and conveying a complex design. *Interfaith Chapel* by Han Dong.

Source: Han Dong, *Interfaith Chapel*, 2011, Physical Model, 3888 x 2592, Cambridge, Canada.

**2.4.2**
Technical knowledge goes beyond construction into other components such as sustainable design. *Aspiro* by Kevin Pu.

Source: Kevin Pu, *Aspiro*, 2011, Digital Image, 3320 x 5427, Toronto, Canada.

own are quickly becoming commodified. While software packages are rapidly becoming more robust in coordinating building information with design intention, the learning curves and user interfaces in these platforms are also making production quite accessible. At the same time, if the incredible outputs from these platforms are not adequate, it is not uncommon for firms to outsource production work at all project phases, from conceptual renderings and models to construction documentation and fabrication. These groups often have extraordinary prowess and productivity that easily outpace those in architecture firms and schools – they specialize in those production tasks. While there are countless certification programs in architectural technology through to design visualization, the point of differentiation one must demonstrate is the ability to utilize those skills in interesting architectural design work. For example, skills with photo-editing software have been commodified in architectural praxis, however rarely is the expectation that renderings generated by architects and students should be photorealistic. What an author should demonstrate is their stylized use of the software in communicating the appearance, use, ambiance, and features of the design. Obviously the greater the quality of technical skill, the greater the range of techniques at an author's disposal. As a result, this certainly improves opportunity for employment with a diversity of firms and validates a great design arsenal for academic pursuits.

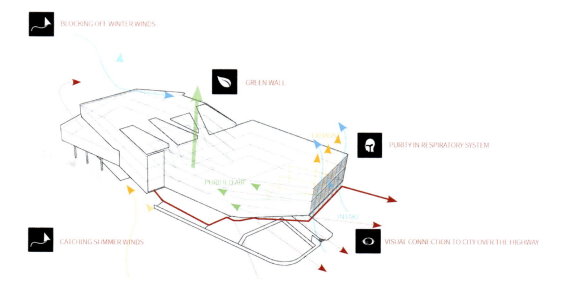

CHAPTER 2.0 | IDENTIFYING YOUR KEY DIFFERENTIATORS

If the first level of technical knowledge in a portfolio refers to the ability to visually communicate and produce architecture, the second level pertains to a comprehensive knowledge based upon how to render these ideas into feasible production. This can range from demonstrated building construction knowledge to sustainable design integration (see Figure 2.4.2). A common problem with students in distinguishing themselves on technical matters is when they defer to and incorporate generic technical materials into their projects simply to demonstrate some level of technical competence. To highlight the use of standard assembly or envelope details in the interest of showcasing technical expertise often has the opposite effect. By including generic materials, audiences infer two messages, that the author: a) does not know how to do things properly and defaults to using textbook details, or b) is so technically weak, she is compensating by padding her portfolio with details to appear competent in that area. Differentiate your work by once again leveraging your innovative design work as a basis of applying your technical knowledge. It might be as simple as taking a design project and thoroughly examining all the details in the assembly and presenting how they would come together in three-dimensional imagery as opposed to conventional working drawing details (see Figure 2.4.3). Alternatively, some design projects have complex geometry that requires equally complex detailing. In such instances, it would be advantageous to show some technical acumen in applying the fundamentals of building construction with a knowledge of contemporary innovations on a project.

2.4.3
Good design work is not defined by imagery alone but its resolution in the details. *Cocoon* by Erik Aquino.

Source: Erik Aquino, *Cocoon*, 2016, Digital Image, 5016 x 2276, Toronto, Canada.

These tactics are useful in differentiating your portfolio work on a technical level. Technical skills are commodities on their own and it is only by applying them to your design work that they are able to articulate their differentiation. Not only is the basis of the technical work unique to each individual's design projects, but this approach also encourages a break from conventional, generic detailing. Differentiation on technical skills in architecture portfolio work is incumbent on design application. Whether in academia or industry, there is a range of technical skills that a candidate must engage on a daily basis. Architectural applicants are not technologists, technicians, or computer animators – they are steeped in architectural praxis and it is important to demonstrate their technical strengths in such a context.

## 2.5 EXPERIENCE

A dilemma faced by applicants with numerous distinctions or visually stunning portfolios is that despite their incredible work, they do not have work experience. People cannot gain employment without experience and cannot get experience without past employment; however, this "Experience Catch-22" paradox is surmountable.

Rarely is a young designer's first employer an architecture firm or even related to the architecture industry. Whether it is in retail or tutoring, there are still relevant experiences that translate from one context to another. Authors must assess and reframe their skills and experiences from their past employment to a relevant alignment for an architecture application. At a very generic level, there are "raw commodity skills" that are applicable to most workplaces or academic contexts. These could range from soft skills and customer care through to financial literacy and marketing. Do not take these skills for granted as they are often critical in determining the appropriate "fit" between similar prospective applicants. For example, excellent interpersonal skills cultivated working as a math tutor assure academic admissions committees that a candidate has the ability to not only communicate well with prospective faculty advisors, but also potentially be able to serve as a teaching assistant upon commencing their graduate studies. These same interpersonal skills would also have a great value to prospective employers, as there will always be a need to not only communicate to clients and contractors on project collaboration, but also when educating colleagues on project information.

A more investigative approach to the reframing of past experience is to write down all the relevant skills that you have cultivated in past work or academic experiences and subsequently group these into categories. The next step would be to draw upon job descriptions or key criteria that the employer or academic institution explicitly request and correlate them to the groupings of experiences you have. Doing this allows you to determine what may be highlighted in your portfolio or résumé for specific audiences.

While this initial exercise may be useful in refining the alignment between your experience and your audience needs, it is no longer enough to simply nominally satisfy baseline requirements. To simply state that you have experience working on a specific building typology or academic field of research does not necessarily offer assurance that you are a strong applicant. To meet criteria outlined by your audience is not enough. Experience, especially in professional contexts, must both showcase proficiency and go beyond conventional tasks or production. Although excellence may be validated via awards and distinctions or even letters from employers and educators (see Chapter 6), the portfolio must contain work that emphasizes productivity acumen and creative capacity from work and academic experiences. In a professional portfolio, where skills are important to showcase, projects cannot be left at conventional, banal levels. If a firm demands photo-editing skills and experience with athletic facilities, a notable portfolio must certainly include these two facets, but must clearly articulate an elevated level of competency and potential innovation. For example, to demonstrate photo-editing skills, a strong portfolio would include projects that do not repeat a comfortable photorealism throughout all the works. It might be worthwhile instead to demonstrate varying levels of photo-editing ranging from photorealistic montages through to more abstract, stylized orthographic drawings (see Figure 2.5.1). To

**2.5.1**
A stylistic, representational render. *Non-Motorized Water Sports Centre* by Timothy Lai.

Source: Timothy Lai, *Non-Motorized Water Sports Centre*, 2018, Digital Image, 6128 × 2829, Toronto, Canada.

best showcase excellent experience with athletic facilities, it would be advantageous to not only showcase a diversity of work, but drill down to specific details or innovations that a candidate had direct oversight or control over. Architecture is a collaborative effort and it may be difficult to isolate a professional task of notable innovation under the oversight of a single person, if not a junior architect or design intern. Despite this huge collaborative undertaking, in most projects, even novices are given opportunities to execute work driven by their own design decisions and as such, authors should highlight these features from their work experiences.

The same approach should be adopted for academic works. Proficiency and exceptional demonstrated knowledge synthesis must be shown in past academic experiences. Every design student will have academic projects to include in their portfolios. To claim that as a notable experience is inappropriate. For academic portfolios, experience with research and design innovation is more than conventional studio work. A more comprehensive and synthetic legacy of investigation must be evident in academic work as opposed to basic fulfillment of project outlines. If an academic portfolio were focused upon pursuing graduate studies investigating architecture in light of rapid desertification, then it behooves the author to not only find design work that highlights arid climate or water-scarce conditions, but also demonstrates strong research skills as applied to design contexts. While a comprehensive building design project on its own may not immediately present itself as a strong sample of design research synthesis, there likely would be innovations in the integration of technologies or strategies that break from the conventional methods of resolution. The ability to investigate and integrate factors ranging from new technologies, processes, or cultural shifts into design work demonstrates academic experience that reinforces a candidate's value on research, innovation, synthesis, and application in architectural design.

Taking the initiative to expand experience is worthwhile but only if it is rewarding and enhances your value. Extracurricular personal projects and design competitions are excellent opportunities to gain experience with specific building typologies, regional contexts, software packages, and levels of resolution that may uniquely position your capacity with employers and academic institutions. For

CHAPTER 2.0 | IDENTIFYING YOUR KEY DIFFERENTIATORS

example, including competition entries for a hypothetical utopian city (Figure 2.5.2) or supertall timber architecture highlight the theoretical and research backgrounds that may be appropriate for academic applications, especially if such competitions pertain to potential academic pursuits. These types of competitions also would be worthwhile if one were seeking employment with firms that engage large-scale master planning or tall timber construction respectfully.

If participating in uncompensated competitions is one method of gaining experience, it should be reinforced that gaining experience with little to no compensation is especially discouraged. Working within for-profit design firms for minimal financial compensation, regardless of the firm's reputation, devalues the individual, the firm, and the industry. To work for anything below a regional minimal salary is myopic. While it might provide an opportunity to gain relevant work experience, the level of responsibility may be limited as employers may be reluctant to give potential quitters

2.5.2
A utopian representation of the revitalization of a riverbed. *Futuristic Award Competition* by Stanley Lung.

Source: Stanley Lung, *Futuristic Award Competition*, 2016, Digital Image, 13007 x 9979, Toronto, Canada.

responsibilities and tasks. It should also be noted that some young architects actively apply to work for famous architecture firms for free simply to be able to add the brand names to their portfolio and résumés. This practice diminishes their own value and that of the industry. While it is interesting to read through applicants with positions at multiple famous architects, it is understood by architectural employers and educators that the experience an applicant has gained within those places is often superficial or inadequate in bringing design ideas into architectural form. As a result, when working for free or undercutting local industry standards, the accrued experience is not especially compelling to prospective employers and educators.

Some uncompensated initiatives such as personal research projects or design-builds also cultivate a level of experience that might not necessarily arise in academic or professional contexts. For example, participating in the design and construction of a market kiosk for a charitable event is not only a worthwhile addition to a portfolio and résumé, but also is an opportunity to demonstrate skills and experience invaluable for audiences such as construction oversight, project management, and leadership experience (see Figure 2.5.3).

**2.5.3**
An extracurricular project coordinated, financed, and managed by students. *Aqueous* by [R]ed[U]x Lab.

Source: [R]ed[U]x Lab, *Aqueous*, 2016, Digital Image, 4207 × 2364, Toronto, Canada.

While work experience tends to be a very weighted component in employment, it has resonance in academic applications as well. The differentiation that arises in applications resides in past experience and the work that goes beyond the status quo. Experience does not have to be completely backward-facing – there are opportunities to cultivate additional experience for portfolios including participating in extracurricular work such as design competitions, personal projects, and design-builds.

## 2.6 ACCOMPLISHMENTS

As degrees become commodities and designations become commonplace, accomplishments have become a critical differentiator for portfolio authors. Currently, it is far more difficult to find someone who has *not* gone above and beyond the minimum expectations and *not* accomplished anything meriting any type of distinction on some level. Accomplishments must be notable achievements that demonstrate excellence and put applicants in a select echelon of candidates. If everyone were to have a litany of accomplishments, it would be a challenge to be distinguished among the crowd of competitors. Fortunately, this is rarely the case. From winning international competitions to overseeing a notable project from initial design through to close out, these types of activities showcase a level of performance that is either validated by a third party or universally understood as significant undertaking in architectural praxis. These activities serve to reinforce the differentiation a candidate has over the standard level of performance from the general pool of applicants. There is a hierarchy of accomplishments: those that are commodities that run the risk of coming across as ways to exaggerate one's value, and those that are truly reinforcing achievements.

Commodity accomplishments are generic – one's competitors have them and likely do not pander to them. Achievements such as tacit benchmarks (e.g., graduation from high school or completion of core architecture courses), participation (as opposed to winning) in activities many others engage in (e.g., mandatory design projects or class-wide travel), or undertaking core tasks (e.g., use of computers in design work or design compliance with building code) are only worthwhile if there is a notable aspect of distinction. Otherwise, mention of these commodity accomplishments reflects poorly on you. For example, if you are extolling your accomplishments to high school, it is clearly a sign that you are desperately filling out your résumé. If your portfolio is preoccupied with showcasing conventional accessibility conformance, it fails to articulate any design ambition or desire to differentiate beyond the status quo.

For accomplishments to be worthwhile, they must have distinction and credibility. Putting such a distinction in a résumé helps, but one must ensure that the reasons for distinction are properly articulated. Given any and every accomplishment, authors must be emphatic as to what the distinctions are for. For example, winning the Seebohm Award may have great prestige and distinction to students in a specific program but the general academic and certainly professional audiences may be unaware of what merits winning the award. If this specific award were presented to graduate students for exceptional digital design work, then such a clarification must be made to audiences at the very least in a few words within in a résumé and certainly in the portfolio as well. By doing this, one can express the notable distinction of the award (such as strong digital design work) while validating the successful execution in nearby imagery within the portfolio. Awards and accomplishments are also only relevant when they have a level of credibility validating the quality of achievement and the volume of participation among other factors. To receive a participation award in a field of five competitors is not a noteworthy accomplishment, whereas winning an international design competition hosted by an accreditation body provides a degree of context for audiences to appreciate the merit of the distinction.

In addition to their distinction and credibility, accomplishments must reinforce excellence in the portfolio of work. If awards or distinctions are referred to in the résumé, they should be evident in the projects in the portfolio. For example, to mention that you received honorable mention for innovations in an international wood construction competition becomes quite unfulfilling when it is not showcased in the portfolio; the articulation of design or technical innovation is initiated in the résumé and then must be demonstrated in the portfolio work. When the wood construction competition project is put in the portfolio, its presentation must highlight the unique innovations that merited distinction, such as parametrically generated optimized geometries based upon maximum flexural stresses. The accomplishment serves as a point of third-party validation on a student's portfolio project.

Once again, another excellent opportunity to distinguish one's work and accomplishments is via competitions. The beauty in participating in competitions is that they provide multiple opportunities to showcase a range of differentiation factors within a portfolio. Competitions offer an incredible outlet for a greater diversity for projects that colleagues and contemporaries do not necessarily engage in. Competition work also offers greater engagement with potential research subjects, financial rewards, and of course widespread accolades and distinctions. One only needs to browse various online repositories of design competitions to quickly find a current or future design challenge that engages topics that may be worthwhile to enter in order to expand your portfolio of projects and experience for an appropriate audience. For example, a prospective applicant for a graduate architecture program with an interest in affordable housing would easily find design competitions for laneway housing through to micro-apartment design (Figure 2.6.1). Undertaking one or more of these competitions not only provide opportunities to garner distinction but more importantly allows the portfolio author to further research, synthesize, and propose design work that would provide a

**2.6.1**
A student design competition for micro apartment design. *In-Between* by Ryerson's CCA Team.

Source: Shengnan Gao et al., *In-Between*, 2018, Digital Image, 3151 x 2607, Toronto, Canada.

2.6.2
A design competition entry for rooftop micro housing in Hong Kong. *A Small Building* by Andrew Lee.

Source: Andrew Lee, *Small Building*, 2018, Digital Image, 3000 × 911, Toronto, Canada.

more robust range of work validating their candidacy for the position (Figure 2.6.2).

In architectural industry circles, it is far less common to find individual employee accomplishment and reward systems in place. In this milieu, accomplishments are often related to roles in a project (such as design architect, integration lead, and project manager) as opposed to explicit awards. To oversee an architectural project is no small feat and anyone in architectural praxis adjudicating an architecture portfolio would appreciate such a role. If such a distinction is necessary in a portfolio, it is incumbent on authors to demonstrate finer levels of oversight, decision-making, and scope of work in the way projects are presented. Beyond seductive imagery that highlights design excellence or conventional technical documentation showcasing expertise, authors with backgrounds in industry may wish to reinforce their leadership roles by presenting a greater scope of work that would neither be necessarily evident in conventional academic work nor comprehensively presented in professional experience generated by an architectural intern. Showcasing concept sketches through to construction photos demonstrates a protracted oversight of a project while documentation such as schedules or millwork imagery elicit the comprehensiveness an author has invested in the creation of a project. For professional applications, this level of presentation is notable in that it quickly and clearly distinguishes applicants with relevant work experience from applicants who, despite potentially having great skills, may not have the depth of work experience that is demanded by industry. This is also relevant for some academic institutions, as many graduate programs value the composition of classes with recent graduates and experienced industry professionals. The demonstrated maturity and experience from industry in a portfolio serves to differentiate and promote an applicant from industry in their endeavors to return to academia.

Accomplishments must have distinction and credibility to affirm the work found in a portfolio. Everyone will have what they believe are exceptional projects in their portfolio. Accomplishments such as awards and citations offer objective validation that propels projects from standard fare to truly unique showcases in a portfolio. Authors should critically assess their portfolio of work and determine where there may be gaps in validation and realize that there are options such as competitions and professional work that afford opportunities to not only receive accomplishment via distinctions but also in further investigating and examining research interests. Given that employers and academic institutions do not wish to accept conventional, mundane candidates, accomplishments play a critical role in guiding portfolio presentation and certainly content.

## 2.7 PASSION

A "regular" workday, one with consistent hours and workload, in architectural praxis is rare, whether it is collaborating with a project team during a deadline at the office or toiling away at refining a studio project. There is an incredible investment and sense of ownership in creating architecture. Whether in hiring or admissions, a portfolio must express its author's passion in their work. Architecture is not a commodity – its production must be driven by a designer's sincere investment of effort. Its inception, development, and execution cannot be done by rote or a mechanical process. Demonstrating a passion behind portfolio work that differentiates from competitors is more than broadcasting a level of enthusiasm behind the work, it must be evidenced in the content and methods of presentation. There is very little desire from employers or educators in architecture to hire or admit candidates who neither care for their work nor are willing to invest additional effort to develop it.

Exhibiting a genuine interest in surpassing mandated deliverables or objectives is an excellent way to showcase a passion behind any given project in a portfolio. Although there is a benefit in succinct and clear presentation, when projects are showcased in a portfolio with the minimal amount of content, audiences may interpret that as laziness in not preparing a full suite of supportive imagery, or that the author only targeted to deliver the bare minimum. In both cases, this reflects poorly on a portfolio author. While a conventional orthographic drawing set and perspectives are the standard expectation for adequate conveyance of a project, supplemental materials demonstrate two notable characteristics: a) an elaboration upon the author's unique focus in a project, and b) their genuine interest and investment in the project. Often, design students submit design portfolios to the same firms at the same time, which results in potential employers gaining familiarity with the projects and quickly determining the standard expectations for deliverables in that particular class. For example, a student may have been tasked to design a restaurant for a studio project and, like all of her classmates, would have produced the same required outputs (e.g., model, orthographic drawings, and perspectives). In order to demonstrate a higher level of investment in the project, she may have decided to illustrate a sensitivity to a specific feature in her project, such as the multiple configurations her interiors could take on through a series of axonometric configuration diagrams. Alternatively she could have demonstrated her attention to a thematic focus in her restaurant and include supplemental design drawings of custom furniture or flatware catering to her restaurant design. In both cases, the student is able to find ways to convey her passion behind her work beyond the conventional expectations in the project. This serves as a fairly clear differentiator in her portfolio that sets her apart from her competition.

Another strategy for showcasing passion in a portfolio is within a range of non-mandated activities available in architectural praxis. Differentiation by highlighting initiatives such as extracurricular work including competitions and design-build projects provides a twofold benefit: doing so a) showcases interests in topics not necessarily covered in academic or professional frameworks, and b) highlights individual interests that distinguish a candidate from others. As mentioned earlier, there are dozens of competitions at any given time that are available to emergent designers, covering topics from the use of specific materials and methods to proposing new typologies. Partaking in such competitions sends the message to prospective

CHAPTER 2.0 | IDENTIFYING YOUR KEY DIFFERENTIATORS

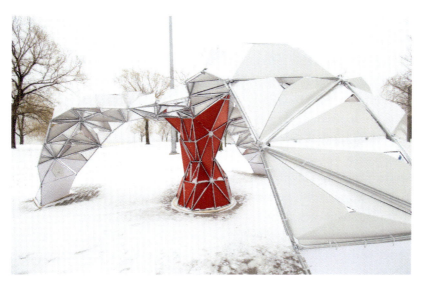

2.7.1
A design build project designed, built, and managed by students. *Tripix* by [R]ed[U]x Lab.

Source: [R]ed[U]x Lab, *Tripix*, 2019, Digital Image, 6000 x 4000, Toronto, Canada.

employers that an applicant's experience may resonate with the firm, while competition work showcases the research interests of potential academic applicants. Extracurricular competition projects highlight an individual candidate's willingness to go above and beyond expectations, which unconsciously registers with audiences.

Design-build projects offer a similar level of initiative and insight but also provide authors an opportunity to reinforce the enthusiasm behind their work as they have orchestrated not only the project's design, but have also overseen its coordinated construction. This is not a small undertaking and is appreciated by academics and industry alike. Rarely do architecture students have projects that are actually built, on account of experience, time, and resources, which makes design-build work in student portfolios quite notable. Even for those in industry, design-build work that is done on the side, such as collaborations with a local community groups in creating a children's play area, demonstrates a level of commitment that in the architecture, engineering, and construction industry is commendable. Design-build projects are robust in their ability to showcase not only the technical strengths in transitioning design ideas to constructed reality, but research interests and a willingness to invest effort into rendering it feasible.

Sometimes the most interesting projects in a portfolio are the ones driven by personal interest. If passion is epitomized by work undertaken outside of academic or employer mandates, then personal projects are invaluable at showcasing one's interests as explored in design work. Some initiatives may be collaborative, such as altruistic efforts for charitable groups ranging from graphic and web design work for children's programs to design-build work (such as Habitat for Humanity or INDEX). While there are various outlets to find ways to apply one's design skills for good causes, it is important to keep in mind that should any activity with any agency be included in one's portfolio, it must be clearly ascribed to what they have uniquely contributed to. As with many design projects, collaboration is essential; however, for portfolio purposes, it is necessary to explicitly articulate what was done by whom. These types of personal projects reflect a genuine interest in topics, processes, or causes that may resonate with employers' portfolio of work or reinforce an individual's range of potential research interests. This is even more abundantly clear in individual personal projects that are solely at the discretion of an author.

While individual passion projects may range from the design of a lamp in a startup through to costume design and anything in-between, they all demonstrate two essential components: a) genuine interest in the topic, and b) interesting design investigation. For academic applications, personal projects can demonstrate strengths in research ability, creative application in design synthesis, and independent productivity. In professional applications, these works serve as an outlet for authors to exhibit design and technical skill in projects that would otherwise not conventionally be done in industry or school. For example, a student may investigate material properties, parametricism, and digital fabrication in the design of a niece's chair. While the product is not an architectural design, it

**2.7.2**

An example of an architecture student expanding their design skills in lighting design. *Absorb* by Brant York.

Source: Brant York, *Absorb*, 2016, Digital Image, 9767 x 4209, Toronto Canada.

CHAPTER 2.0 | IDENTIFYING YOUR KEY DIFFERENTIATORS

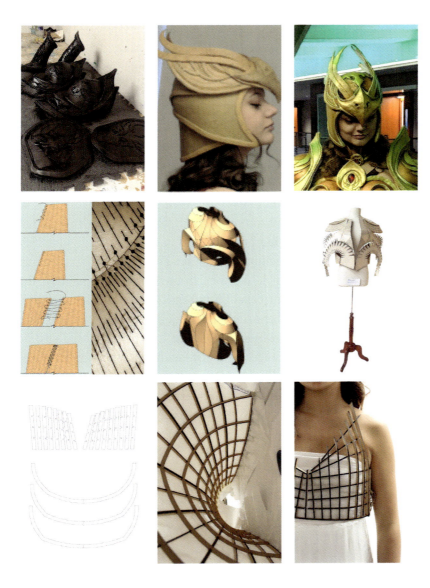

2.7.3
Clothing and costume design using digital fabrication by architecture students. *Cosplay Design* by Alyssa Carere; *Jacket Design* by Connor Gagnon; *Dress 708* by Jessica Feng and Zeenah Mohammed Ali.

Source: Alyssa Carere, *Cosplay Design*, 2019, Costume Design, 4488 x 6171, Toronto, Canada. Connor Gagnon, *Jacket Design*, 2018, Clothing Design, 4488 x 6171, Toronto, Canada. Jessica Feng et al., *Dress 078*, 2018, Clothing Design, 4488 x 6171, Toronto, Canada.

demonstrates a robust set of skills that might be of interest to prospective employers.

A caveat to the inclusion of any personal projects would be to do so only if it is appropriate in demonstrating an alignment with an audience's interests and needs. To saturate a portfolio with incredibly powerful and beautiful personal projects but neglect providing content to convincingly articulate suitability for core criteria is not going to be successful. Personal projects are very potent in expressing an applicant's passions and motivations, but it is important that a portfolio adhere to addressing what an audience's core requests are. If personal projects fulfill this need, then they should be integrated but not at the detriment of other parameters such as page count or project limits.

There is unfortunately not a standard guideline for artworks and creative initiatives undertaken as hobbies in a portfolio. On the one hand, if done well, they provide a good opportunity to leave a memorable impression that resonates with an audience. Alternatively they may be met with a negative reception as, at worst, filler material or, at best, irrelevant and non-sequitur work. Based upon interviews with academics and employers alike, if art projects are to be included in a portfolio, they should be presented to reinforce individualized alignment with the institution or role. For example, a portfolio author may include quick sketches from their travels around the world to emphasize their capability to quickly capture architectural ideas which a firm may have outlined in a job description or is known to integrate in their workflow (see Figure 2.7.4). This would also be useful for academic instances, as many faculty members prefer to see students capable of quickly visualizing design ideas, especially in an era saturated with photorealistic renderings. A word of caution on these art projects is that, as with architecture projects in a portfolio,

2.7.4
Sketches done while traveling exploring the tectonics of the architecture. *Travel Sketches* by Shengyu Cai.

Source: Shengyu Cai, *Travel Sketches*, 2015, Hand Sketch, 4976 × 2984, Toronto, Canada.

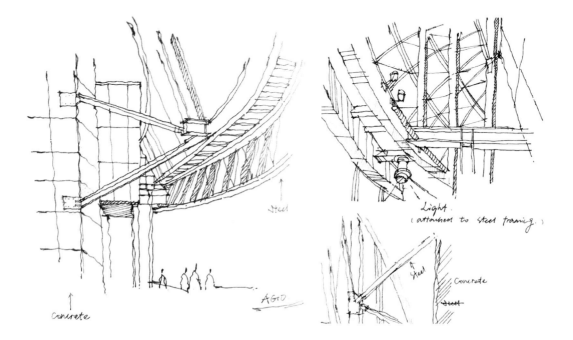

these works should be drawn upon from a bank of layout spreads to insert in a customized portfolio catered to specific stakeholder needs on skill (e.g., model making, sketching, etc.) or experience (e.g., furniture design, art installations, etc.).

Unless there is a clear reason to include such artwork in a portfolio, as evidenced in a job description or academic application criteria, it is best to refrain from extraneous work. Portfolio real estate and effort are best invested in addressing stakeholder needs. There is no point in showing incredible watercolor painting skills to a prospective employer searching for candidates with experience with transformable environments. Instead, those available pages are best assigned to a supportive project such as a kinetic studio canopy design or a multi-configurable residence that would validate alignment.

Passionate and sincere engagement with one's work is an incredibly valuable characteristic that is often unaccounted for when creating a portfolio, although it serves as a strong point of differentiation. When hundreds, if not thousands, of applications are annually vetted by a firm or academic institution, a portfolio's ability to validate a willingness to exceed expectations and take the initiative to undertake work strengthens the case for accepting its author.

# CHAPTER 3.0
## WHAT TO PRESENT IN A PORTFOLIO

**3.1** Aligning Yourself with the Audience    73

**3.2** The Balance: Design and Technical Skills    80

**3.3** The Three Things *Not* to Show: Ignorance, Laziness, and Pride    85

THE ARCHITECTURE PORTFOLIO GUIDEBOOK

**CHAPTER 3.0**

# External Perspectives

**STUDIES HAVE INDICATED TWO KEY PREDICTORS OF SUCCESS IN CONTEMPORARY PRACTICE: CURIOSITY AND A CAPACITY TO LEARN NEW THINGS. WOULD YOU AGREE WITH THIS?**

**ON:** Curiosity – the desire to learn something new is important. Capacity, I would go with as long as a candidate is capable. But I'd like to add a third one – attitude. They have to have the aptitude to grasp the opportunity and want to learn – to show the passion that they have for architecture – it's really about that. In my experience I have had hires from around the world where the person on paper and in the traditional way of hiring wasn't hirable. But there was something about him or her that really interested us. *We* were curious. And then we hired them and the result was fantastic. Attitude is very, very important. Some applicants are actually a bit delusioned, wanting to be a Pritzker Prize winner in two years and some of them are not engaged at all and they want direction all the time so it's really important to have the right balance.

**GS:** Yes. I mean curiosity equates to always looking and continually learning. We expect that during the time they are to stay at the office, and everybody keeps up with current architects and magazines on what's new. Getting out there and seeing things with your own eyes – you see things in reality and that's quite different. We expect that everybody is continually learning, not just whatever is being done in the office, and that would be helping someone develop into what they want to be.

**NT:** Yes, I would agree. Someone who is in our field should always be curious. You're always downloading visual data and trying to figure out "How is that done?", "How did they do that detail?", "Why did they do that detail?", or "Why does the space feel comfortable?"

CHAPTER 3.0 | WHAT TO PRESENT IN A PORTFOLIO

**RD:** I actually think for career longevity, something even better than passion is curiosity or inquisitiveness. Do they ask questions? Whether it's their idea of storytelling or whether it's the way that they pursue materiality. We don't expect them to come in knowing everything, but if they've taken a construction course, however rudimentary or abstract, what does that say about whether they are building on their knowledge and experience versus just taking required courses as one-offs? Did they just survive school or did they really get something out of it? I find that through the filter of curiosity and inquisitiveness, I've gotten students that stick and even employees that stick.

**CHAPTER 3.0**

# What to Present in a Portfolio

## 3.1 ALIGNING YOURSELF WITH THE AUDIENCE

Architectural praxis demands exceeding expectations and rewards innovative resolution to design challenges; however, this is often prioritized over addressing the actual project at hand. Ensure your portfolio aligns with your audience's needs. Investing resources and time into revisiting excellent design projects, recreating imagery, or showcasing particular acumen or experience is only worthwhile if doing so is relevant to your prospective employer or admissions committee. A spectacularly successful portfolio for application to one company may be completely inappropriate for another. To apply to both organizations with the same document makes little sense. As mentioned at the outset of this book, a successful portfolio showcases that the author not only understands her audience's objective needs, but also her awareness of how to demonstrate her capacity to meet these needs.

With subsequent portfolios and résumés, it will be easier for authors to develop a confidence and outline of skills and differentiation features they have. It is important that you understand your value proposition to your audience and know how to present it. As described in Chapter 2.1, there is a range of baseline commodity assets that are essential to gaining traction within architecture firms and academic institutions, as well as unique features and accomplishments that position you and your work and differentiate you from the field of other competitors. Assessing your own list of commodity skills, your acumen with them, and your points

3.0
*Stomata* by [R]ed[U] x Lab.

Source: [R]ed[U]x Lab, *Stomata*, 2019, Digital Image, 2500 x 1667, Toronto, Canada.

of differentiation are necessary to develop a portfolio strategy that aligns with targeted demands from your audience. Comparisons between assessed audience needs and one's own identified traits allow authors to target their audience's specific touchpoints and what may be needed for improvement where there may be deficiencies.

A simple and objective way of assessing alignment, and ultimately where an author would focus their energy, is to create a quick chart of outlined needs and fulfillment options in an Alignment Chart. Summary headings pertaining to a) the audience's expressed need, b) the author's ability to fulfill the need, c) how fulfillment is showcased in the portfolio, and d) the work required (if any) present an opportunity for authors to objectively and honestly determine their alignment with their audience and how to best organize their portfolio. Rarely does a candidate, and certainly their portfolio, perfectly align with an audience's needs. At best, reassessing presentation may be needed and at worst, gaps in alignment may emerge. If there are a couple of gaps that may be addressed, then this may be remedied by reframing how some work may be displayed or require additional material. However, if there are several notable gaps, the costs in time and effort may not merit the prospective benefit of applying to the agency. It is not impossible to succeed with them, it simply might not be worthwhile at this point in one's career.

In the Alignment Chart presented in Table 3.1.1 for a prospective candidate applying to a design firm, there are only a couple of gaps in the applicant's portfolio of work that require a modest amount of new work (in this case, the supplemental work of using additional digital fabrication techniques to use a CNC router demonstrating additional fabrication skills) or pivoting (demonstrating stakeholder consultation in extracurricular activity contexts rather than directly in a workplace environment). In the sample Alignment Chart, there are a few notable gaps in the candidate's assessment of her alignment pertaining to fabrication familiarity and working experience. Under the "Work Required" column, there are clear steps that she may wish to embark upon specifically with an idea of how existing work and experience may be leveraged appropriately in the portfolio. This column is essential as it outlines what work must still be done and the potential investment in time and energy to do so.

The same approach may be adopted for application to academic institutions; however, it should be noted that architecture programs,

**Table 3.1.1** One could assess their alignment with an audience by determining what the audience needs and how to achieve it.

| | ALIGNMENT WITH COMPANY ABC | | | |
|---|---|---|---|---|
| | Professional Audience Expressed Need | Author's Ability to Fulfill Need | How Fulfillment Showcased in Portfolio | Work Required |
| SKILLS | • Strong Revit skills<br>• Excellent productivity with Adobe Suite<br>• Experience with digital fabrication | • Revit: Good sampling of studio projects<br>• Adobe: Consistently used in all studio work<br>• Fabrication: **GAP**: Only experience is with 3D printing | • Revit: Renderings, drawings, and diagrams from Revit on two studio projects<br>• Adobe: Photoshop in montages, Illustrator use in diagrams and drawings, InDesign in overall layout of work<br>• Fabrication: 3D print from recent studio project but could be improved | • Revit: Configure presentation of work for portfolio and check legibility<br>• Adobe: Configure presentation of work for portfolio and update to reflect edits from final studio review<br>• Fabrication: **GAP**: Update site model with CNC terrain and document for portfolio |
| EXPERIENCE | • Experience with multiunit residential<br>• Experience with stakeholder consultation | • Residential: Multiple studio projects with residential programming<br>• Experience: **GAP**: Has never worked in firm | • Residential: Use first- and third-year studio final project<br>• Experience: **GAP**: Refer to lead in design-build extracurricular project | • Residential: In portfolio emphasize lobby and residential units of studio final projects<br>• Experience: **GAP**: Show structural documentation on design-build installation and site photos from inspection by city authorities |

**Table 3.1.2** An exercise that allows one to assess their portfolio to see what needs to be fixed.

| ALIGNMENT WITH ARCHITECTURE ACADEMIC INSTITUTION XYZ | | | | |
|---|---|---|---|---|
| | Academic Audience Expressed Need | Author's Ability to Fulfill Need | How Fulfillment Showcased in Portfolio | Work Required |
| DESIGN STRENGTH | • Design ambition in intention and expression<br>• Comprehensive design capacity<br>• Innovation in design work | • Ambition: Clarity in design projects<br>• Comprehensive design: **GAP**: Modest resolution in conceptual projects<br>• Innovation: **GAP**: Standardized components and conventional design work | • Ambition: Thoroughly shown in consistent level of work<br>• Comprehensive design: **GAP**: Revisit two studio projects for technical resolution<br>• Innovation: **GAP**: Prospectively undertake a competition to showcase work | • Ambition: Select best presentation of work from studio<br>• Comprehensive design: **GAP**: Thoroughly document and detail two studio projects<br>• Innovation: **GAP**: Complete a design ideas competition project showcasing innovation |
| ACADEMIC POTENTIAL | • Academic excellence<br>• Ability to conduct research<br>• Ability to teach | • Excellence: Academic award winning projects<br>• Research: Researcher for faculty project<br>• Teaching: **GAP**: No teaching experience | • Excellence: Highlight features of merit for award winning project<br>• Research: Present contributions of research work<br>• Teaching: **GAP**: Mentoring team members in group project on technical requirement | • Excellence: Ensure work focuses on and presents celebrated features<br>• Research: Collect image-based evidence of research work<br>• Teaching: **GAP**: Gather graphic evidence of complexity of task and teammates' outputs |

CHAPTER 3.0 | WHAT TO PRESENT IN A PORTFOLIO

**3.1.1**
Undergraduate students gaining experience constructing an extracurricular design piece. *Tripix* by [R]ed[U]x Lab.
Source: [R]ed[U]x Lab, *Tripix*, 2019, Digital Image, 7163 x 4547, Toronto, Canada.

**3.1.2**
Student competition entry demonstrating innovation in heavy timber construction.
Source: Ernest Wong et al., *Timber Competition*, 2019, Digital Image, 21154 x 10629, Toronto, Canada.

although typically all accredited by professional bodies with consistent standards of quality, have quite a range of criteria for selecting their candidates. In this case, an academic institution may ask for a demonstrated comprehensive building design as an admissions criterion or even teaching experience (given that many graduate programs use students as teaching assistants for their undergraduate programs). What is notable in the following example is that there are quite a number of gaps that emerge that may indicate that at the very least the portfolio will require a great deal of work, if not a reconsidering of applying at all. To undertake this quick alignment exercise allows authors to honestly assess the prospective success of their portfolio with a target audience and also determine what additional work needs to be done and how to present it appropriately.

While there are several different traits portfolio audiences wish to see in their applicants, ranging from professional certifications (such as LEED or PMP) to teaching and research skills, there tends to be a different prioritization of backgrounds that each group has. For employers, the two most common traits are experience and technical skills, whereas within academic applications there tends to be a greater focus upon demonstrated design strength and academic potential.

In professional applications, this is best addressed in job descriptions issued by employers. Job descriptions explicitly outline to candidates the criteria that need to be addressed by potential applicants. From specific software skills (e.g., parametric modeling or simulation) through to experience with certain tasks (e.g. BIM coordination or specifications) or knowledge bases (e.g., familiarity

3.1.3
Parametric modelling tools used in the production of a design build. *Parklet TO* by John Benner and [R]ed[U]x Lab.

Source: John Benner et al., *Parklet TO*, 2016, Digital Image, 3334 x 2389, Toronto, Canada.

with a particular typology or construction method), a job description presents a concise outline of expectations for successful candidates. It is imperative that a portfolio demonstrates the best alignment a candidate has with respect to these components.

When assessing alignment with an employer's needs, be mindful of both the required experience and skills as well as the manner they are presented. Conventionally employers present required backgrounds or familiarity that would benefit their business trajectory. These could range from a specific number of years working with a particular building typology (such as medical facilities or performance venues) or even a knowledge base with tasks (such as digital fabrication or project scheduling). It is not uncommon for applicants to lack an explicit background or experience. For example, a candidate may be interested in applying to a company that specializes in performance spaces, but she does not have any projects that fall within such a typology or, worse still, she has never worked in an architecture firm. All hope is not lost. Although a clear alignment would be fairly strong (e.g., a candidate's project that showcased a familiarity with similar typologies and methods of production as potential employer), a candidate's portfolio could instead draw upon past school work that may exhibit features common to the performance hall typology such as a school design. Between the two typologies, characteristics such as large assembly areas, public spaces, back-of-house facilities, and clear wayfinding are among the shared features that provide evidence of a candidate's relevant design experience.

As businesses, design firms require employees to have a comfort with not only the type of work, but also the technical skills in their workflow for its production. Different firms have different workflows. While it is increasingly the rarity, some firms expect employees to have incredible skill at manually conveying design work including sketches, hand drafting, or physical models. What is more commonplace is the software compatibility between a firm and a potential employee. Although it is quite difficult to assert mastery over the ever-changing landscape of available software packages used in contemporary design practice, authors should at the very least demonstrate in their portfolios that their architectural outputs are excellent regardless of the software platform. Excellent work will always garner attention and speak volumes of a candidate's skill. That they may have created the content within a different workflow may be overlooked as candidates may also showcase the promise of their ability to quickly adapt to new software and integrate into an office's workflow. While there is increasing consolidation of software by a handful of companies, applicants should not be worried as the thinking and basic operations of the packages are similar and the outputs are nearly indistinguishable in adept hands. For example, an author may showcase their familiarity with a particular BIM package in their portfolio knowing full well that the company they are applying to uses a competing, alternative package. In most cases, this is not a deal-breaker. So long as a portfolio demonstrates excellent technical acumen, adherence to conventions, and strong presentation of their BIM work, an author need not worry about falling short of meeting an employer's software needs.

Regardless of a potential employer's demand for software or traditional design skills, one must ensure that there is evidence of relevant experience and technical skills in a professional portfolio.

## 3.2 THE BALANCE: DESIGN AND TECHNICAL SKILLS

As outlined in Chapter 1.3, a strong portfolio showcases a combination of design innovation and technical skill; these are not mutually exclusive. Even the most theoretical academic studio project cannot rely solely upon a novel idea; its success relies upon the technique used in powerfully presenting the key message. At the same time, a well-detailed design of a simple box would be inadequate in presenting a candidate's capacity for innovative design. Balancing design capacity with technical acumen is often a subjective exercise, but a good starting point to assure oneself is to look at each page of a portfolio and validate that the design of the project is interesting and that there are at least two technical skills at play in the presentation of that work. While this is in no way an exhaustive list, here are some criteria for innovative design characteristics, as well as technical acumen and skills that may be evidenced in the work.

This is not an exhaustive list by any stretch of the imagination and it will only expand as new technologies and new architectural challenges emerge. What should be emphasized is that an "interesting design dimension", is not necessarily programming. A functional program is simply the mandated activities that happen within the

CHAPTER 3.0 | WHAT TO PRESENT IN A PORTFOLIO

| INTERESTING DESIGN DIMENSION | TECHNICAL ACUMEN | |
|---|---|---|
| Typological evolution | Digital modeling | Detail / construction resolution |
| Shifts in scale of operation | Digital fabrication | Photo-editing and montaging |
| Innovation in material/methods | Graphic design and illustration | BIM coordination |
| Social context responsiveness | Technical and regulatory compliance | Rendering / visualization skill |
| Physical site responsiveness | Physical model making | Fine hand rendering |
| Adaptive reuse | Mixed reality representation | Embedded technologies |
| Sustainable design advancement | Systems coordination | Coding |
| Projected futures | Architectural documentation | Advanced simulation |

**Table 3.2.1**
Technical acumen that can be found within design characteristics.

design, whereas an interesting design dimension serves as a differentiator. With this approach, students can gain confidence in their designs despite the fact that their peers also have the exact same projects in their portfolio of work. Honestly looking at how your design work is unique also creates a guideline that serves as concise project statement and allows you to be extremely focused in how the work is presented. For example, if your studio project was to design a cabin in the woods (Figure 3.2.1), you must identify what sets it apart

3.2.1
A first year cabin design focused on engagement with views to landscape. *Cabin* by Shengyu Cai.

Source: Shengyu Cai, *Cabin*, 2015, Digital Image, 3000 × 1487, Toronto, Canada.

as unique from the rest of the class. You may decide that the focus of the work is engaging the landscape to create specific views, which is an examination of physical site responsiveness. Where all the projects have the same program, your design sets itself apart, and its developed resolution makes it unique. The design work should adhere to and emphasize the design concept using the various technical skills at your disposal. From utilizing 3D modeling and visualization software to demonstrating modest construction and detailing knowledge, the suite of imagery produced would collectively reinforce the showcase of design and technical skills.

While this is elaborated upon in Chapter 5.2, on how to conduct a 30-Second Flip Test, tempering a portfolio's showcase of design and technical skills ensures audiences retain a balanced impression of an author's works even if they cannot retain specific project information. After leafing through your portfolio, your audience should comfortably articulate that you have a strong design capacity, with the appropriate technical skills to render them possible.

To emphatically articulate what is considered acceptable or successful design in a portfolio is not the intention on this chapter. Architecture is personal in its conception and subjective in its reception. Regardless of the design decisions or aesthetics behind a project in a portfolio, authors must ensure that the document presents a clear design focus and that it permeates all major presentations of its design facets. Architecture distinguishes itself from buildings as it aspires for more with a greater design ambition and intention. This is what must be evident in any strong design project, let alone an architectural portfolio piece. In a portfolio, the design intention must be graphically clear and in some instances, merit a sentence or two to provide insight on the work should audience members wish to read more. Whereas the earlier example of the simple cabin adhered to a consistent design intention, often design work is presented as simply a decorated building project rather than architecture. Aggressive scrutiny on portfolio projects should objectively question if the project is simply a building with an aesthetic veneer or if there is truly an underlying and consistent design intention that is encapsulated by the work. If there is not a strong design idea, the project may not be a strong portfolio piece. This does not necessarily completely eliminate the work from the portfolio as it may still be an excellent showcase of experience or technique. However, if it only demonstrates a single technical skill well, then it should simply be dismissed as a procedural exercise that offers little value in a portfolio. At best it would come across as a thin project and worse still, it is interpreted as a sign of desperation that someone would have to round out their portfolio of work with rudimentary assignments.

Employers value design capacity as it is a critical task in the architectural profession. Without strong design thinking, technical tasks undertaken by new hires require constant supervision and micromanagement. Hiring a candidate with demonstrated design capacity affirms a trust between employers and employees that small decisions may be made without persistent oversight. Within the academic realm, design thinking is vital as it serves as the basis for the majority of discourse in architectural pedagogy. Whether in undergraduate or graduate levels of study, design is where the majority of time, resources, and academic credit is found. In undergraduate architectural studies, the material from many different courses funnel into a studio project, as it ensures a real design-based synthesis and application of the material. While this happens in graduate studies as well, design skill is even more invaluable as students embark on graduate research and thesis investigations. Unlike the preordained, assigned projects found in undergraduate programs, the thesis work undertaken by graduate architecture students typically require a precise design thesis to research and develop a design that demonstrates the major tenets of the thesis. Design aptitude is essential in not only understanding a discrete facet of architecture, but also in synthesizing innovative proposals to add to the larger discourse of the discipline.

Technical skills are the currency of architectural praxis. Although architecture has always been a discipline open to adoption of new technologies and techniques in the design and construction of the built environment, the past five decades have witnessed incredible strides in design visualization, fabrication, optimization, and collaboration. Now more than ever the tools of architectural production are shifting at an unprecedented pace, which is why students and emerging practitioners alike are expected to have a full arsenal of tools at their disposal. From the conventional (such as physical model making and drafting) to the contemporary (including digital fabrication tools and BIM packages), the expectations by academics and employers placed upon applicants are increasing in breadth and depth. Where decades ago, the ability to draft in basic CAD, sketch designs, and create models from cardboard was a standard benchmark for praxis, contemporary demands have grown exponentially. In industry, the diversity of technical skills is advantageous given the absolute range of tools used by various architecture firms. Having a greater coverage of technical skills provides greater access to more potential employers. It also creates an arsenal for graduate applicants to better convey their ideas. It is important to bear in mind that while the portfolio validates the acumen one has with software, in some instances the portfolio is not the final metric of technical capacity.

It is not uncommon for organizations to require a test exercise to be performed in tandem with an interview when hiring. These exercises often assess a candidate's ability to conform to office standards, productivity expectations, and other performance metrics. This also affords employers to correlate outputs from the exercise to work found in a portfolio, so it is always advisable to be upfront with prospective employers when discussions arise on time taken to create certain content in the portfolio. For academic applications, technical skills are still also invaluable to showcase, given that this assures audiences that applicants have the capacity to communicate their design ideas as well as investigate new directions for innovation. Unlike those of their professional counterparts, academic expectations are slightly different, given that students are often still learning techniques or software packages in school. For those applying to graduate architecture programs, the benchmark for technical skill is high, given that there should be evidence of acumen with tools in the design, investigation, and production of thesis work. While a great range of technical skills is important to have, it is also vital for a portfolio to showcase great acumen in the projects. It makes little sense to include crude parametric modeling work in a portfolio if it looks like a generic exercise put in simply because an author wanted to showcase their diversity. It is better to leave underdeveloped skills out of a portfolio than to validate it to an audience with mediocre work.

## 3.3 THE THREE THINGS *NOT* TO SHOW: IGNORANCE, LAZINESS, AND PRIDE

There are a litany of poor decisions, errors, and problems that can inadvertently emerge in a portfolio. The most egregious fall into three major categories: a) demonstrating ignorance, b) highlighting laziness, and c) exhibiting arrogant pride. None of these are characteristics employers or academics need or want; they are portfolio poison. While these traits are not necessarily consciously inserted in a portfolio, they often are unconsciously communicated to an audience. Whether in the communication of the work or its resolution, portfolio authors must be vigilant about removing all evidence of such traits.

Ignorance in a portfolio is simply any instance where an audience's opinion of an author's knowledge base is diminished. Within academic settings, there is more leeway, given that mistakes are often made on the most complex or avant-garde of projects. This is in no way an endorsement of such errors in a portfolio; if there are mistakes in a portfolio, they must be fixed to a student's best ability. While academic portfolios often have varying levels of technical resolution, a high degree of value is placed upon a candidate's capacity for research and innovation in their design work. While some projects in an academic portfolio may be steeped in theory and have minimal ties to reality, it still should clearly connect to a firm design idea likely drawing from precedents. An unfortunate scenario that often emerges from certain portfolios is the incredible photorealism and excellent presentation behind rather vapid design work. While such

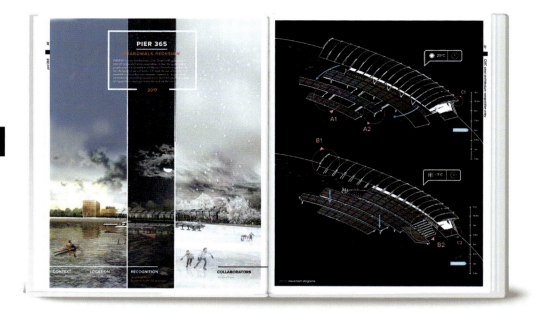

**3.3.1**
A project that uses the changing water levels in different seasons to create a floating platform. *Pier 365* by Tatiana Estrina and Martina Cepic.

Source: Martina Cepic et al., *Pier 365*, 2017, Digital Image, 4600 × 2869, Toronto, Canada.

portfolios may have traction with some employers, the lack of truly compelling design ideas, ignorance of precedents and theory, and fixation on seductive imagery compromise an academic portfolio's success.

When applying to potential employers, authors should ensure that their portfolios demonstrate not only a strong knowledge of architectural design, but also integral components such as feasibility, detailing, and context (see Figure 3.3.1). Whereas academic portfolios prioritize design capacity and thought over the tools of production, professional portfolios demand a strong demonstration of technical skills and technique. To have underdeveloped drawings, convention gaffes, or negligible resolution in portfolio projects only highlights an applicant's ignorance of the knowledge required to succeed in professional practice.

When determining whether one's portfolio exhibits signs of ignorance, they should ask these basic questions.

*Does the portfolio present errors?* Scanning through projects in a portfolio only to see inconsistencies among drawings, an inability to adhere to conventions, or technical flaws quickly erode at an audience's ability to form a positive opinion of a candidate. This is only compounded when work in a portfolio that would have received

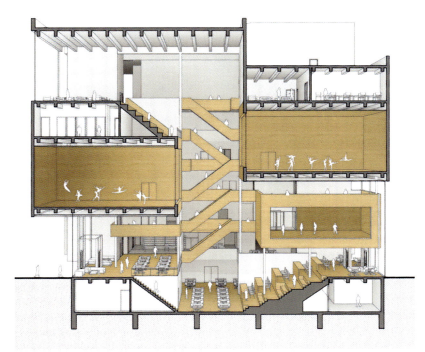

**3.3.2**
Early student work tends to require additional revisions and development. *Unfolded Ribbon* by Jeff Jang.

Source: Jeff Jang, *Unfolded Ribbon*, 2016, Digital Image, 2505 x 2144, Toronto, Canada.

critical feedback lacks any implementation of improvements. In both cases, the portfolio emphasizes a candidate's incompetence at doing things correctly, failure to understand core knowledge, and inability to positively participate in the iterative design cycle. Employers and educators wish to engage with people receptive to implementing feedback in order to develop a superior product; the iterative design process is fundamental to design professions. Glaring mistakes such as poor line weights or oversaturated renderings are easily remedied with digital edits so finding them in portfolios demonstrates an inability to properly present or produce even basic test prints. Modest changes such as technical or detailing errors are also salvageable by consulting or researching best practices and incorporating this into the work. The types of errors that often need a greater investment in time often pertain to fundamental design parameters. This could be the conspicuous absence of a required fire stair in a multiunit residential project or an underdeveloped lobby in a concert hall. These errors require redesign, remodeling, and re-representation in some manner that rarely can be finessed in a single image. In such instances, an appropriate allocation of work and resources should be made in order to ensure that the project is feasibly included in the portfolio.

*Does the work fail to meet audience standards or expectations?* A common approach to portfolio creation is to compile content from the past without any editing, updating, or reassessment. The belief is that audiences will appreciate work as dated and from a particular point in an author's career, and therefore tolerate errors. While there is a greater level of flexibility on this with academic applications (admittedly some institutions deliberately request a chronology of work), the reality is that if every project in a portfolio is good work, then permitting underdeveloped or novice work is typically an excuse for mediocrity and ignorance. To convince yourself that a project with errors should remain in a portfolio because "it was done in first year" is dangerous. For employers, the projects are understood in aggregate as a representation of a candidate's current skill and potential contribution to the firm – they do not care if a project was from your first-year studio (assuming they even read that somewhere in

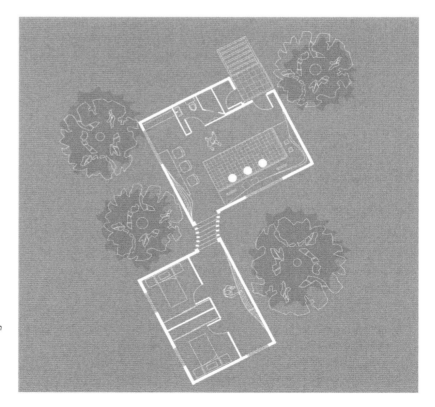

3.3.3
First year work may have good intentions and ideas, but often require revisiting. *Cabin* by Gloria Zhou.

Source: Gloria Zhou, *Cabin*, 2017, Digital Image, 5031 x 4850, Toronto, Canada.

the document). Employers are more interested in what experiences you have now and what you can do for them. All projects in a portfolio should demonstrate an author's current ability to align with audience demands.

*Is there an adequate breadth and depth of knowledge exhibited in the works?* It is tempting to present a homogenous portfolio of work. Unfortunately, doing so compromises an audience's ability to discern an author's extensive and robust body of work. If anything, the only consistency within the portfolio should be limited to layout and not the projects. Some portfolios will only showcase a handful of residential projects, while others only use renderings to convey the design work. In both scenarios, the limited typology and modes of representation undermine an author's value to employers and educators alike. While in certain instances for entry into industry, a portfolio's contents may gravitate towards a prospective employer's body of work, there should remain a level of confidence in diversifying a portfolio to reflect individual creativity and experience. The

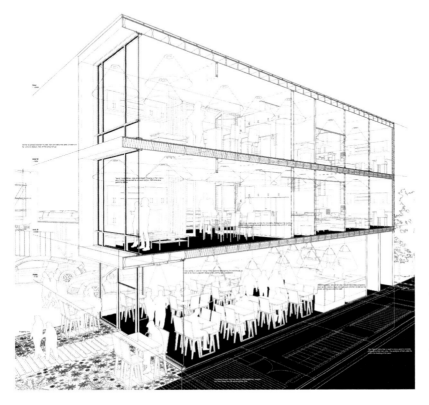

**3.3.4**
Portfolios should aspire to have at least a few projects that demonstrate an adequate breadth and depth of knowledge. *Duplex* by Andrew Lee.

Andrew Lee, *Duplex*, 2015, Digital Image, 1888 x 1873, Toronto, Canada.

scale and scope of projects in a portfolio should be both diverse and properly paced. For example, concentrating all the large-scale residential projects towards the front of a portfolio and saving smaller-scale works for the back half does little for a candidate to successfully convey the breadth or depth of work. The consistency in the projects (despite the shift in scale) also does not attest to the depth of knowledge a candidate may have. Consistently presenting renderings in a portfolio is dangerous. A diversification in the level of resolution, such as in details or interior elevations provides a greater sense of depth to a portfolio. This showcase of knowledge is invaluable as it distinguishes a candidate as an architectural professional as opposed to an efficient CAD technician or an incredible visualization artist. While those are very good traits individually, an architecture portfolio must exhibit a diversity of meaningful work and skills in totality.

Laziness in a portfolio is the lack of any additional effort in presenting one's work. If one fails to show their willingness to put effort into their own portfolio, they are messaging to their audience that they would do the same with that employer or institution. Laziness in portfolios arises in two major ways: a failure to revisit and improve content, and a failure to take the initiative to properly present it. Within professional contexts, laziness is poisonous. Not only does laziness result in poor quality work, but the financial costs and impact on workplace culture are extremely detrimental. Design firms are increasingly demanding that employees are invested in their work; laziness is completely at odds with that. At an academic level, laziness presents candidates at a disadvantage as design programs are quite demanding and require commitment in producing a great deal of work. This is even more pressing in graduate studies, as the individual research and thesis investigations in such a context typically necessitate a great deal of independent work. Laziness in design programs, specifically graduate studies, informs academic institutions that an applicant is not capable of managing their own work and time, and will inevitably require greater levels of guidance, support, or time. This is not what academics are seeking.

While it is clear that an inability to edit and improve past projects when assembling a portfolio demonstrates ignorance, it is also symptomatic of an unwillingness to invest energy into fixing work. Ignorance is the lack of knowledge, while laziness is the lack of effort.

CHAPTER 3.0 | WHAT TO PRESENT IN A PORTFOLIO

Common lapses in judgment such as the use of default screen captures or the use of generic details in a portfolio highlight an applicant's carelessness and lackluster capacity. Why would architects want to look over generic parapet details they see daily in a potential hire's portfolio? Why would academics wish to see wire frame models in a candidate's portfolio? At the very least, these types of images should be critically assessed for content and presentation. If the content is of low value, it should not be in the portfolio. If the content is useful, a portfolio author must invest time into making it look better not only for the sake of clarity, but in order to showcase that they are going beyond the minimal expectation of performance.

Laziness is directly correlated to presentation. Errors in a portfolio such as scaling down presentation boards to a portfolio booklet size or using model photos candidly taken with cell phones reduce an applicant's chances not only on account of demonstrating laziness but also the ineptitude of understanding quality of presentation. To take a project from one scale of medium to another requires a significant investment in time to ensure legibility and clarity are preserved. It makes no sense to simply scale down an A0 presentation board with a great layout to a letter-sized sheet – the hierarchy of line work and legibility of text will disappear, mismatched sheet proportions will result in awkward spacing, and worst of all, the narrative of the presentation will not come through. Take the time to reorganize imagery and text to cater to the portfolio medium, whether digital or hardcopy, and in some cases, new imagery creation may be required (see Figure 3.3.5). Similarly, take the time to properly document oversized sheets,

3.3.5
Rearrangement of boards to adapt to portfolio spreads. *Uproot* by Tatiana Estrina.

Source: Tatiana Estrina, *Uproot*, 2018, Digital Image, 8003 x 3537, Toronto, Canada.

**BOARD**
(24"x25")

**SPREAD**
(11"x17")

models, and installation work. It is quite frustrating for audiences to see potentially great work tarnished by poor imagery. Should there be photos that cannot be retaken, authors must find ways to capitalize upon what they have available. Photo-editing software is capable of not only addressing this problem but also opens up an opportunity to once again showcase great technique or skill in the portfolio.

Pride is the worst of the major messaging problems in a portfolio. Nobody, whether an employer or an educator, enjoys collaborating with obstinate, arrogant colleagues or individuals. It is frustrating, unproductive, and typically results in poor quality work as critical feedback is often ignored. For academics, overseeing a student (regardless of level) is trying if they are unreceptive to feedback and only attend to their own insights on guiding a design. Architecture does not exist in a vacuum and neither should those in the discipline. It is only via feedback from diverse opinions that projects gain greater depth and resolution.

Strong academic applicants demonstrate a willingness to accept and integrate feedback. This is why it is not uncommon for academic portfolios to have a higher level of developmental work (although it occasionally comes across as superficial filler) – it showcases an evolution of an idea ostensibly via feedback with reviewers. Often there is a desire to show only a "final" iteration of a design project, which has value in professional applications; however in academic portfolios, evidence of a willingness to develop and integrate is more important. Additionally, errors in a portfolio come across as arrogant gestures, whether in their presentation or focus. Sometimes, it could be as minute as a poor, hyperbolic title choice or a claim that a design is unprecedented when it clearly has connections to past precedents.

Professional portfolios rely upon a demonstrated currency of skill, whether it is digital modeling through to technical knowledge. While some portfolios are successful in showcasing some of these

**3.3.6**
Various physical model iterations. *Axial Housing* by Jeff Jang.

Jeff Jang, *Axial Housing*, 2014, Physical Model, 3543 x 987, Toronto, Canada.

skills, authors must be mindful to present their work without coming across as arrogant. A portfolio saturated with renderings may be useful for application to an architectural rendering firm, but it has limited value to an architecture design firm as it projects a message to employers that the author only needs renderings to generate a design. Similarly, when professional portfolios have quickly sketched, unintelligible "parti" drawings taking up an entire page of the document, it presents the author as quite self-absorbed. You cannot afford to present yourself as arrogant to employers. Do not present yourself as entitled. You might be an incredible designer; however, in many cases, you would be employed with people who are equally skilled and have also proven themselves within the firm over the years – you will do the same. If you truly are that good, employers will notice and you may move through the process quicker than others.

Pride is also a culmination of the ignorance and laziness that may be exhibited in a portfolio. As mentioned earlier, often a portfolio is the first and only opportunity for a candidate to communicate with their audience. Ignorance and laziness are symptoms of unappealing potential candidates. Exhibiting one of these symptoms is distressing enough but when both are evidenced, the audience tends to wonder if it is due to pride that errors and poor decisions are not only made but retained. Although stories abound of overconfident and arrogant architects, they should not be held as iconoclasts. Even in their nascent careers, they had to put aside their pride to learn from their superiors to develop their design principles and put them into their respective practices. Your portfolio will have a greater reception if you are able to remove any vestige of arrogance from it.

In summation, if one critically examines their portfolio they will find that any given shortcoming or error is a function of ignorance, laziness, or arrogance. For example, poor legibility of imagery could be due to a failure to understand line weights, a lack of effort to reorganize work to suit the medium, or simply a belief that it would neither matter nor be detected by an audience. Similarly, a design flaw in a project could be a result of a genuine obliviousness to fundamental design knowledge, a reluctance to put energy into fixing such a noticeable error, or worse still, a conceit that others should accept the error as it is acceptable by the author. A portfolio is the compilation of your best work highlighting to audiences your capacity to fulfill their list of needs; ignorance, laziness, and pride are unlikely to be on that list.

# CHAPTER 4.0
## HOW TO PRESENT YOURSELF IN A PORTFOLIO

**4.1** Layout and Imagery ............ 101

**4.2** Text ............ 117

**4.3** Interactive Media ............ 125

THE ARCHITECTURE PORTFOLIO GUIDEBOOK

## CHAPTER 4.0

# External Perspectives

**SOME APPLICANTS HAVE A PARTICULAR DESIGN AESTHETIC OR "STYLE" THAT IS CONSISTENT IN THEIR PORTFOLIO OF WORK. IS THIS ADVISABLE WHEN APPLYING FOR POSITIONS IN THE INDUSTRY?**

**GS:** There's no there's no need for somebody to gear a portfolio to match the office in style. Our office doesn't necessarily believe in style, whatever a project becomes is due to its own reasons. Whether that is defined as style is debatable, but in offices there are tendencies. In our office, the range of aesthetics is quite varied.

**RD:** There are good stories, enticing stories, and then there are stories that just don't move you or don't interest you. The stories that I'm looking for show a level of development where you're not necessarily repeating yourself from project to project, studio to studio, but you're exploring something in architecture. It's not a story that goes, *first I did this, then I did this*; it's a different type of story where you can go back and forth in time to show how your interest grew in a material, building type, or approach to architecture.

**WHAT SHOULD APPLICANTS BE CAUTIOUS ABOUT WHEN PRESENTING CONTENT IN THEIR PORTFOLIOS?**

**NT:** Layouts with generic, preordained templates. People will overkill with bullet points, gradient backgrounds, and different types of weird fonts and sizes – even if it is "just graphics," this reflects the design sensibility of a person. I feel like sometimes there isn't an understanding of the images an applicant is presenting, so hierarchy of the images is missing. Don't use too many images on one page when you could actually just us one really good image that tells the idea, and one or two supporting images. Self-editing is necessary, and says a lot about the mind of the applicant.

**RD:** Too much text, having the text font too small or text that doesn't say anything. I'm looking for the emergent professional to have some empathy for the person who's reading the text. The level of empathy also shows for how well they will eventually work with clients. They'll reshape the presentation when they think about the people they're actually presenting to.

**AB:** Too much graphic design, unnecessary lines and masks and amateurish graphics. There is just something about having very clean pages with clean information and breathing space around the images that demonstrates control. We're actually looking for architectural skills not graphic design virtuosity.

## AS A PROPONENT OF ARCHITECTURE AS A CONVERGENCE OF SKILLS AND MINDSETS, HOW DOES ONE SHOWCASE THIS IN A PORTFOLIO OF WORK?

**PB:** If you've done something really special, you put it in, otherwise avoid generic things. Show you know the fundamentals of not just the rendering, but how to make it come together. We can see through the trends and imagery in a portfolio. I think that's a telltale sign of this convergence – if you can resolve the image into how you would really make it. We hired some people in the past and they were the top of their class and they had this crazy parametric stuff. We asked them if they could put together a permit set and they could not. That's fundamental. I don't care about what you can do with a parametric façade and renderings if you can't show how it comes together in a portfolio.

**AB:** I actually don't think that having a huge variety of work is necessary, but what you show needs to be very clear and very high quality. It's about editing – being tough enough on yourself to take out the images or text that aren't absolutely necessary. If you have a particular drawing or model that you think is fantastic, then headline that image

## THE ARCHITECTURE PORTFOLIO GUIDEBOOK

or that model so that you can talk about it rather than burying it in an arrangement of images. I think that drawing out the things that students are passionate about in the portfolio is more important than running through and giving a very comprehensive description of a project. For collaborative projects, I'm looking for a commitment to the work, which may mean two individual pieces of work that each person authored. You have to be convinced of your authorship and demonstrate your commitment through that and being honest about what you've done.

**RD:** I've been incredibly impressed by students and prospective employees who diagram their workflows. Little diagrams in the margins or Venn diagrams off to one side of the portfolio. The detail isn't as important as the fact that these diagrams signal that they're aware of workflows, that you can combine technologies, which tools talk to which tools, or a plugin to get obstinate tools to talk to each other and in doing so, help you and your team to be more productive. Usually diagrams tell top administrators and employers that they're capable of meta-thinking – thinking about thinking. We definitely appreciate this part of the story that they tell about themselves and we'll recognize that they'll be an asset to our organization because they'll be more productive.

**CHAPTER 4.0**

# How to Present Yourself in a Portfolio

## 4.1 LAYOUT AND IMAGERY

Layout is akin to the air we breathe, it is essential, yet taken for granted, and only noticed if it is off or, worse still, missing. The thoughtful organizational design of materials in a portfolio is just as critical as the content itself. For design portfolios, there are several major considerations when developing a layout scheme, among them: consistency, legibility, image-prioritization, image diversity, and audience sensitivity.

This is neither a book on graphic design nor layout; however, it is worth presenting some ideal strategies without compromising individual aesthetic sensibilities. If anything, layout serves as a platform to diversify and distinguish. This is particularly important for students as they often share the same projects, technical requirements, and deliverables; layout and presentation provide an outlet to express individual aesthetic tendencies and technical comfort with graphic design.

Portfolios should have a consistent organizational scheme, as this unifies the document under a clear sense of order and highlights a modicum of design intention in visual communication. Layout consistency does not have to be dogmatic and confining, nor does it have to be heavy-handed to the point where graphic design compromises the messaging of the document. For some authors, layout consistency resides in the use of a base grid or proportioned breakdown of page real estate, whereas for others the constant allocation of a two-page spread rendering with a block text to mark the start of a new project provides

**4.0**
*Tripix* by [R]ed[U] x Lab.

Source: [R]ed[U]x Lab, *Tripix*, 2019, Digital Image, 3903 x 5854, Toronto, Canada.

**4.1.1**
Mistakes and effective techniques for layouts in a portfolio.

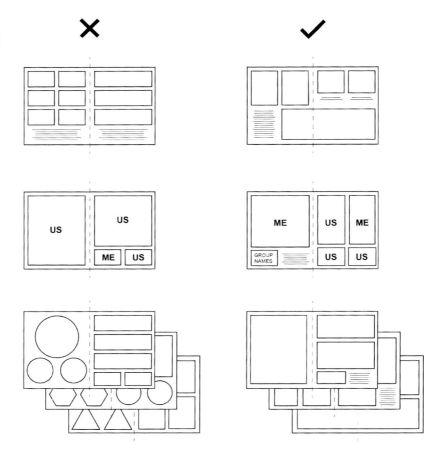

that uniformity in the portfolio (see Figure 4.1.1). Some authors feel compelled to create a new type of ordering or layout template for each project in their portfolio such that there is consistency within the presentation of a project but also potentially several opportunities to demonstrate a range of graphic design and layout skills. This is not advised as it is quite jarring to shift from project to project and also undermines the author's core messaging – that they are applying for an architectural position, not a graphic design position. In some cases this may be merited, such as a professional application for a posting that has a range of tasks including extensive graphic design; however, this is rare and even less useful a strategy when applying for academic contexts.

A consistency in layout does not necessarily impose monotonous regularity. If anything, establishing a consistency in layout throughout a document only highlights the projects that deviate from the order. This can be used effectively both at the macro level of a document (such as emphasizing a final project or innovative personal work in the compilation of other projects) or even on a simple layout spread (where a single image may serve to punctuate an idea). Authors should remember that the human eye is quick to recognize patterns and when something is inconsistent with established patterns, it draws greater attention. Authors should consider capitalizing upon this in their layouts.

Legibility refers to how accessible the portfolio is. While initially legibility would refer to simply the ease with which an audience can read the text in a document, it also describes the clarity in the graphic communication of the imagery.

Architecture portfolios should keep text to a minimum; however, when it is used, it should convey information that is not readily conveyed in the imagery. This does not, however, give authors license to use overtly complex language to describe their work. If an audience needs to read any sentence more than once in a portfolio, it is a failure in communication. It is either too convoluted, verbose, or tangential to the project. Text that is concise and direct in a portfolio is greatly appreciated. To spend five seconds reading a sentence should merit the same level of impact as looking at an image for the same amount of time. If it does not, then the legibility, regardless of font size or text length, is not present.

Legibility of imagery is determined by its clarity and conveyance. Similar to its text counterparts, imagery in layouts can neither be too small nor too vacuous. On one end of the spectrum there are layouts that attempt to cram over a dozen images on a page (see Figure 4.1.2), whereupon none of them clearly showcase the design work, while on the other end, layout may consist of a two page spread of a single parti sketch (Figure 4.1.3) or a satellite view of a building so far away that the actual project is the size of a dime on the page. These examples all highlight the way imagery content may be compromised by layout decisions. It is also quite difficult to read imagery when it is set atop of either a background that is too dark or too light. Occasionally, authors will create layouts where night renderings are presented on equally dark layout backgrounds, which results in difficulty understanding both the imagery content and the author's design layout skills.

Imagery conveyance pertains to the messaging behind any graphics put into the portfolio. When considering portfolio layout, authors must be just as economical with imagery as they are with text. Images should not be simply included because they exist or are available; instead they should be included if they emphasize an alignment of skills or experiences with the audience. For example, an author from industry looking to shift to work for another firm

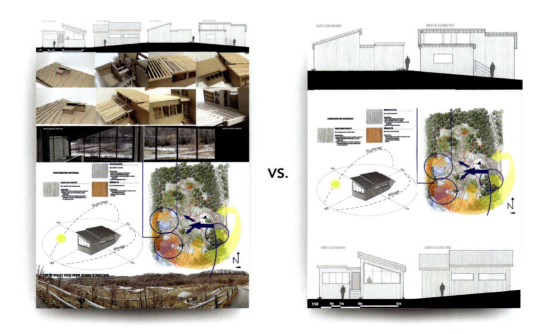

**4.1.2**
A juxtaposition between a dense layout and one that allows the images to be more easily read. *Cabin* by Destiny Megan Mendoza.

Source: Destiny Megan Mendoza, *Cabin*, 2017, Digital Image, 7082 x 4514, Toronto, Canada.

**4.1.3**
Axonometric view which does not immediately emphasize the design of the project. *King Street Art Cafe and Residence* by Kristen Sarmiento.

Source: Kristen Sarmiento, *King Street Art Cafe and Residence*, 2018, Digital Image, 1650 x 1183, Toronto, Canada.

CHAPTER 4.0 | HOW TO PRESENT YOURSELF IN A PORTFOLIO

would unlikely include every single floor plan of a 40-story condominium tower project; however, they may opt to showcase the site plan, ground floor, amenity level, typical floor level, and penthouse level instead. The elevations, sections, and renderings would provide enough information to understand the design while distilling the page real estate to showcase a handful of plans. This type of mentality frees up additional space that may provide opportunities in a layout to highlight unique components of a project that an author may wish to convey. For example, a student applying for a graduate architecture program may wish to set aside a long experiential section that conveys the narrative sequence through a design that goes beyond conventional orthographic drawings and renderings. By ensuring a layout scheme is flexible enough to ensure such imagery can be included in a portfolio is quite important (see Figure 4.1.4).

That a portfolio should prioritize imagery is tacit in its creation. Architecture is heavily governed by graphic communication, whether in sketches, drawings, computer renderings and simulations, or physical models. The discourse and production of architecture mandates the ability to not only think in spatial terms but to also conceive of and communicate it to others. A portfolio that does not prioritize imagery will not adequately convey this capacity. In an academic setting, portfolio imagery serves as the reassurance to admissions teams that a student

4.1.4
A layout which allows for flexibility in various sizes of imagery. *Parallel Divergence* by Ariel Cooke.

Source: Ariel Cooke, *Parallel Divergence*, 2016, Digital Image, 4846 x 2798, Philadelphia, USA.

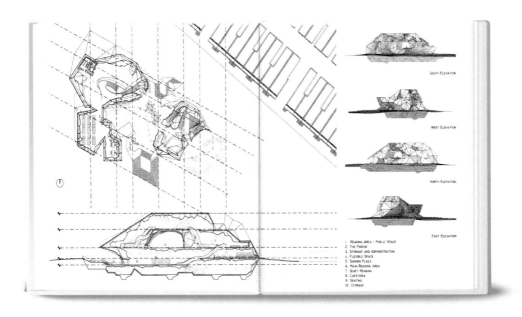

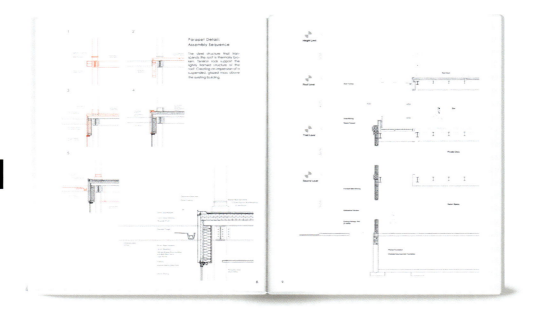

**4.1.5**
An over emphasis on the detailing in a portfolio spread without any design context. *Distillery* by Ernest Wong.

Source: Ernest Wong, *Distillery*, 2018, Digital Image, 4748 x 2865, Toronto, Canada.

is able to design and represent their ideas with comfort, such that they may transition into the next phase in their architectural education. For employers, imagery is necessary to qualitatively validate those skills and experiences listed in a résumé. Imagery in a layout must be impactful and should directly address either the unique features of the project or the author's prowess in its generation. If an image fails to accomplish either of these tasks, it is not a strong candidate to include in the layout of a project. Layouts should serve to emphasize the potency of the imagery whether in the scale of the image or its sequencing in the presentation. These are important decisions when organizing the presentation of imagery in a portfolio.

Beyond simply prioritization of imagery, strong portfolio layouts demonstrate a multifaceted diversity in imagery. This is in no way advocating that authors throw a cacophony of imagery in their portfolios, but strong layouts include a range of imagery in terms of type, scale, and visual appeal. To assemble a portfolio of solely orthographic drawings or BIM documentation might not be sufficient as it tends to depict the author solely as a draftsperson (see Figure 4.1.5). Similarly, to showcase only photorealistic renderings or advanced parametric modeling conveys an applicant's suitability as a visualization artist (Figure 4.1.6). In both cases, these are commodity

CHAPTER 4.0 | HOW TO PRESENT YOURSELF IN A PORTFOLIO

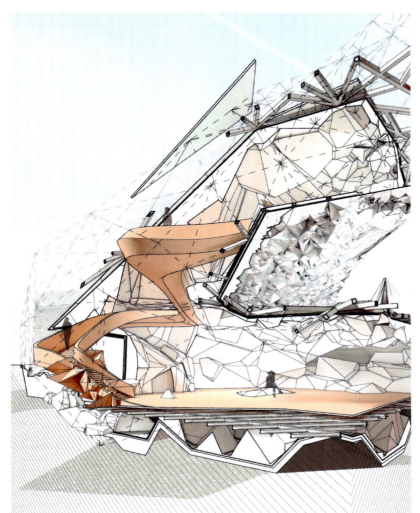

**4.1.6**
Complex geometry and intricate design work mandates some technical resolution to go beyond simple, fantastic imagery. *Parallel Divergence* by Ariel Cooke.

Source: Ariel Cooke, *Parallel Divergence*, 2016, Digital Image, 5100 x 6600, Philadelphia, USA.

skills that can be readily outsourced and do not showcase the synthesis of design capacity, technical acumen, and passion in architecture necessary in both academic and professional settings. Authors should take it upon themselves to ensure that there is a good balance among physical models, drawings, renderings, and any other types of imagery that highlight the robust range of creativity and production skill they offer potential employers and academics. The same procedure should be adopted for the types of projects that are included in a portfolio. Unless catering a portfolio for a very specific target audience, a portfolio should not dwell solely on one typology. Some prospective employees opt to cater their portfolios to only showcase

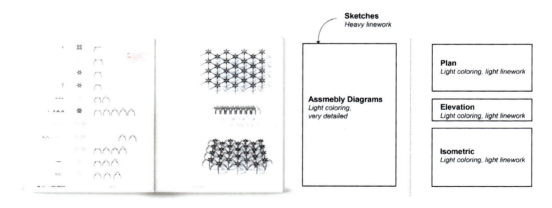

**4.1.7**
Sample Layout Configurations: *Precarious Medellin* by Han Dong; *A-Voidance* by Rachel Law; *Terrera Fabricata* by Sam Ghantous.

Source: Han Dong, *Precarious Medellin*, 2013, Digital Image, 4016 x 6142, Cambridge, Canada. Rachel Law, *A-Voidance*, 2016, Digital Image, 4016 x 6142, Toronto, Canada. Sam Ghantous, *Terrera Fabricata*, 2013, Digital Image, 4016 x 6142, Toronto, Canada.

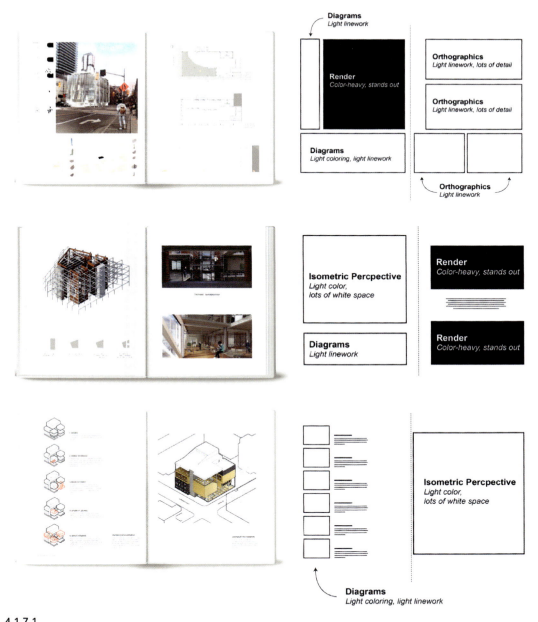

**4.1.7.1**
*TCA* by Shengnan Gao. *Unfolded Ribbon* by Jeff Jang. *Idea ++* by Ruslan Ivanytskyy.

Source: Shengnan Gao, *TCA*, 2017, Digital Image, 4016 x 6142, Toronto, Canada. Jeff Jang, *Unfolded Ribbon*, 2016, Digital Image, 4016 x 6142, Toronto, Canada. Ruslan Ivanytskyy, *Idea ++*, 2015, Digital Image, 4016 x 6142, Toronto, Canada.

multiunit residential projects, which is unfortunately challenging for the audience to discern when one project starts and another begins. Even the best layouts cannot fix such a scenario.

The diversity of imagery is not simply isolated to content. Authors should feel comfortable creating a layout that addresses images of variable size and proportions. A strong layout should be able to engage long, horizontal sectional drawings of transit stations that spread across two pages, through to slender, vertical elevations of office tower perspectives, while at the same time being able to accommodate square, proportioned imagery for diagrams and text blocks. Another important consideration when curating imagery in a portfolio layout is the saturation and color density. It is often off-putting to open a portfolio with a white background with a constellation of simple, black on white orthographic drawings apparently floating haphazardly on the page. While a structured layout template may have been used, the white background of the imagery with the white background committed at least two errors: the layout design was not clearly articulated and uninspired, and the compilation of solely plain orthographic drawings present the author as a draftsperson. To remedy this type of situation, authors must consider the prospect of using a range of image types including perspectives and conventional orthographic drawings on a layout such that there is a diversity of imagery to engage the audience. This also allows larger, darker images such as perspectives to anchor layouts so that drawings do not seem to be indiscriminately placed on the page.

The final component of a strong layout is ultimately the successful alignment with the needs of an author's audience. Portfolios should cater to their targeted audience. This does not mean that authors should agonizingly toil away for weeks at customizing every single portfolio, but instead, if a master portfolio of work were kept, an author could curate the content and determine which projects would suit that audience best. For example, a recent graduate may wish to apply for a smaller architecture firm specializing in single residential work. By selecting and emphasizing pieces that could align with the firm such as a modest cabin, a treehouse, and housing competition entry, the author would showcase her ability to address that scale of work. She could still include other larger-scale studio projects such as a multiunit youth shelter or an art school to showcase other skills, but should ensure that the projects that would resonate with the smaller firm are punctuated and elaborated upon in the document. If the same student were to apply for a larger firm

CHAPTER 4.0 | HOW TO PRESENT YOURSELF IN A PORTFOLIO

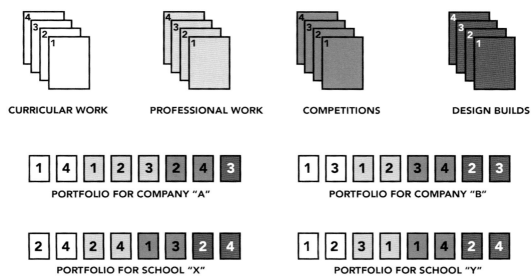

4.1.8
Illustration of how a master volume of projects can be used to create different portfolios that cater towards different firms and schools.

that might never undertake small-scale residential projects, the student could easily pivot and assemble a portfolio using the same content but rearrange the portfolio to emphasize the relevant work (Figure 4.1.8). This could mean including more drawings and technical documentation on account of the scale and scope of work that would resonate with an employer engaged with that range of projects.

As mentioned earlier, some firms have a range of responsibilities, which may include duties pertaining to graphic design and layout. In those instances, an extra level of care should be placed in crafting the document to showcase an author's strength in that capacity. Occasionally, authors may be tempted to emulate the graphic style of a firm or even academic unit to demonstrate some level of admiration, research, or capability. This should be discouraged, as very rarely is this successful. If anything, it only has the potential for negative perceptions (e.g., the author has stalking tendencies or is simply only capable of copying others). Your audience knows what they are and what they want, your portfolio's layout should highlight your complementarity not your copying capacity.

**Imagery**

Although this book is neither focusing upon layout or imagery, it is worthwhile to explain the perspective of potential audiences in order to understand what strategies are appropriate. As a preface to this section, it should be tacit that authors should ensure imagery is their own (or at the very least used with team members' permission) and not misrepresentational (for example, employees will often put renderings of a project in their portfolio despite only working on contract documents that are created at completely different stages of a project). It is also understood that screenshots of software are rarely very useful in a portfolio. If catering a portfolio, what value is raised by showing screenshots of software that employers and educators see every day? While procedural imagery may be useful in emphasizing key requirements in job descriptions, it is rarely useful to place generic imagery as filler in a portfolio.

It is quite frustrating for authors and audiences alike when an incredible effort has been put into interesting work only to have imagery compromised on account of a discrepancy between what is onscreen and what is printed in hardcopy. In such instances, it is recommended that authors consider printing a baseline line test sheet with samples of line weights, hatches, text, and colors (see Figure 4.1.9). These usually

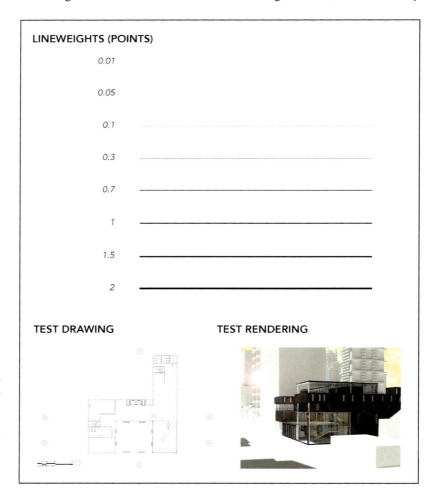

**4.1.9**
Sample figure sheet for test printing. *Homeless Shelter* by Destiny Megan Mendoza.

Source: Destiny Megan Mendoza, *Homeless Shelter*, 2018, Digital Image, 1962 x 2331, Toronto, Canada.

consist of a line weight sampler, a drawing, and a dark and light rendering on a single sheet that authors may use for calibration based upon the range of printing capacities at their disposal. To print out a test sample sheet on a printer and adjust file settings before printing out an entire document could save a great deal of money.

Drawings should follow basic drawing conventions. Faint or exaggerated line weights compromise legibility and demonstrate ignorance on using the basic language of architecture. It is difficult to read drawings when on a full sheet, let alone a letter-sized portfolio, so it is always recommended to test out line weights both on screen and in print. Depending on the screen resolution and anti-aliasing issues, occasionally line work in renderings is inconsistent or broken; however, this situation is becoming the rarity as displays on both desktop and mobile platforms are constantly enhancing resolution. In print, line work that is scaled down either disintegrates or dramatically thins out on a page.

As articulated earlier regarding layouts, there should be a diversity and hierarchy of imagery. Key to this is to ensure that portfolio authors should essentially look at any given layout spread and recognize what image is prioritized and if it aligns with audience needs. To have a dozen small images, regardless of the level of photorealism or attention to detail within them, is quite counterproductive as any one of them could have been made larger for the audience to focus on. To read a two-page spread in a portfolio with one dominant image, such as a perspective that quickly conveys the context, scale, and design of a project followed by a couple of orthographic drawings such as a ground plan and a section, followed by a supplemental interior perspective, may prove to be more than enough in succinctly presenting the fundamental ideas behind a project. Although this is not a default template to work with, it does not overwhelm its audience and provides great legibility on the page. Prioritization should

4.1.10
Unnecessary representation of simplistic evolution of the massing. *Toronto Architecture Center* by Monika Mitic.

Source: Monika Mitic, *Toronto Architecture Center*, 2017, Digital Image, 4657 x 1664, Toronto, Canada.

also be made on communication clarity and audience alignment. It is common to find in architecture student portfolios a strange fascination with inserting parti sketches or models that appear to be post-rationalized and overwhelm more than half a page in their document.

At the other end of the spectrum, photorealism in visualization of design work is equally dangerous. With software progressively increasing accessibility and output quality, photorealistic imagery is essentially a commodity in portfolios. Combined with the global connectivity and ease of outsourcing visualization tasks, photorealistic rendering is subservient to architectural skills. While it is important to demonstrate this capacity, authors are reminded that they are creating portfolios showcasing architectural capability, as opposed to their visual effects prowess. The degree to which demonstrated visualization skill is prioritized in industry is variable (as firms of all scales are capable of outsourcing or retaining these services in-house) and as such, authors should investigate what paradigm a potential employer uses. Applicants to academic institutions should especially be wary of reliance on photorealism as educators are often skeptical of an applicant's potential when there seems to be a prioritization of photorealism over design excellence. They are not

4.1.11
Photorealistic imagery is not needed for potent design conveyance. *MSc. ARCH GRADUATION THESIS* by Ailsa Craigen.

Source: Ailsa Craigen, *MSc. ARCH GRADUATION THESIS*, 2018, 9449 x 6125, Digital Image, Delft, Netherlands.

CHAPTER 4.0 | HOW TO PRESENT YOURSELF IN A PORTFOLIO

mutually exclusive; however, architectural educators and professionals alike are able to see beyond the montaged people, downloaded furnishings, parametrically driven foliage, and manipulated lighting to quickly conclude that an architectural proposal is simply a poorly proportioned box.

Authors must ensure imagery articulates the design intention and does not necessarily serve as clichéd marketing renderings (although in professional settings this may be a component of a job description). The creativity both in the project and its presentation are critical to good imagery in a portfolio. With the latter, as described already, straying from the photorealistic or market-driven imagery is an opportunity to project individual aesthetic sensibilities. While there are conventions behind orthographic drawings, there are stylistic nuances that designers put behind their drawings and even more so in their three-dimensional drawings. A Frank Lloyd Wright perspective (even if drawn by an apprentice) or a Lebbeus Woods rendering are not readily identifiable by formal stylistic tropes, but instead they are characterized by their respective consistent representational techniques.

Some projects lend themselves to imagery that is not conventionally used in architectural contexts. Such images are often welcome in a portfolio as they serve to break the monotony and pacing. This is especially useful in more investigative projects, where authors may prioritize other

**4.1.12**
Effective diagram displaying the design evolution. *Bodies of Water* by Yekaterina Korotayeva.

Source: Yekaterina Korotayeva, *Bodies of Water*, 2019, Digital Image, 12000 x 8100, Toronto, Canada.

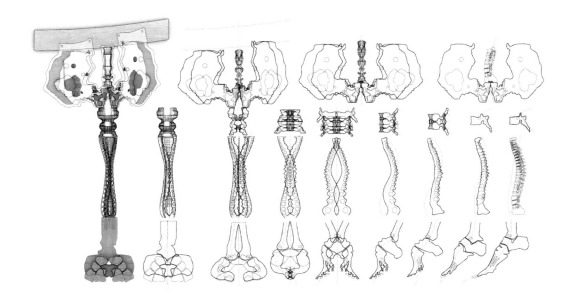

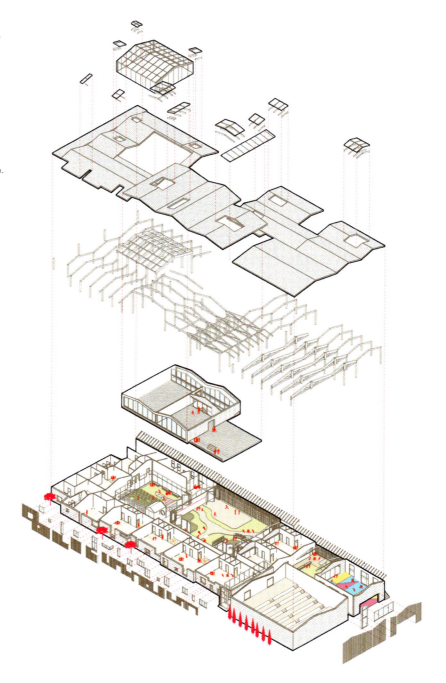

**4.1.13**
A diagram of structure in a heavy timber construction project. *Timber Competition* by Julianne Guevara, Jimmy Hung and Ernest Wong.

Source: Ernest Wong et al., *Timber Competition*, 2019, Digital Image, 1367 x 1772, Toronto, Canada.

dimensions of a design such as experimental fabrication techniques or experiential qualities. To showcase these types of works not only impacts pacing and serves as an outlet to highlight stylistic differences, but also allows authors to emphasize their points of differentiation. Individuals applying within an academic context may wish to highlight their research potential through process imagery of their works, whereas in professional instances, an author may emphasize their familiarity with designing for elderly populations by using a suite of imagery focused upon geriatric experience in a building. In both examples, there is often a requirement for supplemental diagramming in order to convey concepts that require greater explanation without inundating an audience with text. Diagrams are invaluable in a portfolio. Once again, these would be uniquely stylized by individual authors; however, they must be legible and accessible. Diagrams only have value when they convey the intention effectively. It may be worthwhile to investigate diagrams in other portfolios or even quickly search other disciplines such as graphic design or technical illustration to find appropriate precedents to integrate.

Imagery is the critical determinant in a portfolio. Without imagery, a portfolio becomes at best a glorified CV. To have images of work is not enough. The potency of imagery in a portfolio extends beyond adherence to conventions and photorealism. Overt facets of portfolio graphics such as process imagery or unconventional diagramming are often kept in mind as authors create their portfolios; however, more passive graphic components such as layout and aesthetic consistency also have an incredible bearing on the way portfolios are received by all audiences.

## 4.2 TEXT

Text should be kept legible, minimal, and impactful. The imagery should speak for itself. There is no point in putting text in a portfolio if it is not meant to be read. If there is a need to elaborate upon a project for than more than two sentences, one of three issues has emerged: the imagery is flawed, the project was inappropriate for the portfolio altogether, or the author is unable to succinctly present their ideas.

While it may be tempting to present a short manifesto outlining the design intention, programming, or parameters, typically audiences are able to distill most of these criteria from the accompanying imagery. Text addresses the gaps imagery may create. Typically a project title presents the typology while conventional drawings and imagery convey other design intentions and constraints. Often, text is successful where explanation may be required as imagery might not convey components of the design such as the ephemeral, experiential, or procedural. For example, a student may have designed a multidisciplinary arts college with the intention of using atria as physical separations, with visual connections among disciplines. While this intention may be discerned from the imagery, the text serves to focus the audience's attention on the efforts made by the author in the project's design. For professional portfolios, there are often stakeholder parameters such as density targets, adoption of a new technology (such as AI-driven building automation), or demographic factors (such as low income or elderly populations) which may not overtly be shown in the project imagery. Similarly, experimentation or integration of new processes may be worth mentioning in the text if it is not readily articulated in the imagery. An interactive installation piece may have a range of responses (from lighting patterns to movement) or be reliant upon a designer's nascent use of coding and physical computing, which in both cases would not always be clear in imagery alone. Aside from these instances, text should not punctuate a portfolio.

As with layout and imagery, text should be consistent throughout the portfolio. Authors should consider a hierarchy for text such as headings, body text, and annotations that visually work well with each other. Opinions on a candidate's design capacity are made based upon a myriad of factors including typographic decisions. As such, it is invaluable for authors to understand a fundamental awareness of typographic terms and strategies for a portfolio.

Fonts are a prime example of a small design decision that has a cascading impact in a portfolio. To use a mix of several fonts is inappropriate in an architecture portfolio. Instead, consider using changes in font size, weight, and underlining, or even color. When deciding on what font to use in a portfolio, consider the legibility and impression it has. Sans-serif fonts such as Arial or Helvetica are clean and legible for titles and short bodies of text whereas serif-based fonts such as Times New Roman or Lucida are traditionally easier to read in large blocks of text. Fonts also tend to leave an impression with an audience whether consciously or not; the use of default software fonts such as Calibri or Times might signal to an audience that the author really did not care or was not aware of the design impact font has. At the same

## Sans-Serif Font
*Very clean look and reads well on screens.*
Rather than focusing on the final product or design, this design school campus celebrates the students' process and education. The building aims to encourage students to make mistakes, be innovative and think outside the box.

## Serif Font
*Works well for blocks of text because the serif on the letters guides the eye across the page.*

Rather than focusing on the final product or design, this design school campus celebrates the students' process and education. The building aims to encourage students to make mistakes, be innovative and think outside the box.

## Decorative Font
*Comes across as unprofessional.*
Rather than focusing on the final product or design, this design school campus celebrates the students' process and education. The building aims to encourage students to make mistakes, be innovative and think outside the box.

## Script Font
*Difficult to read.*

*Rather than focusing on the final product or design, this design school campus celebrates the students' process and education. The building aims to encourage students to make mistakes, be innovative and think outside the box.*

## Geometric Font
*Very bold and competes with the imagery, which should be the focus.*

**Rather than focusing on the final product or design, this design school campus celebrates the students' process and education. The building aims to encourage students to make mistakes, be innovative and think outside the box.**

time, deliberate use of kitschy fonts (such as Comic Sans or Impact) or overly stylized fonts (such as Script or Blueprint) undermines the prospect of academic and professional audiences from taking the work seriously. Regarding font size, the general starting point for text is to use a conventional font at 12 pt for standard text and 10 pt for any annotations (including callouts and labels on drawings) and then shift up or down size based upon the font and text parameters.

*Tracking* is the standard space between characters whereas *kerning* is the specific space between two characters that often overrides tracking spacing to maintain legibility. This is why the word "Architecture" takes up less space than the word "Unquenchable" even though both are 12-letter

**4.2.1**
Samples of font types and uses.

## THE ARCHITECTURE PORTFOLIO GUIDEBOOK

**4.2.2**
Comparison of different
trackings of text.

# Typography

*Tracking set to 0.*

# Typography

*Tracking set to 100.*

# Typography

*Tracking set to 150.*

# Typography

*Tracking set to 200.*

words. The relationships between the letters in the latter are quite generous and consistent whereas in the former, the spaces on either side of the letter 'i' are reduced. *Leading* is the space between lines in a paragraph; *alignment* is whether or not the text is anchored to the left, right, or centered. Rarely is the justified alignment very useful in a portfolio as it creates irregular spaces between words in the interest of bringing characters to the boundaries. As tempting as it might be for authors to use unique fonts in order to align with their overarching portfolio style parameters, it is highly recommended that they test the tracking and kerning between characters in order to not disrupt legibility.

The measure (the length of a line of text) should reinforce legibility rather than fatigue or frustrate the audience. While there are some preordained parameters (such as the Robert Bringhurst formula) for text measure that are used in typography, the key is for text to not run horizontally too long in a row but also not too thin for a text column to only be three words across.

Another typographic portfolio tactic is to avoid *widows* and *orphans* as they often compromise layout. Widows are the dangling words that run over to the next line at the end of a paragraph whereas orphans are the dangling words that run over from one column or page to another. Wherever possible, revising the text is the best solution; however, adjusting font type, sizing, spacing, and measure length are options, although they may be distracting when read by the audience. As with any component of a layout, authors must keep in mind that the human

Rather than focusing on the final product or design, this design school campus celebrates the students' process and education. Aimed to encourage students to make mistakes, be innovative and think outside the box, the architecture of the building showcases studios where students work rather than galleries.

← **Widow**
*One or two words on an additional line.*

Rather than focusing on the final product or design, this design school campus celebrates the students' process and education. Aimed to encourage students to make mistakes, be innovative and think outside the box, the architecture of the building showcases studios where students work rather than galleries.

← **Hyphenation**
*One word spread over two lines.*

Rather than focusing on the final product or design, this design school campus celebrates the students' process and education. Aimed to encourage students to make mistakes, be innovative and think outside the box, the architecture of the building showcases studios where

students work rather than galleries.

← **Orphan**
*One or two words in an additional column or page.*

**4.2.3**
Illustration of various text justification mistakes.

**4.2.4**
Comparison of font legibility on different backgrounds. *A-Voidance* by Rachel Law.

Source: Rachel Law, *A-Voidance*, 2016, Digital Image, 2225 x 528, Toronto, Canada.

THE ARCHITECTURE PORTFOLIO GUIDEBOOK

**Title** ← Larger size, bold, jumps out at reader

*Subtitle* ← Offers additional information, less bold

**Label**  **Label**  **Label** ← Smaller size, should not stand out from page

Body  Body  Body ← Smaller, easily readable in paragraphs

**15 Point font**
*Very large, overpowering.*

**12 Point font**
*Legible, standard.*

**8 Point font**
*Very small, could be illegible to older readers.*

**4.2.5**
Comparison of text size.

**15 Point font**
*Very large, overpowering.*

**12 Point font**
*Legible, standard.*

**8 Point font**
*Very small, could be illegible to older readers.*

Rather than focusing on the final product or design, this design school campus celebrates the students' process and education.

Rather than focusing on the final product or design, this design school campus celebrates the students' process and education. Aimed to motivate students to make mistakes, be innovative and think outside the box, the architecture of the building showcases studios where students work rather than galleries.

Rather than focusing on the final product or design, this design school campus celebrates the students' process and education. Aimed to motivate students to make mistakes, be innovative and think outside the box, the architecture of the building showcases studios where students work rather than galleries.

**4.2.6**
Sample of text hierarchy.

eye is quick to identify patterns and consistency; because of this, it is just as quick at noticing anomalies and errors.

Clarity is a priority over creativity in layout. While the focus of the portfolio is on imagery, text is often required to supplement the audience's understanding of work. If text is present, it must make an impact. To have text in a portfolio only to have it lost in the background image or a gradient of colors reflects a lack of basic design skills. Establishing a strong contrast, such as black text on white background, is far more legible and less distracting than, for example, red text on a green background. The same rule applies for text atop imagery. Wherever possible, text should be placed over a solid, consistent tone that is a contrasting color to the background image. Where this might not be possible, the annotation or text could be placed below the image or boxed in a discrete frame atop the image.

Given all the nuances and features of typography, there is a simple rule for its presentation: If text is present, it must be legible, especially in a

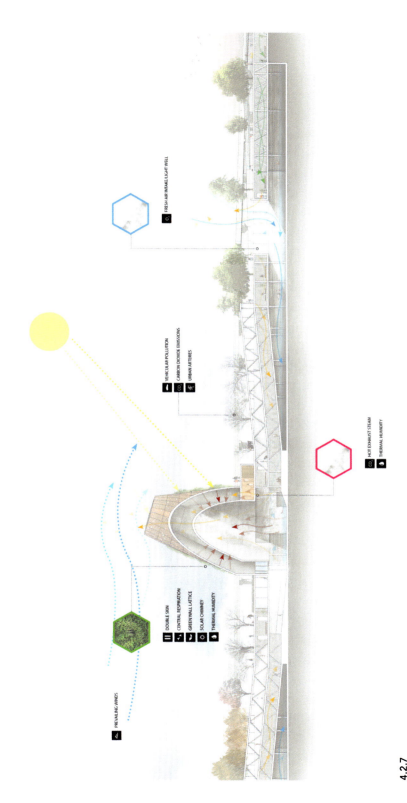

**4.2.7**
Image showcasing the air circulation within a design. *Adult Center* by Kevin Pu.
Source: Kevin Pu, *Adult Center*, 2011, Digital Image, 6128 x 2916, Toronto, Canada.

hardcopy portfolio as there is no ability to digitally zoom into the document. Wasting space to describe in text what imagery conveys better simply compromises the size and legibility of other parts of a portfolio.

While text should be kept to a minimum, didactic elements such as the name of a project, its site, when it was done, its context (if professional, the name of the firm that the work was done under and if academic, the year or term the project was submitted) are the standard components to include for a project.

While the imagery of orthographic drawings must be legible as described already, key tags such as where sections or details are taken must especially be visible and labeled appropriately on corresponding images. It is extremely frustrating for an audience to look at incredibly complex and beautiful building sections only to struggle to essentially guess where the sections are taken from in a plan. Similarly, while the author may be aware of the ordering of the floor plans in a design, it is imperative for them to label which floor is presented on the page. Text on conventional drawings such as room names on plans or assemblies in wall sections must be legible. It is lazy and counterproductive to simply scale down drawings with text labels in order to fit a sheet size, only to completely undermine its value on account of poor legibility. In such instances, as one would with line weights on a drawing, it is worth the effort to change the font size to accommodate the reduced sheet size.

Annotations are also important for imagery especially if they are not conventional drawings. Images that are not orthographic projections need labels. Perspectives, axonometrics, diagrams, and parti sketches should all generally have labels as it is extremely difficult for an audience to guess as to where certain views are taken from and in some cases, what the images actually represent. Like their conventional counterparts, text must be legible; however, there may be additional text to support the messaging, such as indications of energy or circulation flows or variable configurations. Combined with strong graphics, the ideas presented in these images are quite enticing and powerful. For many projects that explore new technologies or innovative design strategies, the annotations on these non-orthographic drawings must be concise and legible as they must clearly articulate ideas that may not be familiar to the audience. Whether showcasing the hypothetical systems at play for an "air filtration building" in an academic setting or explaining complex levels of circulation of a public library to a general audience in a professional setting, a level of discretion and care must be taken when publishing these types of drawings with text.

Although often neglected in portfolios, it is worth briefly mentioning the value of page numbering. It might be stylistically a taboo, but in an increasingly globalized world where follow-up interviews are completed via teleconferencing, it is often helpful for parties to quickly reference work by keying specific pages. Some layouts have overt integration of page numbering in their templates, which are great for portfolios that are able to adhere to such a navigable and intuitive interfaces.

## 4.3 INTERACTIVE MEDIA

Online portfolios are the standard for many professional applications, at the very least they provide a first glimpse into a candidate's work before follow-up interviews, and are gradually becoming commonplace in academic submissions as well. Online platforms provide a diversity of media for audiences to better understand an author's design and technical capacity.

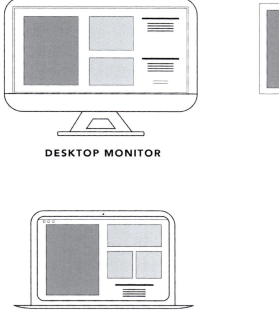

4.3.1
An applicant must keep in mind that the legibility of a portfolio depends on the medium of presentation and the device on which the content is viewed.

There are many online services that serve as a platform for hosting online documents such as portfolios. As PDFs have become an evolving standard for online documents, it comes as no surprise that these online platforms have come to such prominence. These websites are often free, intuitive, and provide a modest level of distribution controls such as permission controls and user. Unfortunately, they also are often supported by online advertisements, optimally display at lower resolutions, and are occasionally unstable on account of their presentation via the technical limitations of a web browser. A note of caution regarding sending PDF portfolios is that file size and intention (including number of projects and resolution of imagery) will often be limited by technology. Whether in correspondence or in display, one must realize the limitation of PDFs. If a PDF portfolio were emailed, it had better be an abbreviated sampler as opposed to a large file with low resolution imagery. While email infrastructures are capable of handling large file sizes, it is extremely off-putting for hiring managers and program administrators to have their accounts clogged with gigabytes of files. Anything larger than 10 MB is best hosted online and linked for later downloading, viewing, and correspondence. Another challenge with PDFs is the display of the medium. While most PDF portfolios are viewed on reasonably sized screens, often they are viewed on screens that are smaller than what would be printed (e.g., laptops or tablets). For example, a portfolio may be formatted for an 11" ×17" tabloid sheet but clearly would have diminished value if viewed on a 10" screen.

Although not quite a conventional linear portfolio, many designers have also opted to host their content as a website. The benefits to creating a portfolio website include the great flexibility in visualization, the range of media presentable, and the high audience accessibility. While at the turn of the 21st century websites were onerous endeavors requiring a level of IT acumen to simply place images and text on a screen, contemporary designers now have a very diverse range of website services that offer an incredibly powerful toolset with an equally user-friendly interface. While these options are quite accessible and provide a diversity of media, they graphically do not provide as many options as a conventional PDF on account of default templates, style sheets, and limitations on browsers.

Regardless of the online platform, whether website, PDF, or something altogether new, interactive content is ever-evolving and serves as a channel to enhance audience engagement and understanding of a project. From the cyclical adoption of virtual reality to the more conventional use of videos and animations in portfolios, portfolio authors have as many methods of design output as they have platforms for their creation. Rather than examining technologies that may quickly date this book, a few key strategies must be considered when adopting new, interactive media on digital portfolios. Three core questions authors must ask themselves when embarking on using a digital medium, specifically those that go beyond the static image, would be whether the medium a) complements the project, b) is seamless and integrated, and c) is accessible.

The first question pertains to whether or not the medium serves to distract or dilute an audience's attention. In some instances, it is awkward to have a design of a kindergarten with an aerial animation where the camera flies and hovers around the building as though it were in a surveillance drone. On one level, the animation distracts the audience from the designer's sensitivities to the design of the interior spaces, and at the same time, dilutes the impact of this level of consideration when presented at such a strange perspective. If this type of medium were to be used, it may have been better presented from a child's vantage point and brought slowly through the entry and classrooms to adequately present the Hertzberger-level of design consideration in the project. The second question considers whether the audience is taken out (literally or figuratively) of the portfolio of work. For example, an applicant's professional portfolio may have a design for an adaptive reuse renovation project with a link to a web documentary based upon the historic relevance of the original building. Although this is related to the project, it violates the first condition of distracting from the core project. Additionally, the linkage takes the audience out of the portfolio to a website with the video, which makes for a cumbersome engagement with the design. In many cases, a video such as a time lapse or phasing animation would be far more useful in conveying the project intentions. Better yet, if the video were either integrated into the portfolio document or website, the integration would ensure the content appropriately complemented the main imagery of the adaptive reuse project. Finally, interactive media in a portfolio should not require extra effort or time in order to remain accessible. A student may wish to include an augmented reality component in their portfolio; however, there are a couple of key challenges with this medium. First, the user must likely download additional software to properly browse the content and, worse still, the audience might not be comfortable or familiar with the medium. For every additional step required to view portfolio content, there is a proportional decrease in an audience's engagement, if not causing outright frustration and thereby losing them altogether.

As technologies increasingly become seamless and more accessible, other new media emerge to provide even more robust depth to design work. While integrating industry standard platforms is the safest approach, new media can certainly be integrated depending upon the audience's comfort with the three components of successful interactive media: complementarity, seamless integration, and accessibility of content.

# CHAPTER 5.0

## PORTFOLIO PREPARATION: TARGETING AN AUDIENCE

**5.1** Pacing     135

**5.2** Passing the 30-Second Flip Test: Impression, Expression, and Retention     140

**5.3** Feedback and Refinement     149

# CHAPTER 5.0

# External Perspectives

## HOW SHOULD APPLICANTS DEMONSTRATE THEIR DIVERSITY AND RANGE OF INNOVATION AND CREATIVITY IN THEIR PORTFOLIOS?

RD: I want to make sure they're avoiding the scattershot approach of trying to be everything to everyone. I want to make sure they edit themselves or better yet have a trusted friend, classmate, or colleague make suggestions as to what should be left out and what should remain. Sometimes we are terrible judges of our own work. There may also be a couple of versions of the portfolio, so that they can customize versions based on the type of firms or the school programs that they're interested in. It probably doesn't make sense, for example, to show a portfolio of vacation homes if you want to work for SOM.

GS: We measure how skillful that person is or how in-depth they think about different things, but when you get to the office, we're not looking for somebody who can take a project and be creative and make it their own thing because that just wouldn't fly in our office. It's an office where the principal architect is the designer and we support them. We know their language and their thinking, and in the end it's their answers. We're also looking for brilliant minds, of course, anybody skilled, but it only goes so far.

## WHAT ARE SOME CLICHÉS OR ISSUES THAT YOU FIND DETRACT FROM AN APPLICANT'S PORTFOLIO?

BK: A badly done drawing, where the line work is poor, and where the composition is badly done. And when there is too much emphasis on "Me! Me! Me!"

GS: I've seen nowadays a lot of the CVs, the skills are just little bar charts. Four out of five or five out of five. I don't know when people

CHAPTER 5.0 | PORTFOLIO PREPARATION

started score charts for themselves – I find that funny. Also the amount of text – when a blurb of text is too big it is too difficult to look at. There may be long descriptions but we really don't have the time to read in detail.

RD: The text in a portfolio is not just a brain dump about the project but actually says, "Here was a problem", and then "This is how I responded to it." So many actually created the problem/solution approach to the text that shows me how they think, how they might approach or tackle an assignment, I want to know – if they were to come on board – will they be able to do this for me as well? If it shows a meta level of thinking in a higher plane that leads me to think that this is something they would be able to apply to this project portfolio as part of the story, that reduces my risk in engaging them either as a student or as an employee.

PB: A pet peeve would be putting garbage in a portfolio because applicants feel as though they have to. Sometimes they think, "Oh, I need to show my first-year, second-year, and third-year work." Why is *everything* there? Also some people like to think they can get hired because they're artistic and put hand drawings and photographs at the end of a portfolio even though it has no role in our production and workflow. I really get antsy when I see stupid details; there are software packages you can pull exploded axonometrics of generic details like the footing. Great. I know half of the applicants have copy/pasted those and if you ask them, "Why is that there?", they cannot answer. Just don't put in the stupid details.

AB: A kind of deal-breaker is when people put in bad sketches.

NT: Poor image choices. Critically looking at the drawings again and editing from the perspective of what a drawing is actually saying communicates a lot about an applicant. If someone hasn't provided a section cut on a project engaging ideas about light and they have cut a section through no windows or no openings, that's a problem. It's not just about the fact that they didn't follow the convention, it shows they don't even understand what the convention should be doing to convey the information.

# THE ARCHITECTURE PORTFOLIO GUIDEBOOK

## IN AN INDUSTRY WHERE DIGITAL AND TECHNICAL SKILLS ARE BECOMING THE STANDARD, HOW IMPORTANT WOULD SHOWCASING MORE TRADITIONAL MEDIA BE IN A PORTFOLIO?

GS: A lot of people put all these flashy images, but there are still some people who present physical models. In our office, we still build quite a few for almost every project.

RD: You might be surprised to hear this, but I actually think sketching, painting, physical models are incredibly important. If I'm hiring them, I trust that they can pick up the technology on their own. They can learn the tools, especially if they have curiosity, what's otherwise referred to frequently as *grit*. If they've proven that they're motivated, curious and inquisitive, I have no concerns or doubts that they'll pick up the tools. I think it's much more important that they're able to sketch, hold conversations while sketching, and to think with physical working models.

## CHAPTER 5.0

# Portfolio Preparation: Targeting an Audience

### 5.1 PACING

Curation and judicious editing of content is critical to creating good pacing in a portfolio. An author should consider their portfolio as a narrative. As with any other storytelling medium, whether literature, music, or cinema, it is the variability and contrast among the content subdivisions that maintains audience interest. A song with all the verses in sequence followed by the refrain repeated several times at the end would make little sense, while a movie with all the dramatic scenes put at the front is just as bad. To simply present content in chronologies (e.g., first-year undergraduate studio work through to graduate thesis) or categories (e.g., models, renderings, technical imagery) without a sensitivity to pacing fails to showcase both basic design awareness and respect for the audience. At the very least, learn from what is successful in other media – start and end a portfolio with the best projects. Start on a high note and leave the audience with something memorable.

Unless explicitly mandated by audiences, portfolios are not chronologies of all the projects undertaken over the course of one's architectural education and professional experience. As a curated document, authors must ensure that projects in the portfolio are top-quality and cater to the key messaging intentions. Often students assembling portfolios feel compelled to create the document as a chronology of their work, which is not the optimum approach for a professional portfolio. Rarely is there a need to show every project done in school, let alone in chronological order. While some early projects

5.0
*Terra Fabricata* by [R]ed[U]x Lab.

Source: [R]ed[U]x Lab, *Terra Fabricata*, 2010, Digital Image, 3000 x 4000, Toronto, Canada.

5.1.1
Portfolio project ordering and pacing methods.

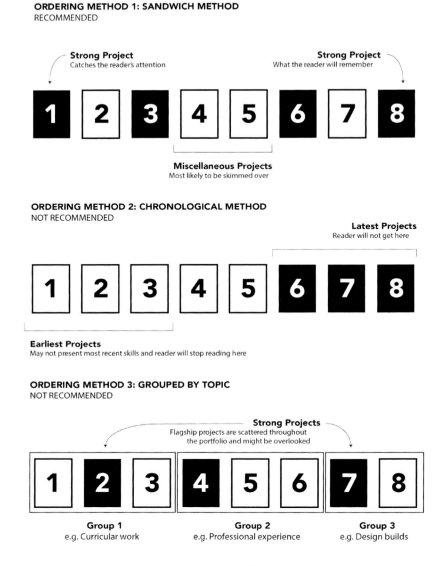

may be worth including, they should be updated in order to reflect greater acumen with visual communication tools and general technical knowledge. As mentioned earlier, audiences do not assume that projects are done years apart and they certainly do not give authors the benefit of excuses. For example, students often include undergraduate work that may lack representational strength or technical knowledge assuming that prospective employers know that these projects were done when the applicant was a freshman. This is not the case. If the portfolio is a compilation of one's greatest work for a current position, it should be reflective of their current capacities. As such, revisiting past projects may be required to provide a degree of consistency throughout the document.

For some emergent practitioners, the temptation is also to include all professional work ranging from drawing edits through to client renderings. This thorough exposition may be helpful in showcasing an ability to bring a project to reality, however it must be presented in a concise manner. Aside from the potential legality of sharing an entire suite of imagery with an external audience, the sheer volume of content would be overwhelming. In both academic and professional scenarios, authors must empathize with their audience on two levels: a) that the audience is already familiar with navigating similar content from their daily operations and b) that the audience is fatigued having gone through dozens of portfolios already. Aside from validating an applicant's demonstrated skills or experience, why would an audience want to pore through sheets of drawings similar to those they see all the time? Will dumping more of the same format and nature of content have any additional benefit? For these reasons alone, pacing is instrumental in maintaining audience interest by strategically sequencing work in the portfolio.

A pitfall for many authors is their assumption that they should solely focus on specific types of projects in their portfolio. For example, a recent graduate applying for employment with a firm lauded for its design work with multiunit residential buildings may feel compelled to only showcase residential projects or work that emulates that of the firm. Similarly, an applicant for graduate studies might feel only compelled to showcase academic work. While including such content is a good idea in both cases, doing so exclusively neither holds the audience's attention nor does it provide a full impression of what a candidate has to offer. To include a diversity of work has two key benefits. The first is the opportunity to demonstrate a familiarity with a range of project types and techniques that an employer or graduate program may consider useful for success. The second benefit is that demonstrating a diversity opens the possibility for an author to align with opportunities emergent with a potential employer or academic institution. For example, by showcasing work ranging from theaters to daycares, an applicant to the aforementioned multiunit residential firm may have greater success as the firm wishes to expand its portfolio into potential performance facilities. Applicants do not wish to be typecast and neither do employers and institutions.

Process and development are good to include in a portfolio but must be extremely concise. It is extremely frustrating to see pages of a portfolio wasted on unrefined, disparate, and illegible sketches and models, especially when the proportion of developmental material is similar to, if not greater than, imagery pertaining to the final product. In some instances such an approach is appropriate so long as there is a clear narrative that allows an audience to understand the intention. For example, a project that may have required a combination of extensive iterative parametric modeling and physical prototyping may merit imagery that highlights the author's design and technical skills involved during the developmental process. The imagery of the project, including renderings, drawings, and final outcome, may be kept to half the allocated space in a portfolio but what is equally valuable are the iterative and innovative methods in its development. Careful curation of the process imagery should communicate how the procedural exploration relates to the final product.

A specific warning should be for screenshots of software. Unless they demonstrate something uncommon in daily praxis or highlight an author's unique technical strengths, they are essentially filler. Screenshots of generic digital models or CAD interfaces are desperate, shallow attempts to show some level of technical skill. Worthwhile screenshots may include complex simulations or procedures that audiences may value such as strengths with advanced parametricism or multidimensional analyses.

When it comes to pacing, authors should feel confident in including non-academic or non-professional work. As mentioned earlier, extra-curricular projects, design competitions, and even personal design investigations are great at breaking up the pace of a portfolio. Self-initiated work is excellent as it provides the audience insights on an author's genuine interests, which may align with those of prospective employers or academic programs. These types of projects often are

5.1.2
A developmental process from concept to reality. *Tripix* by [R]ed[U]x Lab.

Source: [R]ed[U]x Lab, *Tripix*, 2019, Digital Image, 10092 × 2407, Toronto, Canada.

INITIAL SKETCHES

DIGITAL MODEL

PROTOTYPE

FINAL PRODUCT

also individually initiated, such as a competition or personal research project, which reflects a clarity on the role an individual played in the work exhibited in the portfolio.

A portfolio is more than a summary of a candidate's skills. One is neither simply good at design nor solely proficient with visualization skills. A portfolio author should have a range of skills that validates their capacity as an all-round strong candidate with excellent communication, collaboration, and critical thinking skills, all of which are instrumental to success in academic and professional contexts. When pacing the story arc of a portfolio, authors should also be mindful that, while their individual projects and showcase of experience are core to the document, they must also reaffirm a holistic message to their audience. For some, it is finding ways to demonstrate excellent experience in the industry or great project management capabilities, while others may opt to convey strong interpersonal acumen or innovative thinking. The portfolio serves as a platform to show one's potential as part of a specific community as opposed to simply one's capacity to complete tasks. In graduate studies, successful candidates are members of a class that share ideas and critically examine each other's work while in professional settings, collaboration and team chemistry are invaluable in getting through deadlines. Any visual

**5.1.3**
Sample of independent student research merging the computer science field with architecture. *Digital Sketchbook* by Sam Ghantous.

Source: Sam Ghantous, *Digital Sketchbook*, 2013, Digital Image, 5013 x 2907, Toronto, Canada.

5.1.4
Self-initiated research on two-way kerfing of wood. *Wood 3.0* by Filip Tisler.

Source: Filip Tisler, *Wood 3.0*, 2016, Physical Model, 1024 x 768, Toronto, Canada.

evidence of passion, multidisciplinarity, or simply personality in a portfolio goes well beyond the skills exhibited in its projects. Pacing is key to eliminate any monotony that would compromise this messaging. Instead, pacing is an invaluable tool to highlight skills, design approaches, specific projects, and even personality.

## 5.2 PASSING THE 30-SECOND FLIP TEST: IMPRESSION, EXPRESSION, AND RETENTION

Although weeks of work may have been invested into creating a portfolio, the unfortunate reality is that in many assessments, both academic and professional, the document will only be looked at briefly in order to process the volume of other candidates. For graduate school applications, a handful of students are selected from the hundreds (if not thousands) of applications. Perhaps more distressing is the number of applicants for a single placement within an architectural firm. While some institutions and employers invest more time poring through portfolios, it is still worthwhile to ensure a portfolio can convey its intent in an abbreviated timeframe. If portfolios are to be successful, they must effectively: a) leave a strong impression of the candidate, b) express an alignment with the organization's goals, and c) provide a clear component for retention.

CHAPTER 5.0 | PORTFOLIO PREPARATION

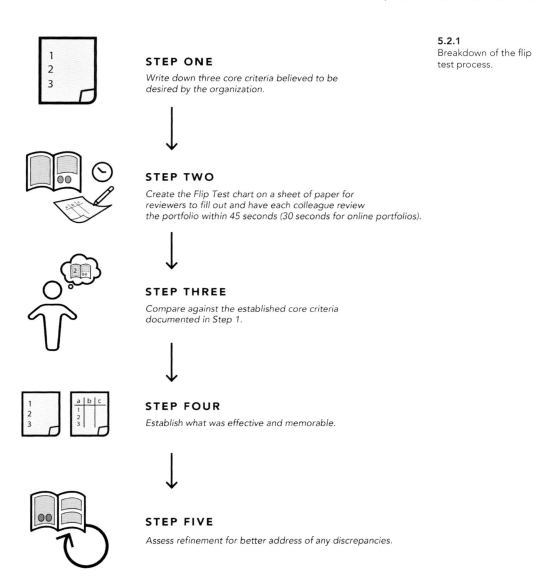

**5.2.1**
Breakdown of the flip test process.

The Flip Test is an excellent diagnostic tool for self-assessment and even better with external portfolio review and critique.

## Step 1: Write down three core criteria believed to be desired by the organization

This is a critical step as it establishes the framework for success.

With employment opportunities, this step should be clearly presented in a job description. Typically firms will explicitly state specific experience or skills that are required for successful candidates.

# THE ARCHITECTURE PORTFOLIO GUIDEBOOK

**Table 5.2.1**
A sample list of traits under various categories that an applicant may want in their portfolio.

| SKILLS | EXPERIENCE | INTERESTS | WORKPLACE FIT |
|---|---|---|---|
| Photorealistic rendering and animation | Previous work experience in the AEC industry | Midrise residential | Group worker |
| Advanced BIM | Design-build work | Infrastructure projects | Good time-management |
| Detailing | Graphic design and illustration | Building technologies | Sense of humor |

This may range from particular software packages and model making skills to previous work with a specific typology or scale of work such as installation art. As outlined in Chapter 4, the alignment between an employer's criteria and an applicant often goes beyond expertise and experience and may extend into other dimensions such as interpersonal "fit" with a company. Based upon an initial reading of the job description, applicants should understand the key traits demanded an employer.

Table 5.2.1 shows samples of different types of traits applicants may wish to focus on showcasing in their portfolios. Although this list is far from exhaustive, as any of these traits would be worthwhile, it would be important to select the traits based upon the job description to emphasize proper alignment.

For graduate programs, it would be worthwhile to initially at the very least visit their respective websites or pore over their materials to address desirable traits. These may be explicitly stated by faculty research groups or agendas such as digital fabrication or sustainable design. Unlike professional applications, many graduate programs may indirectly use this as a venue for applicants to identify what they see as an alignment between students' research interests and the resources within their institution such as faculty, research centers, or facilities. This will vary based upon the institution as well as the individual applicant's interests. Worse still is that often in graduate

CHAPTER 5.0 | PORTFOLIO PREPARATION

| SKILLS | EXPERIENCE | RESEARCH FOCUS |
| --- | --- | --- |
| Parametric design | Architectural intern | Interactive architecture |
| Design communication | Study or experience abroad | National identity in architecture |
| Teaching and research | Conference and publication record | Architectural resilience to climate change |

**Table 5.2.2**
A sample list of traits that one applying to a graduate program may want in their portfolio.

portfolios, institutions tend to set a page limit, which forces another layer of curation.

Again, Table 5.2.2 is simply a sample of different categories that would be relevant for architectural graduate studies. Unlike the professional application where candidates would specifically address criteria outlined in a job description, graduate programs are more open and it is better to address components in multiple categories that provide a clear alignment and independent initiative.

**Step 2: Create the Flip Test chart on a sheet of paper for reviewers to fill out and have each colleague review the portfolio within 45 seconds (30 seconds for online portfolios)**

On a separate sheet of paper, simply create three columns that outline the following categories: a) key traits presented, b) memorable project, and c) overall impression. This is essential as it effectively encapsulates what others synthesize as the messaging from a portfolio. If the messaging intentions outlined in Step 1 are not echoed by reviewers, then a reassessment of curation and expression in the portfolio must be performed.

The average time spent initially flipping through a physical portfolio is under 60 seconds and approximately 30 seconds for online documents. Regardless of medium, employers and graduate admissions committees must go through hundreds of portfolios to determine ideal candidates for their respective employment opportunities or academic placements, which means very little time is

THE ARCHITECTURE PORTFOLIO GUIDEBOOK

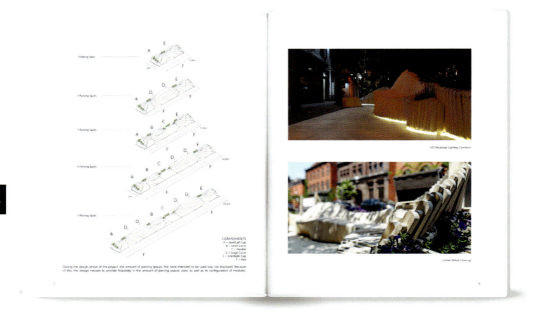

**5.2.2**
The presentation of this project emphasizes the technical considerations beyond the final product. *Parklet TO* by John Benner and [R]ed[U] x Lab.

Source: John Benner et al., *Parklet TO*, 2016, Digital Drawing, 4714 x 3156, Toronto, Canada.

spent going through each page extensively. As outlined in earlier sections of this chapter, imagery must be impactful, text kept to a minimum, layouts must be clear, and pacing must maintain a steady level of audience interest and engagement. All these strategies must be adopted in order to effectively reinforce a candidate's alignment capacity with a company or institution (see Figure 5.2.2).

Have a series of external reviewers assume the assessment role and independently fill the columns. The feedback should be drawn from an appropriate background and as candid as possible. This is elaborated upon at the end of this chapter (5.3 Feedback and Refinement). The ideal reviewer would be someone from the actual organization one would apply to. For professional applications, reviewers should include upper-year students (especially those with work experience), faculty, and people currently in industry, especially if they have any familiarity or affiliations with the desired firms. For those with aspirations for graduate studies, the portfolio review should certainly take the same approach; however, a focus on students currently enrolled in graduate studies (especially if they are in the program one seeks to gain admission into) and faculty would be invaluable.

## Step 3: Compare against the established core criteria documented in Step 1

After quickly performing a Flip Test (or better yet, several with a group of assessors), it is important to compare what the various reviewers understood as the key traits presented, the memorable project(s), and the overall impression of the portfolio. Strong portfolios will unsurprisingly demonstrate a match between anticipated core criteria and reviewer's assessments. Any significant discrepancy between the portfolio intentions and the assessors' responses should be considered a failure of the Flip Test. If a portfolio is unable to leave a distinctive memory with any particular project, it can be addressed by highlighting specific components of its presentation. If a portfolio cannot leave a strong impression, it may be a matter of adjusting the content and its presentation. Often, portfolios that come across as generic or uninspired hold a great deal of potency, however their presentation may have compromised it. Similarly, a failure to address an alignment with the key traits (the first column criteria) would be considered at best a generic, and at worst a weak portfolio.

For professional application, portfolios are focused predominantly on skill sets that provide support for a firm's productivity and success. Whether it is a candidate's technical skills as support to the production workflow or their experience with particular typologies, firms actively look for an applicant's ability to bring their ideas to reality. If there is ambiguity in reviewers' responses, applicants should explicitly inquire about the confusion. For example, one of the core criteria listed was "Advanced 3D modeling" but reviewers responded by stating "Rendering" or "Visualization" – although those criteria are related, they are not the same. If possible, clarification from reviewers would be invaluable in determining what the confusion was and how it could be remedied. In this example, the problem may have been that the renderings of the complicated 3D model were so photorealistic that the design was subverted by its presentation. A way to address this could potentially be creating supplemental imagery or diagrams that emphasize the complexity of the form that mandated "Advanced 3D modeling" skills.

Ideally, academic portfolios should pass the Flip Test; however, it is often difficult to project a strong, direct alignment with graduate pursuits. Although it may be possible to successfully present skills and experience, it is often a challenge to precisely present research interests on a topic that may not be fully investigated; after all, that is what graduate studies would facilitate. As it is difficult to provide precise support in a single project, the portfolio would benefit by showcasing a variety of projects at varying levels of refinement to best convey both a prolific and productive investigation and interest in a particular research topic.

### Step 4: Establish what was effective and memorable

A portfolio that leaves a good overall impression and is memorable for particularly noteworthy work is quite promising. Following the strategies presented in Chapter 3, each project should showcase a combination of creative design excellence and technical skill in its execution. This approach is an excellent method to ensure that the overall impression presented in the portfolio is both positive and aligns with the goals outlined by the organization. An additional strategy to develop potency in the portfolio is to ensure that it is memorable. Generic responses to strong portfolios often refer to the overall quality, whereas notable portfolios often have a key project that assessors can recall.

In professional pursuits, this distinctive capacity often lies in the remarkable creativity of a particular project or the level of development and depth showcased in a work. With the former, it is often a subjective criteria that may be lost on assessors. To succeed in showcasing distinctive creativity, it is imperative to understand a reviewer's mindset and background in order to present ideas that challenge or go beyond what would conventionally be done. For example, applying to an architecture firm with extensive ecologically sustainable design projects, a notable creative project that goes beyond conventional sustainable strategies (such as LEED guidelines) and adopts a different approach such as onsite biomass waste-to-energy concepts would be notable for a prospective employer. The innovation aligns with the reviewer's needs, showcases the applicant's skill set and awareness, and – on account of its innovation – proves to be a memorable component in the portfolio. Alternatively, if such investigations and innovations are not necessarily reflected in a project, it may be worthwhile to

CHAPTER 5.0 | PORTFOLIO PREPARATION

identify a strong project in the portfolio and showcase a high level of articulation and consideration beyond the conventional project presentation at a schematic design state. For example, an applicant may wish to select distillery museum design in their portfolio and supplement the work with diagrams, renderings, and details that showcase the design's flexibility to accommodate different types and scales of sporting events. Going beyond the conventional expectations of development in a project provides assessors a greater insight on applicants' ability to investigate design work with greater thoroughness and comprehensiveness.

For academic pursuits, once again there is a mandate to use the portfolio to not only present a strong overall impression of a candidate's aptitude and ability, but also project a sense of confidence in a candidate's ability to succeed in graduate studies. As graduate work is often a self-motivated exploration in research and innovation, portfolios must demonstrate both these facets. Often in an undergraduate portfolio, students have a few projects

5.2.3
A project that exhibits an understanding of detailing and program. *Condenser Distillery* by Jessica Gu.

Source: Jessica Gu, *Condenser Distillery*, 2017, Digital Drawing, 9518 x 7313, Toronto, Canada.

(whether from academia or industry) that allow them to explore their interests in graduate studies. Where possible, it is important to emphasize the increased level of development put into these projects. For example, a portfolio of an applicant interested in applying for graduate studies in parametric design in architecture should not only have projects showcasing this type of work, but should have a memorable project that examines a critical challenge that paradigm faces, such as resolution of design work via digital fabrication. Demonstrating engagement with research material and explicitly investigating innovative solutions make for both a strong impression, as well as creating confidence in a candidate's genuine interest and potential success in graduate studies with a particular institution.

### Step 5: Assess refinement for better address of any discrepancies

The first method of addressing discrepancies is to speak with the reviewers and understand the gaps between intention and expression in the portfolio. Based upon the expertise and experience they bring, their feedback will allow candidates to refine their portfolio work. In most instances the projects may require greater precision in presentation and curation. This might entail drawing attention to specific imagery or eliminating others. As described earlier, it is not mandated that applicants put every single drawing of a project in their portfolio. A common problem with portfolios is inundating audiences with complete drawing sets from landscape plans to construction details. Although these types of drawings are appropriate in certain applications, populating a portfolio with all that content dilutes the potency of the document. For example, in a professional application portfolio a candidate presenting a multiunit residential tower should present key plans such as the site, ground, podium, and typical residential plan and rely upon the 3D renderings and diagrams to convey the rest of the design.

Occasionally, there may be a need to supplement or add content. For example, in an academic portfolio, if the intention were to convey advanced digital fabrication, rather than showcasing a finalized, fabricated piece, it may be essential to showcase the steps in fabrication to highlight this knowledge and skill. Similarly, for a professional portfolio, a candidate that professes an ability to use BIM software may need to present comprehensive drawings from the software beyond simply 3D renderings of a design that would be inadequate in conveying an awareness of the robust features in that paradigm.

## 5.3 FEEDBACK AND REFINEMENT

Given that architectural praxis is built upon gaining critical, constructive feedback in the interest of refining a design, then that same mentality extends to the iterative production of a portfolio. As outlined in Chapter 2, each architecture firm and institution is different and likely requires a different portfolio that embraces a different positioning statement (however nuanced) for each application, as outlined earlier in this chapter. While an author may have a range of projects, skills, research interests, and experiences, they would consider invaluable in an application – it is imperative that others are able to provide feedback to refine and reinforce the document. Refinement is objectively implementing the feedback not to simply improve the portfolio, but to ensure it is focused on addressing the needs of a specific target audience. Strong and diverse content is great but an aligned focus is essential in a portfolio.

Strong feedback is core to good editing. It is too easy to suggest what else can be added into a portfolio; however, it is the insight to prioritize potency through reduction that is truly invaluable. From interviews with employers and academics from around the world, a consistent component of and necessity for strong portfolios is good editing. Content must be deliberate, succinct, and impactful. This means more than simply distilling design ideas to key representative imagery; it also necessitates a strong control over consistency and style. Where limitations such as page counts and display size impact what and how things may be presented, the inclusion of content must clearly reinforce messaging alignment. If it does not, it only detracts from an author's intent. While it is tempting to include developmental iterations of a project in a portfolio, it may undermine the preoccupation with final outputs in a professional portfolio, while developmental content in an academic portfolio may only serve as filler content that dilutes the resolution of the actual project.

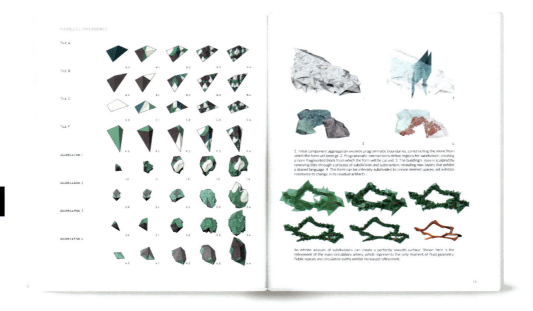

**5.3.1**
An example of how showcasing too much process can distract from the main purpose of the project. *Parallel Divergence* by Ariel Cooke.

Source: Ariel Cooke, *Parallel Divergence*, 2016, Digital Image, 4784 x 2962, Philadelphia, USA.

This is not to say that developmental work should be disregarded. In some instances, it can support an author's dexterity with specific skills an audience may be interested in or the thought process behind a design project. While some stakeholders require portfolios to include developmental work, authors must be aware of the limitations on defined requirements and variable parameters (such as audience attention span and needs). It is counterproductive to have a collection of postage stamp-sized developmental imagery on a page that ultimately reduces the potential size, and more importantly, impact of key imagery. The same may be said of simply placing imagery of the same type on a layout (see Figure 5.3.2). As editing is a critical component of portfolio production, it is important for authors to utilize and integrate appropriate resources to gain as much feedback for editing as possible. The same content has greater impact with feedback on layout and curation of imagery.

Resources for feedback range from colleagues to mentors. Just as with conventional architecture studio projects, each reviewer has a different perspective on one's portfolio and its alignment to their own sensibilities; and just like any studio review, one must be attuned to the value of their insights and how they may be reflected in any editions to the work. While it is perfectly understandable to have

CHAPTER 5.0 | PORTFOLIO PREPARATION

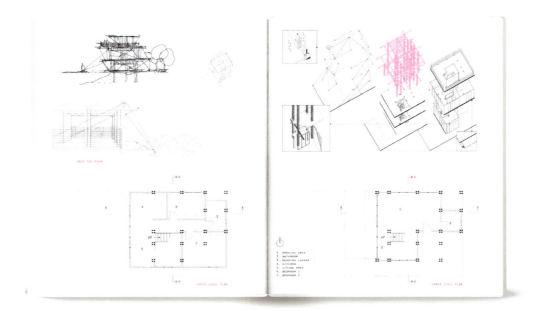

5.3.2
Spread before feedback was provided. *Cabin* by Shengyu Cai before feedback.

Source: Shengyu Cai, *Cabin*, 2015, Digital Image, 4775 x 3017, Toronto, Canada.

young architecture students ask any of their professors for feedback on their portfolios in pursuit of their first architecture job, the insights from a professor familiar with current industry demands or operating a practice would likely have more relevant impact. Better yet, if the firms that the student were applying to operated at a certain scale (multinational versus boutique), scope (such as specific building typologies), or locale (geographic location), then a professor not only familiar with industry but experienced with similar conditions would be a key advisor on portfolio feedback. For students seeking employment, opportunities to engage industry often come about via events such as guest lectures, school networking events, and studio reviews. Although it may seem intimidating at first, students should have the confidence to speak with these industry contacts; after all, they have made the effort to set aside time to visit academia and often are open to dialogue as opposed to one-sided communications.

The same could be said of mentors for offering feedback on academic portfolios. Beyond some of the parameters outlined for employment portfolios, academic resources can also provide insights on ways to best connect existent work in a portfolio to notable research and thesis directions. To ask professors for feedback is the easiest and most obvious of outlets. They are ideally familiar with particular

THE ARCHITECTURE PORTFOLIO GUIDEBOOK

5.3.3
Spread after feedback was provided. Smaller images were removed and a feature render was added to complement the line work. *Cabin* by Shengyu Cai after feedback.

Source: Shengyu Cai, *Cabin*, 2015, Digital Image, 4820 x 3050, Toronto, Canada.

topics in architectural studies, have overseen successful graduate students in undertaking research work, and are well connected to research networks that could offer greater development of graduate work. Having a professor pore through an academic portfolio has the potential to dramatically reframe not only how projects are presented in it, but also present additional opportunities or facets to display in work. They can offer familiarity with how projects may be presented better, insights on notable works that may serve as precedents, potential corrections to less overt errors, and invaluable constructive feedback in supporting an articulation of a student's thesis pursuits.

Architects are often guilty of generalizing and typecasting. From building typologies and technologies to ideas and aesthetics, architects and academics are quick to define individuals based upon the work they produce. This is unfortunately true when seeking resources to provide feedback. Those producing academic portfolios must look to a greater diversity of resources. If academics have the credibility to offer insights on students applying to professional placements, then it is quite a surprise that it is not reciprocated. While professors may offer insights on academic matters, there are many in industry incredibly steeped in theory and advanced ideas on architecture who

CHAPTER 5.0 | PORTFOLIO PREPARATION

carry as much credibility, if not more, than academics in certain facets of praxis.

Within the workplace, academic candidates may find that coworkers may be a good source of feedback. It is common for senior architects within a firm to be called in as an external reviewer at thesis defenses. While they may not necessarily have the depth of research expertise faculty have in specific architectural topics, they still have both an awareness of the interplay between architecture and other topics that define the breadth of architectural education. In some cases, senior coworkers may have backgrounds in specific facets of architecture that a candidate may pursue, such as sustainable design or urban morphology.

There are three general levels of portfolio review, each with their respective knowledge bases, duration, and targeting. Although these are not rigid criteria, these general guidelines establish a refinement in feedback from general, quick impressions to focus improvements on optimizing alignment with targeted audiences (see Table 5.3.1).

**Table 5.3.1**
The three general levels of portfolio review.

| LEVEL | WHO | EXAMPLE | DURATION | TARGETED FEEDBACK | WHY |
|---|---|---|---|---|---|
| BASIC | Peer | Classmate or coworker | < 30 minutes | General feedback on impression based upon legibility and impact | Familiarity with projects and presentation methods |
| INTERMEDIATE | External | Senior student or coworker | < 60 minutes | Aforementioned feedback in addition to insights on methods of differentiation | Familiarity with larger pool of applicants and can offer insights on differentiation |
| IN-DEPTH | External Knowledgeable | Professor or knowledgeable professional | Multiple sessions | All of the above but specific support on alignment with targeted audience | Familiarity with specific work or research |

The basic level of portfolio review is a quick assessment of work by a colleague that addresses obvious points of improvement including legibility and errors, as well as the general impression of the document. The 30-Second Flip Test described earlier is a sample of this quick and informal feedback model of this type of review. As colleagues are familiar with the exact nature of the projects, methods of presentation, and parameters around a project, they can offer an informed insight on how to best present work. Unfortunately, this level of review is not necessarily objective as familiarity breeds empathy.

Although the basic portfolio review by a colleague is beneficial at a general level of impression, the unconscious awareness of project challenges does not provide objectivity. Reviewers may be aware of project details such as the workflow challenges (such as a tight timeline or restricted resource access), additional requirements not necessarily included in a portfolio (such as scope creep demands by a client, or technical components required by a studio instructor), or the author's capacity on the project (whether it was done as a first-year studio project with nascent design skills or if it were a professional project where the author was the design lead). An intermediate review not only comes from an external source to provide an objective assessment, but also offers additional feedback on methods authors may adopt to reinforce differentiation. A level of detachment from a senior colleague ensures feedback is unbiased. Without an awareness that other peers may have, an intermediate portfolio reviewer's feedback will build upon the comments made by the basic reviewer and proceed to elaborate upon ways to improve the portfolio in its differentiation. On account of their experience, these reviewers can provide a greater objectivity and feedback, as they have seen a range of methods of presentation that can better articulate an author's intentions. What is especially useful about intermediate reviewers is that they can be instrumental in identifying possible directions an author may explore in validating their ability to separate themselves from competitors. Beyond simply stylistic methods to distinguish a portfolio, an intermediate reviewer may offer insights on distinct traits that an author exhibits that should be reinforced whether with additional content or presenting content in a more conspicuous manner. For example, an intermediate reviewer, based upon her experience with a similar pool of candidates, may recognize in an author's portfolio parametric design strengths that she believes are necessary in industry, especially well developed in her portfolio projects, and that the work should be highlighted in the author's portfolio.

An in-depth portfolio review not only continues the feedback support on general impressions and methods of differentiation from basic and intermediate reviews respectively, but forces authors to identify strong alignments with the firms or institutions they are applying to. Aligning with a targeted audience's needs is core to the purpose of a portfolio. Whether emphasizing a resonance with a potential employer's approach (to materials and methods, design ethos, or typologies) or a potential academic group's resources (including research facilities, faculty scholarly activities, or program strengths), the portfolio serves as a validation of both an author's distinction from her competitors but also her suitability for admission into an organization. Continuing the example of a student who was able to leverage the intermediate feedback in developing her portfolio to highlight her parametric design strengths, it may be quite evident that this distinctive trait fails to present a compelling case for acceptance to the institutions she wished to join. An in-depth reviewer such as a professor or senior partner within an architecture firm would be able to provide the potential methods of refining a portfolio to cater to particular institutions or employers respectively. For example, if this applicant were to use the portfolio in pursuit of a graduate program with a focus on her thesis interests in architecture's role in helping indigenous populations, she might have to work with the reviewer in identifying an appropriate method of ensuring her potential is realized by an admissions committee. Although her advanced parametric skills may be appropriately highlighted in distinguishing her from the pool of competitors, she still would need a method to validate her thesis pursuits. Through discussions with an in-depth reviewer, the author may receive feedback that suggests demonstration of the application of parametric design in some facet of an indigenous design project in the portfolio (whether it is new content or generated to complement existing portfolio work is at the author's discretion). This reaffirms to an audience that the candidate has an excellent range of experience and skills, unique characteristics that set her apart from her competitors, and more importantly reinforces her alignment with the program. The same approach could be utilized for application to professional groups. If the same student were applying for employment with a small firm focused on private residential work (that might not even use parametric packages, although it is still her key point of differentiation), she may wish to consult with her in-depth reviewer on what methods would be best to secure a position. Feedback from such an experienced reviewer may necessitate a supplemental image highlighting the use of parametric tools on a modest residential studio project or perhaps the ways parametric tools could automate workflows on such small-scale projects. In all cases, the feedback from the in-depth review is dyadic. Multiple sessions may be required in order to generate iterations, discuss approaches for different targeted agencies, and allow for time for authors to synthesize and produce appropriate content for subsequent in-depth reviews. A portfolio is a document that affects the next several months or potentially years of an author's life and warrants an appropriate investment in thought, effort, and time.

# CHAPTER 6.0

## THE PORTFOLIO AS A SUCCESSFUL REINFORCING DOCUMENT

**6.1** Letters: Cover Letter and Letter of Intent — 163

**6.2** Résumé/CV: Outline of Your Potential — 169

**6.3** Transcripts: External Assessment — 178

**6.4** Letters of Recommendation: Validation — 182

THE ARCHITECTURE PORTFOLIO GUIDEBOOK

## CHAPTER 6.0

# External Perspectives

**HOW WOULD YOU RANK THE FIVE CONVENTIONAL COMPONENTS IN AN APPLICATION (RÉSUMÉ/CV, TRANSCRIPTS, LETTER OF INTENT, LETTERS OF REFERENCE, AND PORTFOLIO)?**

BK: The portfolio is the most important, of course; second in importance is the statement of interest. The third in importance is the letters of recommendation, fourth is the transcript, and last comes the CV. I first review the portfolio to get a sense of the applicant and what their strengths and weaknesses are. Then I look for confirmation in the transcript. If somebody comes across as being a strong design wise and if it turns out that the studio grades are Bs, then we wonder what's the cause of the discrepancy. We had cases in the past, where we had issues of fake portfolios, which we started to pay a lot more attention to, especially in portfolios from overseas.

NT: Reference letter – number one. Because we are just a small office and so it's hard to take the risk if it's a total cold call when I'm relying solely on my own intuition. But if there is a friend, someone at a university I've known for a long time or former colleagues that recommend someone, that's always helpful because they have a sense of my office and how it functions. Then I would look to experience in the portfolio and the CV. After that would be transcripts and letters of intent.

GS: Transcripts we never see, so that's at the bottom. The next one is the reference letters, CV, and then portfolio with the most important being the letter of intent. It's the most important thing because when the person or the candidate passes through the directors, we check the portfolio to ensure that it's strong enough. When gets to the final decision, we bring that up to our principal architect for his check, then he reads the letter. He looks at the CV and everything as well, but he just wants to find out what your reasons are for joining and what does this person want to get out of it. That's a personal letter of how they feel, put directly to our firm, not through the work because that was done at a different time, whether that's through the school or through other projects. A lot of times, with portfolios, it's stuff that you've worked on in the past few years that you were in school and you don't get to choose the projects you get to work on. If your site was somewhere in Western Europe, that may have nothing to do with why you're applying to the office – that was a project that you were given to do in school. So, the intention behind the letter of intent is directly catered to the office alignment, which is why it's probably the most important piece.

RD: I just start with the transcripts, to make sure that the GPA is good. I put their references and letters of reference into one category, so I look at those second. Once the transcripts cancel the first round I look at everything equally, there isn't really an order and there isn't a hierarchy either. I don't want to exclude students that don't express themselves very well in writing, where even if their portfolio isn't really up to speed, you can see the little things in their work that hint at the fact that they would succeed in our program.

ON: First, I would look at the portfolio. Second, I would review the résumé. Third, I would look at the transcript. Fourth, I would look at would be the letters of reference. Then I would look at the letter of intent. We don't often look at those because they are often copy/paste. There are so many tricks online on how to write them to be interesting and appealing. It's fabricated – to me it has no value. I'd rather see the intent in a face-to-face meeting in an interview where I can easily pin down what the intent of the person is.

PB: The résuméis number one, looking at the experience of past offices where they have worked. Then the cover letter is important. When we find somebody we find interesting from these letters, we send them an email asking them, "Why us?" So if you're applying for a specific role, you should cater your cover letter based on that rather than something generic. "I'm passionate," "I love architecture," "I saw your works," "I really want to be an architect" – avoid those things. The next item would be the portfolio. It's important and we ascribe a great value to it but not much time. Then it would be references to check their experience, we don't ask for transcripts for positions in our firm.

## HOW SHOULD APPLICANTS INCLUDE GROUP WORK AND COLLABORATORS IN A PORTFOLIO?

NT: You're almost going by an honor system at that point because they are listing all the people that were involved. Always acknowledge the group unless you're designing and running the whole show – but in practice is never that. You would never just put your name there and not list any of the team members, whether it's in your office or it's your consultants. In an interview, if the person can just talk about the project coherently, if you can ask specific questions to which drawings or technical details they were responsible for, that to me shows that they did their part in the group work. You can reveal a lot through the detail in the answers you give; it can be very obvious when someone is vague or hazes over aspects of group work that they've taken credit for.

AB: People often have images in their portfolio and they show the CGIs of the project that they've worked on along with a few drawings. It's very hard to know what they authored and I think this incredibly irritating. They will show a professional CGI, then they'll show lots of images of the finished building, and a sort of list of what they did. But it's very hard to know, when people are part of a team, what they actually did. I think that being honest about what you did in a team and showing the work that you did rather than showing pictures of the finished building should be a requirement. I think there's a lot of dishonesty in portfolios of people who work in practices as part of team and don't actually clarify their work, what they authored and their role. Weaker students hide in group projects a lot! You can say that actually imitates real life, but it's quite tricky for prospective employers.

PB: I would say to put group work in, but when we are looking at a portfolio and see generally weak individual work and then uncharacteristic design work, we immediately think "Oh, this person didn't do that project." When you see five or six projects in a portfolio, you can

CHAPTER 6.0 | THE PORTFOLIO AS REINFORCING DOCUMENT

see a consistency of the graphic and design approach. If you include a group project in a portfolio, make it clear what you did on it.

RD: I ask myself, "Is this all their work or did they work with groups on projects and did they make that clear?" Some students, I find all the time, under-represent their contribution, while others claim to have done the entire thing themselves. Did they take a divide and conquer approach on a team or did they truly collaborate together? You can tell even without any conversation. You can tell by the way that they show their narrative, by the way that their project works.

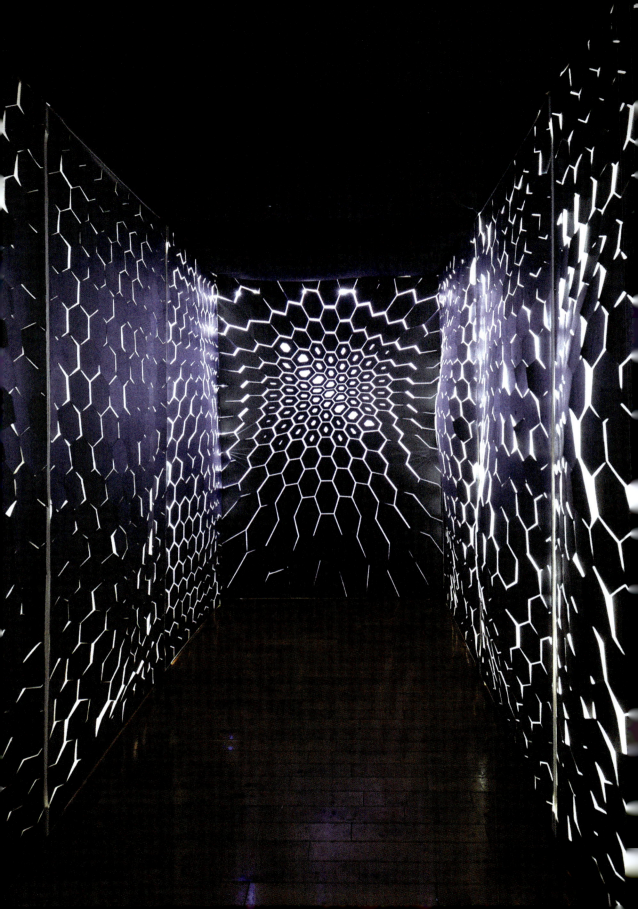

**CHAPTER 6.0**

# The Portfolio as a Successful Reinforcing Document

### 6.1 LETTERS: COVER LETTER AND LETTER OF INTENT

While in design disciplines, especially architecture, the portfolio is the most invaluable component in an application for employment or academic pursuits, letters are also an essential document in an application, which establish the framework for the entire submission. Letters serve as the expression of interest, outline of capacity, and affirmation that a candidate is suited for a position within a firm or academic program. Letters are the first presentation of suitability and the only opportunity for an applicant to explicitly articulate their case to potential employers and admissions committees. Résumés and portfolios may present curated samples of experience and work; however, with these components, direction is at the discretion of the audience. Transcripts and references are external sources for assessment but they do not always necessarily serve to validate an applicant's messaging. The letter is not a perfunctory component of an application – it is influential, effective, and the only opportunity for one to directly make their case to an audience.

While templates are easily found online and in workshops, their formulaic, fill-in-the-blank approach is nothing more than an architectural mad lib. Letters are best written in a professional manner but still retain hints of personality and individuality much like a portfolio. Although reflecting individuality, letters should still aim to a) introduce the author, b) outline alignment with the audience's program, c)

6.0
*Fraktur* by [R]ed[U]x Lab.

Source: [R]ed[U]x Lab, *Fraktur*, 2018, Digital Image, 2000 x 950, Toronto, Canada.

# THE ARCHITECTURE PORTFOLIO GUIDEBOOK

|  | ACADEMIC | PROFESSIONAL |
|---|---|---|
| AUTHOR INTRODUCTION | Positioning statement highlighting research-related intentions and notable accomplishments *If applicable: Articulation of thesis* | Positioning statement emphasizing appropriate skills and experience |
| ALIGNMENT | Demonstrate researched awareness of program-specific resources that align with research interests/thesis | Clear identification of applicant's fulfillment of employer-requested skills |
| EVIDENCE | Projects, research, and extracurricular work that reinforces genuine research interest and potential in program | Successful projects that emphasize good acumen or innovation with requisite skills and experience |
| SUITABILITY CONCLUSION | Reaffirmation of potential success in program and prospects of impact on praxis beyond graduation | Reiteration of positioning statement and capacity to contribute to the employer's success |

**Table 6.1.1**
Key points that may be written in an academic and professional cover letter.

provide some notable, key evidence, and d) reiterate one's suitability in a conclusion.

Author introductions quickly assert why an applicant is ideal for a position. Letters of intent and cover letters both start with academic and professional positioning statements respectively. While the professional cover letter directly addresses experience and skills that an applicant has to offer a potential employer, a letter of intent in an academic application often requires greater positioning on the potential one has. In a professional application, an introduction may indicate that a candidate is the best intern for design visualization on account of her dexterity with specific software packages in various award-winning projects. This addresses specific needs an employer has in their company's workflow with an opening that instills confidence and assurance with the prospective validation found in sample projects. Specifically in a professional setting, applicants should explicitly restate any terms, skills, or names of software that human resource administrators are looking for. This is important to note as in some professional situations, a human resources staffer or outsourced hiring agency is enlisted to pore through applications. As they may not have an awareness of the nuances in presenting skills, it is best to use the terms from job descriptions to improve one's chances. With some hiring protocols, software is used to quickly isolate terms in digital applications to assess applicant suitability. Using the terms issued in a job posting demonstrates that the applicant a) actually read the job description, and b) is objectively better able to transition into the company's value chain. Unfortunately this clarity is not necessarily the case with introductory statements of intent in academic admissions letters

In academic letters, the introductory declaration goes beyond stating research intentions and academic suitability. While a similar approach may be undertaken as professional letters in articulation of a positioning statement, academic letters typically mandate a succinct presentation of a thesis intention. This is often why an academic letter of intent is at least twice as long as a professional cover letter – there is simply so much to elaborate upon. Rather than expanding the scope of this book on thesis abstracts and intentions, what is absolutely critical in a letter of intent is a position a thesis may take. Far too often thesis proposals fall into one of three tropes: a) extreme ambiguity (e.g., a "thesis exploring sustainability" is quite generic and does not address any particular sustainable challenge architecture faces), b) fixation upon a project (e.g., a student may erroneously believe that a "thesis" project would be renovating her parents' home or designing a generic community center), or c) prioritization of another discipline at the expense of architecture (e.g., focusing upon digital fabrication or urbanism in a thesis while subverting architecture).

A strong presentation of a thesis intention in any academic letter requires a direct position on architecture in the first paragraph. For some, it is possible to establish a strong position by asking what is inherently problematic in contemporary architectural praxis and how things could be done better. For others, generating a thesis position is presenting a blind spot in contemporary praxis that merits research. Whatever the method in generating a thesis, the crux of a thesis is to establish a well-supported position on architecture that, through design and research, can bring about new perspectives for future praxis.

Once an introduction is made in a letter, the next major component is to articulate alignment in tandem with supportive evidence. Within a professional cover letter is a clear and succinct articulation of an author's experience and skills that align with employers' needs and validation in projects that may be referenced in the portfolio. In a cover letter, it is important to present criteria that are outlined in job descriptions that may not necessarily show up clearly in a portfolio. A key dimension in an employer's job description may be a need to lead in team settings. A portfolio, with the exception of photos of group members working together or a list of team members' names on group projects, will rarely explicitly show this. A letter of intent is an excellent opportunity to describe an author's role on a strong project that might be referenced in the portfolio. The imagery in the portfolio would speak to the design ability, technical skills, and even group collaboration capacities an author may have, but a cover letter would give an author the chance to focus attention on the key success factors not necessarily visible in a portfolio. Similarly, there may be experiences and tasks that might not directly manifest in a portfolio that employers may demand of potential applicants. It is not uncommon for firms to request experience with specific typologies or programming, such as a type of medical facility. Rather than solely rely upon imagery of a new pediatric oncology ward in a portfolio, it may be worthwhile in a cover letter to make mention of the various stakeholder consultations and refinements to functional programming that were undertaken to make the project. This presentation of alignment with supporting evidence adds value to the work in the portfolio as it gives an opportunity for an author to guide the audience with information beyond the imagery. This alignment with evidence renders a cover letter as a supportive document that improves the success of an application.

This is also the case with academic letters of intent. The articulation of alignment between an applicant's work (and typically thesis pursuits) and academic suitability with the resources available in an institution must be presented in a letter of intent. In most instances, work in a portfolio is understood as simply done because it was assigned by an instructor or commissioned by a client. While this tends to be the case, it is important that applicants are able to use the letter of intent to guide admissions committees in understanding that there are threads of skill, experience, and best of all, critical thinking for academic pursuits found in the portfolio. For example, an applicant to a graduate architecture program interested in the role of mass-customization in architectural praxis may mention how elements of bespoke prefabrication were integrated in a façade design for studio, as well as components of an extracurricular design-build project. While the projects in the portfolio may clearly show this consistency of interest throughout the applicant's work, the letter of intent allows the author to reaffirm this to the admissions committee. It is also worthwhile for academic applicants to use the letter to emphasize their alignment with potential resources at an institution. The letter of intent is likely the only place where an applicant can present this. Continuing with the same example, an academic applicant may wish to also position her mass-customization academic pursuits within the backdrop of advanced computing and fabrication resources or outstanding faculty researchers that would potentially complement her graduate pursuits. Once again, the ability to frame the discourse and articulate issues not necessarily present in the portfolio to validate alignment with evidence is an invaluable capacity of a letter of intent.

To follow proper form, all letters, whether academic or professional, should have a conclusion that goes beyond the perfunctory parting contact and follow-up information. The author should reiterate to the audience the positioning statement emphasizing their suitability for the position or program. With a professional cover letter, it is incumbent on the author to reinforce their ability to fulfill their needs in the interest of contributing to the firm's overall success. In an academic letter of intent, the author must emphasize not only their suitability to the program but their ability to succeed in their program and succeed in architectural praxis beyond graduation.

Unfortunately, even if professional cover letters or academic letters of intent contain all the correct information, they may still come across as banal and mechanical. Although the content may go beyond boilerplate templates, it may lack engagement or passion. This is where another layer of insight is required. Personalization is key. Generic letters receive little follow-through and come across as disingenuous. Personalization is often found in either: a) demand fulfillment – the direct alignment of a candidates' experience to specific audience parameters or alternatively, or b) complementary fit – demonstrating a candidate's alignment to the resources available with a potential employer or institution. These are not mutually exclusive.

With the former, candidates may read a job description that demands experience with a particular skill, software, or experience and, therefore, opt to showcase parameter alignment through distinguished works such as award-winning projects with past employers or excellent design studio work. In this case, the author presents how they align with their audience's requirements. The critical issue with personalizing *demand fulfillment* in a letter is to not simply articulate meeting outlined criteria, but instead it is incumbent on authors to present individuality that distinguishes them from their competitors. In a professional application, this might simply be articulating specific experience working with specific typologies (e.g., three years working on hospitality projects cited in the portfolio) or specific skills, software, and roles (e.g., a role as the office's BIM coordinator) in a letter to validate an applicant's qualifications. Scouring a list of skills in a job description will often highlight a few core competencies that employers would wish to have that should be present in a letter of intent. In academic contexts, demand fulfillment could include stating previous experience (e.g., two years of professional internship on specific projects with a notable firm), degrees (e.g., a pre-professional architecture degree on the Dean's List versus a general Bachelor of Arts), or grade point averages that may be established requirements for admission. These criteria are typically outlined in admissions and program websites but it is best to demonstrate exceeding them and distinguishing the author's application.

With the *complementary fit*, it is the author's mandate to present how the audience is best suited to their application. This is a bit of an inversion to demand fulfillment. Rather than have an author's letter seek to fulfil criteria set out by a potential employer or institution, this level of personalization emphasizes the audience's suitability for the author's goals. In a professional context, this could be stating that a potential residential architecture firm is the best place for a candidate to apply their thesis research work on micro-housing. An academic example of personalized complementary fit would be describing specific faculty with appropriate knowledge bases or facilities at an

CHAPTER 6.0 | THE PORTFOLIO AS REINFORCING DOCUMENT

institution that would allow a candidate to thrive. Once again, this is an excellent opportunity for authors to embark on fundamental research into the alignments with resources with their prospective employers and graduate programs. In both cases of personalization in cover letters or letters of intent, the purpose is to not only to differentiate from competitors but to show a genuine desire to contribute to the organization. If skills and experience are commodities that are outlined in résumés and CVs, then the letter of intent is the one opportunity to emphasize the passion one has for the next step in their career.

## 6.2 RÉSUMÉ/CV: OUTLINE OF YOUR POTENTIAL

If a letter is the initial presentation of an author's potential and intentions with their audience, then the résumé serves as an outline of the critical experiences and skills that would make them suitable for admissions or employment. As with the portfolio and the letter of intent, the résumé is a document that is curated and created by an author to present a message that aligns with an organization's needs. This is most evident in a professional setting where a job description typically explicitly outlines mandated and desired capacities (e.g., technical knowledge, software familiarity, level and nature of experience). The priority tends to be on the capacity to add value to a firm, whether it is in experience with a particular typology, efficiency with a certain workflow, or familiarity with a type of client or site. At an academic level, everything in a résumé is a listing of not only the capacity and skills one has to create architecture, but also the experience and maturity to explore it further in graduate studies. Beyond the production and work experience typically found in a professional portfolio, an academic portfolio should show promise for other duties including research, publication, and academic leadership. These are additional tasks that architecture students undertake as graduate students. In both academic and professional scenarios, everything in a résumé outlines an author's achievements and skills that demonstrate the successful potential they have whether in industry or pursuits in architectural education.

A résumé is not a curriculum vitae (CV). The former is a list of relatively recent accomplishments that makes one qualified for current position. The latter is a far more detailed document that serves as an exhaustive record of a great deal more than the conventional education, experience, skills, and accomplishments found in a résumé. Where a résumé is the succinct, one- or two-page document that serves as a synopsis of those aforementioned criteria, a CV is an extensive record that also includes, among other things: professional designations, member affiliations, publications, exhibitions, projects, courses taught, grant funding, and extracurricular service. As such, authors should not feel obliged to put down every single accomplishment in a résumé – that would be best reserved for a CV. A résumé is a sampler, so it is best to outline points of distinction such that they may be elaborated upon in an interview at the very least and, at most, may provide direction when the audience refers to the portfolio.

It should be noted that, similar to portfolios and letters, résumés are customizable documents that cater to different audiences and reflect both the individuality and creativity of an applicant. Like portfolios, résumés not only present facts and achievements, but serve as a venue to demonstrate graphic design and layout skills. In many instances, a résumé may literally be the only thing adjudicators leave with. If understood as an introductory preview of an applicant's suitability and skills, including design, the résumé should be just as curated, concise, and creative as a portfolio. Unfortunately, this is often neglected. A résumé is often stylistically connected to the aesthetic of an applicant's portfolio, and in many instances is included as an introductory component of a portfolio.

Like portfolios, there is neither a standard successful template on what to put in nor a baseline for how materials should be presented. The following are guidelines that authors may consider and adopt in their own résumés.

When compiling a résumé, there are a range of topics that authors feel they must address. In general there are four major groupings for these topics including:

- **Education**, including the architectural degree or program one has completed and any relevant courses or notable academic experiences (such as workshops with distinguished instructors and abroad programs)
- **Skills**, including knowledge bases and familiarities (e.g., construction knowledge or code compliance), traditional media (such as physical model making or freehand sketching) and digital

media (including software, digital fabrication, and advanced visualization)
- **Experience**, including professional experience, internships, notable work with various projects or firms, and extra-curricular work (such as design-build projects, roles in student governance, etc.)
- **Accomplishments**, including publications (e.g., proceedings, journal articles, citations, conferences and exhibitions), distinctions, and awards

These are general categories that can both be rearranged based upon type of application, as well as broken down into subsections. For example, a professional résumé likely prioritizes skills and experience over accomplishments as employers are more interested in skills alignment first and foremost. An academic résumé, however, may start with education and experience and then subsequently create headings to emphasize publications, research work, and awards.

Within each of these headings, authors must consider the best strategy to document their notable accomplishments and skills. The same guidance on text in a portfolio holds true for that in a résumé. Keeping it concise and precise is essential. Although stylistic parameters may prioritize different features, a résumé should provide an audience a sense of what the applicant can do, who they did it for, when they did it, and how it is aligned with the audience's needs. For

6.2.1 Juxtaposition of the headings emphasized in a resume for professional applications and academic admissions.

example, an intern applying for a junior architect position at a firm specializing in religious architecture and uses Software 123 may state in her résumé:

---

**PROFESSIONAL EXPERIENCE**

**01.2025–09.2026 XYZ Architects Inc., Lagos, Nigeria**
While working here, I used many software packages on several projects in the office. I was responsible for several design competitions but my primary responsibility was working on implementing changes to the ABC Church from schematic design to the design development phase for the last ten months of my internship.

---

Although the example is successful in presenting who the applicant worked for and when, as well as what they did, there are ways to refine this for greater potency. The first recommendation would be to remove the sentences and state things with bullet point(s). It is good that she uses an active voice, but it would dramatically help if she did not use a first-person voice. Blocks of prose in a résumé will unlikely be read and take up a great deal of space. The written statement also fails to address what she actually did with any precision and how it could be relevant to supporting her suitability for her prospective employer. While she addresses her past experience on a church project, it is not overtly emphasized. Like all applicants with résumés for an architectural audience, she should cater the text to reinforce her relevance to the firm's needs.

---

**PROFESSIONAL EXPERIENCE**

**01.2025–09.2026 XYZ Architects Inc., Lagos, Nigeria**

- Used various software packages, including Software 123, on four design competitions
- Revised design documents with project architect for ABC Church from schematic to design development phases

---

While the wording seems similar, the revision is more direct and emphasizes alignment with the workflow, role, and typology that is asked for in the prospective job description. This one example demonstrates the potential need for minor refinements to each résumé to suit each prospective employer or admissions committee. Authors can take solace in the fact that once the content has been put in place, the finessing of content for different, subsequent applications is easier.

When assembling a résumé, regardless of the headings and their ordering, there are some mandatory components that must be clearly presented. There is no point in creating a résumé if there is no ability for employers or admissions committees to follow-up with an applicant or take additional action to investigate further. Surprisingly, basic elements such as including one's name and contact information (email, phone, address) are often neglected. Imagine the absolute frustration for reviewers to identify a strong candidate only to have to spend additional effort in identifying who they are and how to contact them. Another requisite component in a résumé is a link to additional online content such as a website or at the very least a digital portfolio. Anyone applying for an architecture position should have an online presence for interested assessors to access. It is no longer an option or preference.

Beyond the baseline content included in the categories, there are a number of finer points that authors may consider based upon the audience they are applying to. Applicants for jobs tend to be reluctant to include work experience that is not design or architecture-related, believing the experience to be unrelated to the profession. While an entire block of text is not required for such jobs, they have the potential to support alignment with firms. Jobs and skills that showcase strength with commodity soft skills (including oral communication, interpersonal skills, teamwork, and time management) and hard skills (such as graphic design, web development, and social media) should not be eliminated from a résumé. While it might not seem relevant to include experience as a shift manager in a restaurant, the soft skills pertaining to communication, teamwork, problem-solving, and interpersonal relations may be a distinguishing component in a résumé. The same could be said about languages and hobbies. In an industrial landscape that is both expansive in the types of projects undertaken and its global reach, these two details occasionally catch the attention of professional and academic assessors alike. For example, a student may indicate that they speak English and Mandarin or have hobbies including cycling. While these may seem foreign and non-sequitur, some companies may hire one candidate over another based upon these types of details. Whether it is due to camaraderie around common hobbies such as cycling or the prospects of expanding work into a Chinese-speaking market, these details may prove to be helpful.

Another finer point that authors may wish to address in their résumés pertains to explanations. As with portfolios, there is no need to use reams of text to explain accomplishments. Bullet points are perfectly fine as they get to the point. That said, whenever there is text in a résumé or portfolio it should be done deliberately and with potency. Wording must be precise. Nothing is as useless in a résumé as generic, clichéd terms (such as "experienced," "utilized," "assisted"). Instead authors should be specific and articulate what they did and the results. For example, a supportive text may read: "Participated in mental health awareness campaign," which offers little impact to the audience. Alternatively, it could be phrased as "Oversaw the budget and assembly of the inaugural Mental Health Care packages alleviating studio stress for 400 students." The same task has impact on account of its precision and outcomes. The same level of precision on employment and activities should be extended to awards. Far too often recipients of awards assume the rest of the world knows what they are presented for. To simply list being a recipient of the "Thomas Seebohm Award" might at best be confused by an audience as it could be in reference to digital simulation or phenomenological design and, at worst, have no meeting at all. Authors should take the time to succinctly articulate what awards are for unless tacit to the title (e.g., "Top studio design award").

As a final note on explanations in résumés, it is absolutely essential for authors to explain their roles on any given project. While a portfolio might have imagery that alludes to the final product, résumés and letters give authors an ability to directly speak to their contributions. Whether on a group studio assignment or a complex airport project in an office, it is important to acknowledge at the very least, the fact that it is a team project, partner names (if the group is small enough), and what the author's role on the work was. With professional work in particular, it is understood that projects are not done as individual efforts so it is important to highlight in a résumé what tasks were undertaken by the author. Failing to articulate one's contributions and role is either a sign of ignorance or the epitome of arrogance (to take complete ownership of a project).

While there are many considerations an applicant may consider to include in their résumés, there are several items that should give authors pause for consideration or not be included at all. One common issue that appears in résumés, particularly those from students seeking their first opportunity to work in industry, is the reliance on clichéd components. As mentioned already, wording should be precise and cannot be left to overused terms (e.g., "responsible for," "great communication skills," "team player") without any clear objectives or goals. Similarly, components such as "objective" or "references available upon request" are also components of résumés that seem to have emerged from a misguided high school student who took their guidance counsellor far too seriously. In some professions, these practices and headings may be standard, however in architecture it makes no sense. Why else would an individual submit a résumé if not to get a job with an employer? Why does one need to be told that the "objective" of the résumé is to get a job? At the same time, why would anyone deem it appropriate to tease an audience by hinting to an admissions committee that an applicant has referees but will only provide them if asked? What could they possibly be hiding? If the intent is tacit, there is no need to put it in writing. If one has quality referees who are informed and ready to validate their suitability, then they should feel free to include them in a submission package.

Clichéd headings aside, another issue often plaguing résumés is the lack of curation. If one considers a résumé as a highlight of recent accomplishments validating suitability for a position (as opposed to an entire CV documenting every single accomplishment with modest detail), then resurrecting distinctions that are neither relevant nor recent only comes across as desperation filler. For example, it makes little sense for a graduate student seeking employment with architecture firms to include "swimming champion" or "painting displayed at high school art exhibition" as notable "accomplishments." Even if a firm were working on swimming complexes or art galleries, these distinctions would not sway an employer to hire an applicant. Of course, this is also a time-sensitive matter. For example, a first-year student may find that it would be worth highlighting some of their high school accomplishments simply on account of the fact that they have nothing else to validate their capacity or passion. In general, a three-year rule should be applied. Aside from notable distinctions (such as a national architecture award) or historic background (such as program and graduation dates or past employers and projects), keeping résumés as a documentation of the past three to five years is ideal. If one were to rely on distinctions over a decade ago with little done to date, it raises questions in a reviewer's mind pertaining to why a candidate has failed to maintain such productivity since.

This is also an issue when potential employees circulate on their résumés a litany of companies that they may have worked for, but for only brief stints. While it is understood that interns may work for brief periods, to have a résumé with only stints of experience (regardless of how famous an employer may be) is a telltale sign that there may be a great range of experience in such a candidate, but the depth would be questionable. In an industry where architecture develops and comes to fruition over years, what degree of experience would a candidate have with merely a few months on a project? To potential employers, a candidate's demonstrated experience and capacity to contribute in the firm's workflow far outweigh a candidate's claim to have worked with well-known architects.

While a résumé is an objective listing of accomplishments and skills that a candidate has that may be further validated in a portfolio, because it is produced by the author, it is *not* completely objective. In some instances, this is as innocent as making assumptions on what reviewers wish to have in a résumé such as formatting "in the style" of a firm or including portraits of a candidate. With the latter, it is a trope that has become ubiquitous on account of everyone having some presence online making it easy to match a name to a face. Unfortunately, in some instances it is frowned upon to include self-portraits in a résumé – employers ideally hire based upon the quality of an applicant over their appearance. No architecture program worth mentioning would accept students based upon their physical attractiveness, and if such a program were discovered, one would have to question what the quality of education offered there would be. If for some reason an admissions committee or employer were interested in finding what an applicant looked like, they could find it fairly quickly in an age saturated with social media and profile photos.

One's physical appearance is not a criteria for acceptance so it is best to stay out of that arena and instead use the résumé space for stating more relevant information.

Finally, when it comes to information in a résumé, one issue that has arisen in the past decade has been the ubiquity of infographics. While these are not inherently bad when presenting an applicant's résumé through a timeline or showcasing on a map the various firms and projects they have worked on, the use of self-rating infographics has become problematic. They are quite subjective and do not provide any objective measure of skill. For example, an applicant may indicate that they have a "4 out of 5" star rating on a particular software package. While the applicant may feel that this indicates their own sense of comfort and acumen with the software, the rating is relative to her own frame of reference and also indicates that there are many things (specifically 20% based upon this rating) that she does not know. How would a second-year student authoritatively have the ability to assess their knowledge of software relative to professional expectations? For an assessor, how convincing is it for them to hire someone who, even when self-assessing, gave herself a modest grade? A self-assessment of skills only serves to highlight one's weaknesses or shortcomings, especially when it is at the discretion of the candidate. Infographics have a great opportunity to succinctly communicate ideas on a résumé but should not serve to undermine a candidates' potential by opening the door to misrepresentation or miscommunication.

One untapped resource for résumé support many applicants seem to overlook is their own academic institutions. While an architecture student may be isolated and spend more hours in studio than with family and friends, let alone anywhere else on campus, every university has a career center that is more than willing to help current students and alumni. Beyond offering general advice and information on academic and professional applications, these supports typically have specialists assigned to different industries and maintain currency with alumni and the profession in order to ensure graduates have the potential to succeed in the profession. As they have their finger on the pulse on the industry, they are familiar with not only what industry demands for skills and experience, but also able to provide access to remedial workshops or resources to build up some skills. For example, a career center may offer exclusive video tutorials or working files for alumni and students to hone their skills. These career centers may also offer one-on-one consultation that may allow candidates to build upon the strategies outlined in this book.

### 6.3 TRANSCRIPTS: EXTERNAL ASSESSMENT

Transcripts are the closest objective metrics that assess one's capability to perform well in various topics or tasks. To a lesser degree, certifications from training seminars and workshops provide an objective validation but do not have the same level of assessment (as they tend to be pass/fail or awarded for participation) nor do they necessarily attest to specific application in an architecture context (for example, taking a building code seminar does not necessarily mean the knowledge was applied by participants in a project, but instead might have simply discussed what the codes are). Unlike a résumé or portfolio, a transcript presents the fine grain of academic accomplishments in every course taken, which at worst can expose critical gaps and flaws in an applicant's knowledge base or at best demonstrate the evolution of a student over time. There is little an applicant can do when assembling this component in an application package but at the very least it is worth understanding how it is assessed by professional and especially academic audiences.

From interviews with employers around the world from firms of all types, it is clear that grades are not the key determinant for successful employment. While certain internship programs may require transcripts or academic validation, it is uncommon for employers to demand official transcripts from applicants entering the industry. Official transcripts are required for academic application and may be requested from an applicant's university or college. In most cases, there is a fee associated with processing and receiving official transcripts so it may be a costly endeavor should multiple copies be required. For some academic institutions, only official transcripts, sealed and stamped by the applicant's alma mater are acceptable for admissions into a graduate studies program, whereas others may be content with physical or digital reproductions. Applicants should confirm with institutions as to what format is required and their associated costs, as timelines for processing vary from institution to institution and the aggregation of transcript costs may be a financial challenge.

For employers participating in an internship program, they may require an unofficial transcript, which can simply be downloaded or requested from an applicant's student profile. If, however, they require an official transcript, then the issues pertaining to cost and timeline must be accounted for. To employers, the transcript typically provides a general idea of what an applicant's knowledge base is (as governed by the program and portfolio of courses taken) as well as where their strengths may lie (as determined by the grades in a course). A firm specializing in sustainable design selecting from a pool of student applicants might quickly use transcripts to determine if students from a specific program take notable, relevant courses, as well as further refine their search by assessing applicants based upon performance in those courses. While in a professional context grades in specific courses may reinforce or even be referenced in a résumé or letter, within academic contexts distinction in courses may emphasize acumen in subjects that may drive research or teaching opportunities during graduate studies. If an academic applicant were to frame a letter of intent around an interest in advances in responsive materials for envelope design yet have poor grades in building science and construction courses, then it draws attention to a discrepancy that may undermine the thesis application. At the same time, an applicant with incredibly good grades in digital design courses may not only find opportunities to affirm this interest in their thesis work but also distinguish themselves to faculty as potential research or teaching assistants.

When looking at transcripts, the simplest measure of academic success is in the Cumulative Grade Point Average (CGPA), which is the numeric average of all courses taken within that degree. For a typical architecture student, that number would include everything from introductory structures and electives through to final capstone studio projects. To compound the complexity, in most architecture programs, the weighting of a studio course tends to be double or triple that of their lecture-based counterparts, which means stronger performance in studios tends to pull CGPAs higher. CGPA requirements for graduate programs in general have a minimum cutoff of 3.0; however, clearing that value is not an assurance of admission. Most graduate design programs are extremely competitive and have hundreds of applicants each year. In some instances the most efficient method of reducing the pool is to simply take the top percentile of applicants based upon CGPAs and subsequently look at other application components such as portfolio and letters. Although some programs may not be at liberty to inform applicants of each step in the admissions process, it may be worthwhile to contact admissions officers for program-specific procedures.

Unfortunately, many students are not able to demonstrate a consistently high performance, especially for those transitioning from secondary to post-secondary school. Changes in lifestyle, pedagogy, or career goals occasionally result in some students' poor academic performance in the early years of a program. Some academic institutions acknowledge this situation by initially referencing CGPAs and then if the score is low, they may reference an applicant's CGPA from the past two years instead. This benefits applicants who have acclimatized to university levels of performance and wish to carry that momentum into graduate studies. It may be worth confirming with program admissions staff on how they assess CGPAs.

Despite the globalization of education, a consistent assessment method and standard across borders and jurisdictions has yet to be developed. All grades are relative. It is not uncommon to have applicants lay claim to incredible "A" grades that result in overly inflated CGPAs. As shown in Table 6.3.1, even the fundamental concept of what is deemed an "A" or a failing grade in a course varies from country to country. Different admissions committees approach adjusting transcript grades independently, so there is no need for applicants to process and adjust their grades for them.

Transcripts serve as an objective record of one's knowledge through the onslaught of assessments undertaken in an architectural education. While grades matter for academic admissions, they do not have a notable impact on professional hiring aside from instances such as internship qualification or determining specialized skill. However, for academic applications, transcripts reaffirm to admissions committees a candidates' sincerity in their letters of intent, their promise of potential thesis excellence, and their potential as research and teaching support.

**Table 6.3.1** Comparison of grade to percentage equivalences from various countries.

| AMERICAN GRADING | | | CANADIAN GRADING | | | CHINESE GRADING | | | IRANIAN GRADING | | |
|---|---|---|---|---|---|---|---|---|---|---|---|
| Letter Grade | Numeric Grade | GPA | Letter Grade | Numeric Grade | GPA | Letter Grade | Numeric Grade | GPA | Letter Grade | Numeric Grade | GPA |
| A+ | 97–100 | 4.0 | A+ | 90–100 | 4.3 | | | | | | |
| A | 93–96 | 4.0 | A | 85–89 | 4.0 | A | 90–100 | 4.0 | A | 16–20 | 4 |
| A– | 90–92 | 3.7 | A– | 80–84 | 3.7 | | | | | | |
| B+ | 87–89 | 3.3 | B+ | 77–79 | 3.3 | | | | | | |
| B | 83–86 | 3.0 | B | 73–76 | 3.0 | B | 80–89 | 3.0 | B | 14–15.99 | 3 |
| B– | 80–82 | 2.7 | B– | 70–72 | 2.7 | | | | | | |
| C+ | 77–79 | 2.3 | C+ | 67–69 | 2.3 | | | | | | |
| C | 73–76 | 2.0 | C | 63–66 | 2.0 | C | 70–79 | 2.0 | C | 12–13.99 | 2 |
| C– | 70–72 | 1.7 | C– | 60–62 | 1.7 | | | | | | |
| D+ | 67–69 | 1.3 | D+ | 57–59 | 1.3 | | | | | | |
| D | 65–66 | 1.0 | D | 53–56 | 1.0 | D | 60–69 | 1.0 | D | 10–11.99 | 1 |
| D– | 60–64 | 0.7 | D– | 50–52 | 0.7 | | | | | | |
| F | <60 | 0.0 | F | <50 | 0.0 | F | <60 | 0.0 | F | <10 | 0 |

## 6.4 LETTERS OF RECOMMENDATION: VALIDATION

A letter of recommendation is a validation by another party of what an applicant states in the other components for submission, most notably the résumé and portfolio. Often, these are considered perfunctory documents that serve as a final validation of an applicant's capability within a program or firm. Letters serve a document from a third party that a) validates what has been stated by the candidate, b) addresses any gaps or discrepancies that may exist, and c) outlines a candidate's potential for the future.

Excellence in past performance is a harbinger of things to come. Within a professional setting, an ideal letter of reference would reflect an applicant's past achievements and capacities such as notable work on a project or acumen with particular software or technologies. Similarly, an academic letter of reference should present a retrospective validation of knowledge and skills as demonstrated in classes and assessments. These letters also have the potential to address any discrepancies in a candidate's application. For example, in a professional context, applicants may be able to explain issues such as early departures or type of work undertaken. A letter from an employer may reference an office-wide reduction of office staff during a recession or a shift in job duties on account of a colleague's maternity leave. These quick explanations in a letter remove any potential negative perceptions that may emerge in future employers' minds. The same could be said of academic letters. A student might have taken an additional year to complete their sophomore year of their undergraduate studies but a referee's letter may emphasize that a candidate was awarded an exchange program position at a prestigious institution elsewhere for that year. This also may prove to be helpful in demonstrating a candidate's ability to improve themselves. A professional reference letter may indicate how an applicant took the initiative to visit sites to improve her knowledge of construction coordination or an academic reference may describe how industrious an applicant was in taking additional coding courses to advance her digital design skill. All these notables from a letter of reference reinforce the prospects of an applicant doing well with an employer or a graduate program. The most basic of letters would simply affirm the first level of support, which attests to skills and work from the past. It is a strong letter of reference that does this while also elaborating upon issues that may be seen as negative all the while ensuring the audience feels confident that the candidate would fit well with their organization in the future.

Despite the incredible imagery in a portfolio, the extraordinary achievements in a résumé, and the strong academic performance exhibited in a transcript, nothing has as much veto power in decisions as at negative assessment by a referee. Ostensibly a referee is selected by an applicant to validate the statements made in the other application documents and portfolio. If this is true, there should only be positive commentary. If the best possible referee, selected by an applicant, cannot speak well of them, then reviewers and employers are extremely suspicious of a candidate's potential. Although a negative letter is essentially a veto on an applicant, the second worst is a tepid, generic reference letter. If a reference cannot say anything notable, then it is best not to have them.

A good reference should be a notable, authoritative contact that can speak to an applicant's role, duration, and level of engagement on any particular enterprise, whether performance in the office or classroom. If a potential referee cannot assess these three criteria, they will be of marginal support. While a general HR manager or professor may easily identify the first two criteria for any given applicant, it is the level of engagement that proves to be a critical factor in distinguishing a referee (and by extension, the applicant) from general acquaintances. These individuals do not need to be personal friends, but instead they should have a high opinion of an applicant and their work. Better yet, they should be able to attest to an applicant's notable accomplishments. In a professional setting, a project architect could recount an applicant's capacity to learn new software quickly to perform precise lighting studies for a project whereas in an academic context, a professor could refer to an applicant's ability to not only excel in their own studies, but to also help classmates by holding tutorials on challenging topics. In both cases, the referee is in an authoritative position to give credibility to a significant level of engagement that goes beyond the status quo.

Applicants should keep in mind that in academic settings, references are not necessarily isolated to letters but often require a completion of a supplemental form that asks referees to assess an applicant's potential and performance in a number of roles that align with tasks that applicants may undertake in graduate studies (see Figure 6.4.1).

# THE ARCHITECTURE PORTFOLIO GUIDEBOOK

**KNOWLEDGE OF APPLICANT**

In what capacity have you known the applicant?

How long have you known the applicant?

To approximately how many students in the past 5 years and at the same level of study are you comparing the applicant?

**SPECIFIC ABILITIES**

| | Outstanding (Top 5%) | Superior (5–10%) | Good (10–25%) | Average (25–50%) | Poor (Lower 50%) | No basis for judgment |
|---|---|---|---|---|---|---|
| Past academic achievement | ■ | ■ | ■ | ■ | ■ | ■ |
| Scholarly promise | ■ | ■ | ■ | ■ | ■ | ■ |
| Independent research ability | ■ | ■ | ■ | ■ | ■ | ■ |
| Creativity | ■ | ■ | ■ | ■ | ■ | ■ |
| Resourcefulness | ■ | ■ | ■ | ■ | ■ | ■ |
| Ability to meet deadlines | ■ | ■ | ■ | ■ | ■ | ■ |
| Overall I would rate this student as | ■ | ■ | ■ | ■ | ■ | ■ |

**6.4.1**
Sample of a university application reference form that many masters programs require during their admission process.

Specifically for academic referees, universities are interested in applicants' capacity for undertaking teaching or research tasks. It may be worthwhile for applicants to look online and download these forms in order to review what criteria will be assessed. This is especially helpful in strategically selecting certain references over others based upon their likely responses to a particular institution's assessment criteria. Given this level of familiarity, it is important to also properly connect with prospective referees for optimal assessment.

A good practice is to contact a potential referee a month in advance of when letters and assessments are due in order to take a moment to draft the letter. Better yet, it is worthwhile to give them a call to chat about the application and discuss key points that would be worth raising in the letter. This is a very important step because of demand and memory. One can imagine that people who are the most suited to serve as referees are often bombarded with requests usually all at the same time (e.g., soon after graduation, just prior to academic admissions deadlines, at the start of the new year). These same people also engage hundreds, if not thousands, of people each year and it may be worthwhile to reach out and remind them of incidents that would reaffirm alignment with a potential graduate program or employer. This could be an excellent time to share your portfolio

CHAPTER 6.0 | THE PORTFOLIO AS REINFORCING DOCUMENT

Saturday, June 29, 2019

To: ▮

**Faculty of Architecture**
**Admissions Committee: Architecture**

I have been asked to write a letter of recommendation ▮ for a placement within your graduate Architecture program. I can write this letter but I cannot recommend her.

Let me be clear about two issues: A) She asked me for this letter the day before your application deadline because she "*could not find any other professor willing to write*" one for her, and B) she is applying to your program because she believes she "*would possibly get into* ▮ *'s Master of Architecture program but it would be too much work.*" As a professor within ▮'s Department of Architectural Science, I have witnessed her work over the past four years and cannot recommend someone exhibiting such arrogance and laziness.

I taught ▮ in several classes in her undergraduate Architectural Science degree including Communications Studio (ASC101), Collaborative Exercise (ASC205 and ASC605), and Digital Tools (ASC755). Her work is generic and shows little design exploration; that she designs based upon "*approval*" is disturbing. Despite her needing "*approval*" to execute her work, in larger classroom settings, she is very focused on her own interests. Her selfishness does not help the pedagogical environment. She only participates when grades are offered and on multiple instances she has abandoned her partners during project deadlines. This inability to see beyond herself is where her largest challenge lies. ▮ occasionally has something to contribute to the classroom but on account of her disposition and inability to relate with others, she will have difficulty working with her peers in your graduate program. Compounding the program is her fixation on what the minimum requirements are for any given exercise. In several projects I can recall her efforts in minimizing and isolating requirements of assignments as opposed to potentially developing a strong design.

▮ is a student who will likely graduate from our undergraduate program at the end of the academic year. Her weaknesses in her interpersonal skills, lack of design innovation, overt selfishness, and academic laziness may be something your program can facilitate moving forward. I do not know if that is within the scope of your program. If your program accepts derivative, superficial design and argumentative, selfish applicants, then she may be a worthwhile candidate. I do not believe this is the case with your respected institution. I cannot in good conscience recommend someone of this caliber to you. She is not a good representative of our program. If you have any additional questions, please do not hesitate to contact me directly.

Best regards,

Associate Chair,
Experiential Learning

T:
E:

185
6.4

6.4.2
Sample of a poor letter of reference.

with them or at the very least stir a memory. For example, project architects in a firm may work with individuals for a couple of years but then are reassigned to another project in a satellite office for a long period of time. They would be a good reference but a discussion would be worthwhile to remind them of past positive activities that may carry forth in their referee submission.

If a potential referee declines a request to serve as a reference, do not push back. They have their reasons and it might not necessarily be due to any negative perceptions of an applicant. As mentioned already, strong references are often busy so they may politely decline simply because they do not wish to produce anything less than a considerate, personalized letter. Harassing a potential referee may instead result in possibly negative sentiments that would undermine an entire application.

One final note regarding letters of reference or applicant's assessments is that non-disclosure matters. When applicants include effusive letters in their submissions or portfolios, reviewers receive them with a degree of skepticism as the applicant has clearly read it and selectively included it. At the same time, many online portals provide referees a choice as to whether or not applicants are able to review their assessments. For some institutions, it is understood that letters of reference that are shared with applicants are essentially invalidated. To have an applicant aware of a referee's assessment of them is almost assuredly going to result in a positive, but potentially neutralized letter. For example, a professor would be far less willing to assess a candidate negatively knowing that their assessment would be disclosed to the candidate, thereby potentially creating quite an awkward situation. An honest reference, free of potential awkwardness or retribution by an applicant, is the best reference to submit. A candid letter is far more valuable than one that has already been curated by an applicant. Applicants should ensure that all referee materials *not* be disclosed to them. It allows referees to comfortably attest to an applicant's strengths and weaknesses, which are far more genuine than those already filtered or "approved" by an applicant.

# CHAPTER 7.0
## COMMUNICATION USING YOUR PORTFOLIO

**7.1** Online: Websites and Social Media     193

**7.2** Complementary Materials     200

**7.3** Interview: The Tipping Point     204

**7.4** Following Up     209

# CHAPTER 7.0

# External Perspectives

## HOW HAS SOCIAL MEDIA AND ONLINE UBIQUITY IMPACTED YOUR ADMISSION/HIRING PRACTICE?

RD: Social media, as with anything, can be misused but there are opportunities to interact with well-known personages, architects, and design professionals that otherwise wouldn't respond to you and add to the conversation. Social media is all about social learning and social knowledge. There's no quicker way to find out the latest things that are happening, the latest developments in terms of technology. I also think that social media provides an emerging professional, even a soon-to-be graduate, with a platform giving them a voice. Everybody is a publisher now, you don't have to wait to get published because you can publish anytime you have a thought. You discover your voice. Then in terms of virtual identity, there is a great way to put your name out there – a face with a name. With that, people are more interested in engaging, working with you, or take you on.

ON: Our team does their due diligence on background checks. But I have to be honest – to me, I don't mind if someone has photos online with his classmate being silly or having fun – that's part of life. To neglect that and see everyone so clean is distorting reality. So, we just like to believe that everybody's in-between. If we are trying to hire somebody, between two candidates, and two of them are really good, then we might consider those sort of things. We don't usually do any social media reading before we hold the interviews. We receive the portfolios that first go to our colleagues and they do a shortlist based upon the understanding of our strategy and objectives. Then, I normally interview the shortlist with teams. We decide as a collective so I never make a decision myself.

NT: I Google applicants all the time. If a candidate's portfolio looks interesting I'll call them in for an interview and I will Google them. Some people in my office found it actually interesting and were

# CHAPTER 7.0 | COMMUNICATION USING YOUR PORTFOLIO

surprised that I did this for them prior to hiring. In this day and age, we have to be conscious of our online presence – so whatever you write or post, don't be surprised if I read it on your Twitter account, and judge you accordingly!

## TO BE HIRED SOLELY ON ONE'S PORTFOLIO AND RÉSUMÉ IS THE RARITY. WHAT IS THE ROLE OF NETWORKING, INCLUDING RECOMMENDATIONS, AND INTERVIEWS IN THE HIRING PROCESS?

PB: Networking is huge. I do it to hire consultants and to get projects, so of course I would answer somebody favorably if I get a referral from their boss. I have all these friends in different universities and firms that I trust. If they say that they have this good grad coming up and recommend them, I look at whether we've got the capacity.

AB: Interviews are critical, we normally do two interviews per applicant as we are shifting through and figure out which one has got the right skills and fulfills all the other demanding criteria I have. An associate will interview the person first and if they pass that test, then I will interview them.

BK: In a recommendation letter, I am looking for confirmation of my impressions. If I have the impression that somebody is a strong student, then I would expect to read in the references that the student was strong. If the student exhibit strengths in certain areas, then I would look for evidence of that in the letters of reference.

NT: You're going from job to job, so that's a network in and of itself. You don't even know if someone next to you at the office might one day be a colleague at another office and literally say, "Hey we need somebody, are you interested?" Even just from slightly shifting roles within the same organization, based on people knowing your skill set, networking matters. Reach out to mentors. They have a different network layer, a different group range where they could say, "This would be a good fit for you." I find now what's happening at my level (principal of a small office) is that people are calling other people. I'll call a former colleague at his office and say, "I can't hire this person with this portfolio that's just come through, but I remember a month ago you were looking for someone and this person looks amazing. You should check this person out." So that's happening as well.

GS: Reference letters – every office is asking for one and I've seen some sent to us from other Japanese offices; they are all the same. Most often, no one is going to refuse a reference letter, as in most cases these are for students who were interning at an office. This is why what's written in those letters is not necessarily important because it's all probably copy and paste – it's more about who it is that may have written. Yet, it doesn't really say too much about who that person is, only where they've been.

## HIRING BASED UPON SKILL ALONE IS NO LONGER SEEN AS A SUSTAINABLE METHOD OF CREATING A STRONG STUDIO CULTURE. WHAT TRAITS ARE YOU LOOKING FOR IN A PORTFOLIO BEYOND TECHNICAL AND DESIGN SKILLS?

ON: The way they think. In interviews, you could get a graduate or an intern where they don't have a lot of experience. They can't talk about experience, they just don't have it. So, to me what is important is their thinking – the way that they look at a problem and the way that they solve it. A question would be "Quality, time, or money, which would you give up on a project?" There's no right or wrong answer to this but it shows a candidate's approach. Another question might be, "If you had to design an underwater airport, how would you do that?" I want to see how the person responds. It's totally random and I want to see the way they maneuver, the way they articulate the question, the way they might challenge you, and how they embrace the challenge. There must be some sort of indication of their passion, their creative thinking, and their problem-solving approach. I am testing these capacities in an interview and then the portfolio, transcripts, and letters are all validated in their responses.

RD: I look for two things: "Will they be a good fit (in terms of firm culture or in terms of the work that we do)?" and "Do they exhibit performance?" I don't expect them to be technically proficient nor

CHAPTER 7.0 | COMMUNICATION USING YOUR PORTFOLIO

to be an excellent designer necessarily, but I am looking for whether they're a fit for the school program or for the employment situation.

GS: At the beginning, we're looking for people who have had work experience. But on top of that, also a wider or broader knowledge of architecture as well. That translates to being able to speak the same language when you get into the office.

**CHAPTER 7.0**

# Communication Using Your Portfolio

## 7.1 ONLINE: WEBSITES AND SOCIAL MEDIA

The ubiquity of a digital identity can serve as an excellent opportunity to reinforce qualities that a candidate wishes for admissions committees and employers to remember. This is also a double-edged sword. From errant social media posts and inappropriate content on portfolio websites to documented failures or errors, what is online is accessible to the general public, specifically potential employers and program adjudicators.

As mentioned earlier, a common platform for presentation of work beyond a conventional online document is a website. While this medium offers a range of benefits in excess of a PDF file, including multimedia (e.g., video, virtual reality, interactive models), open navigation, up-to-date content, and a more robust design platform in general, websites require an extremely vigilant, editorial mindset. Similar to a portfolio, curation is key. Websites can be generated fairly quickly with little experience; however, they must ensure they still pronounce the appropriate message on design capacity, technical skill, and passion behind each and every project.

While the content of a website is critical, it is also important to acquire an appropriate web address name. Although these are easy to purchase, names should be brief, if not memorable and direct. Addresses that are prone to typographic mistakes or are simply difficult to recall are neither useful nor demonstrate an awareness of the medium in general. Even if one were to find an ideal name, there are no guarantees that it has not already been taken. If putting up a

**7.0**
*Flummox* by [R]ed[U]x Lab.

Source: [R]ed[U] x Lab, *Flummox*, 2016, Digital Image, 5184 x 3456, Toronto, Canada.

website, authors should have a backup plan for alternative website names as well as locational extension suffixes. While a website name may be already taken as a ".com" extension, authors should also confirm if the name is taken in local conditions (such as a ".de" extension for Germany).

The same nomenclature concerns should be clear for social media accounts as well. In design, words and names matter. In addition to the various accounts one may have, it is important to curate one's social media presence, specifically during the ramp up to applying for employment and graduate school. While it is important to not to outright censor and over-sanitize one's personality on social media, all prospective applicants should consider removing provocative, inappropriate, and malicious content that could compromise their candidacy. Instead, social media, on account of its condensed nature, should project the most positive traits one has in the most direct manner. Whether limited by character count, video duration, or simply image size, one's social media presence should be governed by the newspaper test – if something were fit for the headline of a newspaper, it could be posted on social media. Whether it is cynical sarcasm or irreverent humor, anything that does not adhere to this guideline should be removed from one's social media. As with portfolios, the brevity of the medium neither affords nuance nor opportunity for clarification, which may result in, at best, negative perceptions and, at worst, outright denial of employment or admission.

For all the effort put into creating a website and curating a social media presence, it is important to ensure that it is constantly updated as well as circulated. Including websites and social media accounts in signatures would be the baseline of operation. It would be incredibly disappointing if an employer were interested in a candidate but could not get their proper contact information to take further action. In an increasingly connected world, many people have been especially effective at leveraging their online presence to professional and academic success. From becoming an online source for information (e.g., posting software tips on a website or sharing architectural photos on social media) to actively engaging in online communities, ensuring a digital footprint connecting to one's core presence on the Internet will be increasingly in demand. As such, any online presence must be constantly updated and cannot afford to be static. For a portfolio of architectural work to have any online impact, authors must ensure that their online presence is: a) available, b) personalized, c) content-rich, and d) memorable.

Inherent to online content is its accessibility and constant avail-ability wherever and whenever possible. It is important to note that once a decision is made to embark upon presenting a portfolio of work online, it mandates a commitment to ensure appropriate, current content is available to an audience. Online portfolio content cannot be inadvertently locked behind passwords, permissions, or paywalls – if content is to be secure, then accessible links or provisions should be provided to relevant parties rather than forcing upon them cumbersome authentication procedures. While it is completely understood that applicants may have unique or secured portfolio content for different audiences, it is highly recommended that authors invest in a few minutes to double-check linkages on a separate device before circulating links to other parties. A few minutes of time potentially prevents the confusion of revising links as well as embarrassing situations where incorrect content is provided to the wrong audiences. When creating a full portfolio website, authors should be mindful that it should also be current and available. There are often unfortunate situations where authors have gone to great lengths to create incredibly robust portfolio websites only to not have uploaded the changes to a current site or, worse still, failed to pay for site renewal or hosting services. Nobody wants to open a link to a website that is either under construction or not available at all. It leaves a poor impression with audiences as it demonstrates an inability to complete basic tasks and worse still, denies an audience the ability to view the applicant's work.

When it comes to social media, this accessibility is easier to oversee (from a technical standpoint as there are fewer steps in creating an account); however, it typically demands a higher frequency of maintenance. Social media provides an excellent outlet for authors to present insights on current issues in general, offer updates on their own work, and ultimately project their personality to the rest of the world. With linkages to various topical news feeds, articles, and media, it is not uncommon for individuals and organizations alike to share secondary content such as links on media that reinforce messaging. For example, an architecture firm specializing in heritage work may post articles on changes to historic designations while a graduate student in architecture focusing on indoor environmental

THE ARCHITECTURE PORTFOLIO GUIDEBOOK

**7.1.1**
This website displays images that allow one to quickly view the range of projects at once. Website by [R]ed[U]x Lab.

Source: [R]ed[U]x Lab, *Website*, 2018, Digital Image, 3500 x 3531, Toronto, Canada.

quality (IEQ) may circulate a recent video on the impacts IEQ on workplace productivity. Social media is more impactful when it is primary, user-generated content as simply recirculating content does not necessarily give credibility beyond the original source. Within architectural contexts, social media is an excellent vehicle to present updates on projects, insights on developmental process, and curation of a message. Typically, architecture firms circulate images of concept sketches, team members on site, prototypes, and developmental work to highlight the accomplishments, process, and notables about their work. Students often post content to do the same, but often with hints of their own personality. While this is often seen as content circulated among friends, if accounts are available to the general public, then content must be filtered for appropriateness. Sarcasm

CHAPTER 7.0 | COMMUNICATION USING YOUR PORTFOLIO

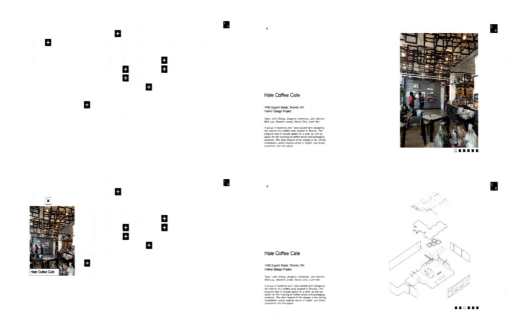

and humor, while good indicators of an individual's personality, should be tempered when posting content at the risk of offending prospective employers and program directors or the public in general. The summation of primary and secondary content ultimately provides a sense of an individual's interest, personality, and capacity. Social media is also used to reinforce this. An organization or individual may post imagery of their participation in a charitable event or recreational activity (such as a company golf-spa day or a school's games night). In other cases, a student or firm may post interesting imagery from a recent trip that speaks to potential interests or upcoming projects. In all cases, the ubiquitous accessibility of social media ensures messaging is constantly available.

Online content, specifically social media, is more than simply a platform to showcase materials that would constitute one's portfolio. It is a platform to express one's individuality and personality that are not necessarily translated in a conventional, hardcopy portfolio. As mentioned already, online content (from social media posts through to a web-based portfolio) and media (such as videos navigating a construction site or producing elements in a workshop) are quite versatile at not only supplementing messages on an author's alignment, but also reinforcing other dimensions including interpersonal skills,

7.1.2
How one would navigate through this particular architectural portfolio website. Personal Website by Liam Hall.

Source: Liam Hall, *Personal Website*, 2019, Digital Image, 4517 x 7500, Toronto, Canada.

interests, and activities. While not explicitly mandated as core components for evaluation, a positive impression in these categories is certainly appreciated and may serve to benefit one applicant over another. While the content curated and posted online by an author may showcase acumen and interests, it is often useful to be explicit about these qualities online and not leave them to interpretation. This is why social media and websites all provide an opportunity to generate an author's synopsized biography in an "About Me" section. To repeatedly post on social media (or in an online portfolio) imagery of an neglected building at a prominent intersection in a city leaves the content subject to interpretation. Is the imagery to indicate an upcoming project that forces the designers to address urban renewal? Is it a casual preoccupation with adaptive reuse in the city? Or is it simply a sample of an applicant's photographic skills? These three different impressions could be addressed with a clear "About Me" statement that better positions a majority of the content generated by their social media presence. This level of forethought ensures audiences appreciate the online content available to them as fleshing out an applicant's qualities beyond what may be articulated in a portfolio or résumé.

Online portfolios and social media not only ensure that content has the potential to take on engaging methods of representation, but also provide a current, extensive insight on the process and developmental work. To create relevant online content is to ensure it is updated vigilantly. As content is increasingly accessible online, it is also equally chronicled in time. Unfortunately, content that is out of date is detrimental to an online portfolio. For example, if the most recent work in an online portfolio is several months old, the immediate question from an audience would pertain to what an applicant has been up to since that last post several months ago. While juggling multiple online platforms may be difficult, there are several free services that automatically consolidate and connect all shared social media platform and web content so a single update cascades across all online media. Rather than leave questions about an applicant's absence over the past several months, she may periodically upload site images while doing architectural reconstruction research on Notre-Dame in France which is posted across all her online platforms, thereby addressing any potential gaps or misinterpretations.

To refresh, add, and edit online content mandates a similar level of curation as creating a portfolio. Unlike a conventional printed, two-dimensional portfolio, online portfolios provide ample opportunity to be current as well as integrate a greater range of media. While conventional portfolios may downplay developmental content to prioritize final production imagery, online content may provide a greater opportunity to integrate a range of robust media including imagery, video, and mixed reality to allow an audience to have a higher degree of engagement. Once again, with the interconnectivity and network accessibility of online content, media (such as an animation through a project) can be posted up online at a high resolution and automatically shared across all social media channels. This accessibility also ensures ideas and impressions on an individual's portfolio of work can be circulated to a wide audience quickly, whether intended or otherwise. If content goes online, it can be shared. As a result, authors must ensure that while online content must be current and robust, it must be heavily curated to reinforce portfolio messaging should it be circulated to a wider audience.

Finally, any and all online content must be memorable. The combination of excellent design work, technical expertise, and passion behind each project must be the mandate for what is posted online; however, the robustness of the media, its accessible reach, and the incredible range of options for personalization are instrumental in creating a strong impression with an audience. Two key components in making online portfolio content memorable are the media and the personalization behind the presentation of work. Both of these facets do not necessarily translate in a conventional portfolio and authors should consider taking advantage of online media to leverage these components. Media on design projects can range from images of schematic and developmental sketches and models to videos of projects under construction that offer additional dimensions that do translate in a conventional portfolio.

Some authors will use interactive media including 3D models or 360-degree rendered scenes, which are all excellent options provided there is a seamless integration and appropriate need. Online content should be memorable for the quality of the work as opposed to the frustration with activating content. Authors should be mindful of how and what is presented with digital media. It is interesting to note that while projects may be the same between an author's hardcopy and online portfolio, there is a higher degree of "stickiness" or time spent by audiences within website portfolios (as opposed to simply a digital format of the hardcopy posted online). This is attributed to the time spent navigating, browsing, and engaging content. This may be used to an author's advantage as greater time investment tends to correlate to a more memorable candidate. Additionally, personalization is instrumental in capitalizing online content. Beyond visual layouts, color schemes, and the type of media integrated in an online presentation, one's personality should come across in online portfolio content. From music selection in videos or how models are photographed to the range of content posted on social media, these elements reflect the personality traits that potentially resonate with employers or admissions committees. While an individual's personality may be well presented via online content, it should not risk coming across as unprofessional, offensive, fake, or disingenuous. Although online identities are better versions of what people wish to be, what is presented online demands fidelity to how people behave in reality. To misrepresent oneself for admissions and employment on personality and interpersonal traits is just as egregious as misrepresentation on skills and experience in an application.

### 7.2 COMPLEMENTARY MATERIALS

A portfolio conventionally satisfies the criteria for determining suitability in getting a position but in some instances, specific representational material may be required. These are typically categorized in four categories:

1. Hardcopy – supplemental documentation that might not conform to a portfolio (e.g., working drawing sets or reports)
2. Onscreen – visualizations that go beyond conventional prints (e.g., animations and 360 imagery)
3. Supplemental technologies – hardware or software (such as VR/AR interfaces)
4. Physical artifacts – tangible objects (e.g., prototypes or models)

Should any of these components be used in an interview, it is critical that their use addresses audience needs and does not break the momentum of the interview. While it may be necessary to bring prototype samples of advanced digital fabrication to showcase alignment with a specific criteria in a job description, the same pieces should not be considered useful for a prospective employer where such skill is not required. Worse still, such an artifact may derail dialog on an applicant's alignment with an employer's needs, as it would be foreign to the discussion.

Hardcopy documents are useful when prospective employers wish to validate comprehensive skill and professional capacity in documentation. For example, some intermediate positions in an architecture firm may mandate in a job description familiarity with BIM documentation and request a sample of working drawing sets be brought in. This would allow employers to determine a candidate's adherence to professional standards and conventions as well as their ability to navigate drawings and documents that would otherwise not be highlighted in a conventional portfolio. Such thorough documentation is not conventionally included in an architectural design portfolio as they often do not reproduce well on scaled-down portfolio pages. In other instances, hardcopy samples of publications (including books, magazines, or posters) may also be necessary as supplemental components to a portfolio in an interview as they reinforce a prospective employee's graphic design skills or a potential research assistant's publication capacity.

Onscreen content is often required when static, conventional imagery will not suffice. Typically a job description would explicitly indicate whether certain skills would be required and an applicant could prepare appropriate content (such as video or interactive media) for presentation. Applicants must be mindful of the media demands and resources available when determining how and what to present onscreen. In some instances, technical resources including appropriate hardware and software are readily available on site whereupon the content may be simply accessed online or via digital transfer. This is a convenient model and provided the venue has a strong data infrastructure for data streaming, hosting the content online reduces potential hassles with media and data transfers (as a backup, applicants should always still have the content available during an interview). Unfortunately applicants do not always have such a convenience and alternatively may be required to bring their own equipment for viewing onscreen content, such as a computer or portable electronic device. Applicants should feel comfortable asking beforehand to assess whether additional equipment or steps must be taken to ensure the content is used and makes an impact. It is extremely frustrating to all parties if conveyance of a core skill such as immersive video production is presented on a small screen or erratically streamed due to hardware limitations or, worse still, is not presented at all because of a lack of resources at an interview. Unless there is a preordained interview format, applicants should be aware of which portfolio projects would be most opportune to integrate onscreen content to the discussion. They should also be mindful of potential transitions to other projects that may also necessitate onscreen content so as to thoroughly showcase onscreen content before continuing with the rest of the interview. For example, an applicant may refer to their design of an urban marketplace on a school project when asked by an employer to speak to their animation abilities. Rather than flipping between the hardcopy portfolio and the onscreen content, an applicant should also have another project that demonstrates video creation as a follow-up to maintain focus on the medium before returning to the conventional portfolio.

Similar to the scenario with onscreen content, occasionally supplemental technologies may be called for in an interview such as mixed reality visualizations. Like its onscreen counterparts, supplemental technologies must be used to address alignment and also properly facilitated. This is especially noteworthy for technologies. There is no purpose to investing effort into configuring hardware and content if it is not aligned with what an interviewer needs. Unless requested or required, to do so leaves an employer with an impression that an applicant is either preoccupied with the novelty of a particular technology or unaware of the workflow and duties outlined in their job description. Ignorance and arrogance are not what integrating technologies should facilitate in an interview. While it is noteworthy to demonstrate an eagerness to learn and a capacity to maintain currency with emergent technologies, unless explicitly required in a job description, this level of expertise is best mentioned in a résumé or succinctly presented as a spread in a portfolio.

When preparing technology-driven content for interviews, applicants should have projects ready for presentation beforehand as opposed to spending time turning on equipment and configuring all the material during an interview. As with the integration of onscreen content, the use of supportive technologies must not compromise

CHAPTER 7.0 | COMMUNICATION USING YOUR PORTFOLIO

the flow of an interview. Portfolio projects that have content leveraging other media should be preloaded to reduce transition times. Applicants should have a list of relevant projects and potentially consolidate the presentation using the supporting technologies to prevent jumping back and forth with the medium. For example, an applicant may bring in a computer and equipment configured for VR display and have preloaded three relevant projects using the medium so that once discussion begins on the topic in an interview, the acumen with the technology may be fully presented concisely. One important note about hardware in a portfolio is that applicants should always have a contingency plan should issues arise (e.g., power or Internet access may not be consistent, interviewers might not be physically able to use the equipment, etc.). Once again, a reliance on an extensive layout in a portfolio is a good measure to take. Although it lacks the impact of the actual experience with the technology, an extensive inclusion in a portfolio with strong imagery can be very useful in lieu.

Artifacts such as models or prototypes should only be brought into interviews if they are requested or if they showcase characteristics that might not otherwise present well in a portfolio. If they are not required, they should not be brought in as they have the potential to become a focal point of discussion as opposed to supplemental reinforcement of an applicant's strengths. When artifacts are called for, applicants should ensure that they align with interviewer's needs and elicit qualities that are not tangible in 2D imagery. Otherwise, strong model imagery in a portfolio is more than adequate. For example, if a job description calls upon the ability to integrate rapid prototyping into furniture design, a candidate may bring in a series of samples of CNC routed components that articulate investigations into craftsmanship, material flexibility, and finish that would not necessarily arise from static imagery. An image of the final product(s) and process documentation included in the hardcopy portfolio as reference for discussion would be helpful but pales in comparison to actual physical prototypes. At the same time, this approach may have a negative impact for a job application that seeks expertise in BIM coordination as having a bespoke, physical artifact might not resonate with such job duties.

For some applicants, there is a preoccupation to bring in models into an interview simply because that is one of many responsibilities outlined in a job description. This is not necessary. Strong images are more than sufficient and allow for attention to be maintained on the portfolio document during an interview. While it might be worthwhile to bring a single sample that is extraordinary on some dimension such as level of detail or method of production, there is no need to invest the effort into bringing a collection of models to an interview (unless for a specific model-centric firm). The same rigor should be adopted when considering developmental work. Strong imagery in a portfolio reduces the need to bring in a multitude of developmental samples that quickly overwhelm during an interview. However if one were to bring models or prototypes into an interview, an additional effort must be placed in its presentation. From the container it is placed in to when it is referenced, the same level of care put in presentation in a portfolio should be carried into a physical piece. Anecdotes abound from employers recounting how humorous or pathetic it is when an applicant pulls a model out of a shopping bag wrapped in paper towels. If the artifact is a reflection of one's portfolio of work, it merits a similar level of respect.

While additional components in an architecture interview are useful when called upon, whether to demonstrate acumen in a professional setting or prospective experience with an academic topic, applicants must ensure that they complement content outlined in a portfolio. They must cater to interviewers' needs and seamlessly complement the presentation of the portfolio of work. Supplemental content should always have a presence in a portfolio, even if it is not as engaging as the pieces themselves, to ensure it is reinforced in an interview regardless of technical or time constraints. The challenge with including supplemental materials and media is to ensure that it does not undermine an interview by becoming the central discussion feature. Applicants must be mindful that what is brought into an interview in excess of a portfolio garners additional attention. It is best to use this conspicuous feature to highlight rather than become a spotlight in an interview.

### 7.3 INTERVIEW: THE TIPPING POINT

Putting an incredible amount effort into a strong portfolio necessitates a comparable delivery. The vast majority of interviews pertain to professional contexts as admissions to academic institutions via interviews are uncommon. While some undergraduate intakes mandate an interview, these are often simply opportunities to assess an applicant's personality "fit" in a program, rather than a developed sense of architectural knowledge. Good programs can cultivate that. Similarly, most graduate programs do not mandate interviews; however, some admissions to doctoral programs request to hold interviews in order to determine a candidate's suitability for their institution. That said, portfolio use in employment interviews is by far the most commonplace context.

Architecture interviews are unique in that they mandate a discussion based upon skills and distinctions found within a portfolio. The portfolio can be understood as a safe haven to use, particularly for those who may encounter difficulty during interviews. Rather than focus on eye contact or interpersonal challenges, candidates should feel confident in deferring to their portfolio to respond to questions. This is a completely appropriate approach in architecture interviews as it reinforces the value of the portfolio as the focal point of validation.

It is in this instance where the impact of the investment in creating a portfolio pays off. From the general physical size of the document, such that prospective employers can quickly discern skills and experience from well-sized images, to the sequencing of projects for admissions committees to understand an applicant's alignment, a portfolio in an interview setting has an incredible impact on a candidate's success. Works in a portfolio are not only able to reaffirm to prospective employers and administrators as to why they shortlisted a candidate, but also serve as a catalyst for conversation to assess other dimensions of an individual's "fit" with a program or office, such as interpersonal strengths or comfort in verbal presentations. In most cases, an interviewer has already gone through an applicant's portfolio and is familiar with the general quality of content. The success of the portfolio opens opportunity for interviews. Any feature in a portfolio becomes a point of discussion during an interview. Interviewers may latch on to anything from ways projects are presented (e.g., rendering style, graphic design, or aesthetics) through to discussions on personal interests or experiences (e.g., shared hobbies, common working or educational backgrounds, or even past mentors or faculty). These types of questions should not be seen as negative. That the interviewer is asking reflects a desire to better assess the candidate's potential as a colleague or coworker.

Authors should be mindful that anything put into a portfolio potentially serves as a catalyst for discussion.

Authors should not forget to bring a sample sheet or at least an extra copy of a résumé, as employers at the interview may not necessarily be the same people who received the application package. A sample sheet serves as a quick highlight of some of the projects from the portfolio. It is best understood as a portfolio-in-a-page and should adhere to the general guidelines presented earlier in this book. This sheet simply serves as a reminder to the interviewer of the author's alignment with a job or program criteria. Upon interviewing potentially dozens of candidates each day over the course of a hiring period, an interviewer would benefit from a succinct artifact reminding them of a candidate's alignment with program or job criteria.

While in an interview, candidates often find it difficult to properly respond to questions. A simple guideline is to answer questions in the first sentence of a response and then support it with notable work from the portfolio. If one considers answering the question in the first ten seconds and then spends another 30 seconds guiding the interviewer with validating work in the portfolio, they will succinctly answer the question and prevent potential rambling. Setting a mental constraint on response time may initially seem difficult and compressed but in reality one would likely take over a minute to verbalize and properly respond. Unlike the rhetoric that occasionally emerges in architectural pedagogy, interviewer questions are directly investigating specific objectives and merit similarly direct answers. An employer may ask questions pertaining to an applicant's experience with energy simulation software while an academic interviewer may inquire about a candidate's familiarity with a specific field of research. In both cases the interviewer seeks insights beyond what may have been simply written in a letter or résumé. Similarly, in both cases, an applicant should be able to confidently speak to their capacity and comfortably refer to a project that best addresses the question. As such, it is highly recommended that portfolio authors are able to ascribe at least two notable characteristics to any given project (e.g., a studio project may highlight excellent rendering techniques as well as mandated knowledge in brownfield remediation). Each project should serve as evidence of a capacity listed in one's résumé. This is why diversity of work and curating projects for inclusion based upon a combination of technical and design capacities is always recommended (see

Chapter 5). At the one extreme, some professional applicants with experience from other offices may have focused solely on multiunit residential, which at some point will offer little diversity and clarity on an applicant's range of skills and knowledge. This is typically not useful in professional interviews as "more of the same" is monotonous; however, it does become useful in instances where such a typological focus is essential to a successful application. This is also relevant for academic applications, where typically diversity presented in an interview portfolio is preferred; however, certain programs may have resources that facilitate specific research agendas (such as advanced digital fabrication or envelope performance research groups) which merit highlighting with similar, relevant works.

Interview questions in architectural contexts fall into four major categories of inquiry: a) factual, b) competence, c) introspective, and d) hypothetical. Factual verification questions arise from items presented in a résumé, transcript, or letter that employers need greater insights on. Questions pertaining to clarification on past job duties, grade point average, or nature of research work are examples of questions that an audience may wish to better understand. These questions benefit from direct, objective responses – anything else potentially undermines a candidate. If a response to a yes/no question (e.g., "Did you produce these images?", "Have you worked with this software?", "Are you licensed?") requires a five-minute preamble, an audience may become suspect of anything else presented in a candidate's application. A competency question refers to past actions and behaviors that validate suitability for new tasks with the interviewer's organization. If factual questions affirm whether certain characteristics are present, competency questions examine their qualitative strengths (e.g., "How comfortable are you with this software?", "Which project best showcases your sustainable design knowledge?", "Please explain your role with the client on this project"). Competency questions often ask applicants to present examples where they have utilized specific technologies, demonstrated knowledge and capacity through past projects. Both verification and competency questions simply call upon a reference to the work from the past documented in the portfolio. Suitable projects can be used to showcase software skills or collaboration in very direct ways. For example, a question on receiving a top studio grade may require verification by referencing the appropriate projects that merited the distinction. A question pertaining to strength with specific simulation software may require further elaboration in a portfolio to demonstrate the level of competency one has with it.

Introspective and hypothetical questions allow applicants to speak to their opinions on their behavior that would inform future actions. Interviewers often ask applicants to give examples of when they were able to deal with challenges, how they would assess their own weaknesses, or what they would deem as their most significant contributions on a project. This type of question may require referral to work in a portfolio, but remember that an applicant should always conclude on a positive note. For example, an introspective question may ask what an applicant's notable weakness is. A good response would be honest and punctuate it with a closing statement about improvement as noted in work in a portfolio. To simply state that one's weakness is in building construction and detailing, although sincere, does not reinforce any positive qualities. Nobody is perfect at everything and admissions committees and employers understand this. Instead, a good response would still state that weakness but use a more recent project as a foil to older work to demonstrate how one's knowledge of construction is improving each term. To further improve upon such an introspective question, an applicant may find it useful to address how they are proactively taking steps to ameliorate this weakness (such as entering additional construction-related competitions or taking supplemental continuing education courses to improve their knowledge base). This insight during an interview speaks to a candidate's ability to not only assess themselves but also demonstrate a positive response to an otherwise potential negative matter.

In employment interviews, questions often go beyond the actual work presented in a portfolio and instead pose "what if" questions to determine future actions and approaches. These hypothetical questions are often harbingers of what an applicant may do within an interviewer's organization or program. Hypothetical questions can range from behavioral (e.g., "If a colleague did not complete their part of a project, what would you do?") to disarming (e.g., "If you were a superhero, who would you be?"). While these types of questions may call upon extemporaneous responses, applicants should first and foremost address the question and, if necessary, feel comfortable in referencing cues in their portfolio (e.g., "I would be Batman because even though he has no superpowers, he relies upon methodical planning and research. I believe I have done this in projects such as X, Y, and Z...”). Once again, the critical part in responding to these questions is to conclude on a positive note. Far too often architecture students easily dwell on the negative and fall prey to self-deprecation, especially in hypothetical questions. With this group of interview questions, where the variety of topics and thinking is quite diverse, there is no real strategy for developing responses beforehand.

The best way to develop familiarity with all of the aforementioned methods of integrating one's portfolio in an interview setting is through practice. Whether asking colleagues, mentors, supervisors, professors, or even institutional resources (such as university career support or architecture associations), practice cultivates one's comfort with responding to questions while referencing the portfolio. Doing so also familiarizes a candidate with locations of projects and how they may flow into one another in conversation. A portfolio in an interview is quite a potent device that reassures prospective employers and admissions committees of a candidate's objective capacities and intangible dimensions. With the latter, practice nurtures a sense of confidence in an applicant and also makes for a comfortable interview for all parties.

## 7.4 FOLLOWING UP

Gratitude is a small investment for potentially large dividends. In academic contexts follow-up with institutions is not necessary, but it means a great deal to referees to be updated upon the status of any applicants they have supported. For all the hours of consultation, letter writing, and effort, at the very least applicants should have the courtesy to inform referees on acceptances regardless of the results. Unlike professional applications, these references typically frontload their investment. Letters and assessments are created and sent to an institution regardless of how strong an application actually is, whereas professional referees tend to be briefly contacted for a few minutes should candidates prove to be promising after assessment.

In professional applications, regardless of discipline, a good follow-up email within 24 hours of an interview is a courteous way of demonstrating professionalism and proper etiquette, while also serving as a reminder to potential employers. Follow-up emails are appreciated by employers, yet numerous studies indicate that the majority of applicants fail to do so. As with referees, those who have taken the time and effort to interview a candidate should be shown appreciation at the very least in this manner.

As with cover letters, this communication is unique to each applicant, however there are four core components that should be incorporated: a) a greeting addressed to those interviewing, b) an expression of gratitude for the time and interest in holding the interview, c) reinforcement of alignment drawing upon notable insights from the interview, and d) an offer to provide additional information. While these components should be addressed, the more personalized the messaging from the interview, the better. Rather than present a boilerplate letter, applicants should include references to points raised in an interview. From shared interests with the interviewer to reiteration of familiarity with specific features of a discussed project, a brief mention of such details in a thank you message reinforces a candidate's professionalism and serves as a distinctive reminder of their interview.

Candidates should not, however, expect a quick response from prospective employers and admissions committees. In both cases, there may be many more candidates to interview, assess, and coordinate making offers. A follow-up message a week after an interview is reasonable and followed by another one a week afterwards if required. If no response is presented over two weeks, unless otherwise noted (such as a glut of applicants or allocation to a waitlist), there is an unlikely chance the organization would be interested in hiring or admitting a candidate. While there may be a glimmer of hope, candidates should invest resources to other opportunities.

In some cases when a response is received from an organization, typically an employer, there may be insights on why a candidate was not successful. Some reasons are beyond an applicant's control (such as a contraction in the market, delayed project start, etc.) and do not reflect poorly on a candidate's application. In other instances, there may be challenges that can be addressed with greater experience (such as familiarity with specific typologies or attainment of key credentials). Again, these are not negative and may offer goals for future development. While some deficiencies may be outside an applicant's control, items presented in interviewer feedback that is both within an applicant's immediate control and quickly recoverable should be integrated into subsequent applications. If an employer's feedback pertains to a lack of demonstrated technical expertise or an applicant's weak verbal presentation, then it is critical to find ways to ameliorate these deficiencies in portfolio revisions or additional interview practice for future applications. That these interviewers are taking a moment to provide constructive criticism should be taken as a genuine desire to help an applicant for the future even if not within their organization. At the very least, applicants should be polite, receptive, and gracious upon receiving such feedback. Despite the global reach and proliferation of architecture firms and academic institutions, the industry is a surprisingly well-connected and small world – burning bridges to prospective employers and academics is never recommended. Applicants should always use the feedback to constantly improve themselves, especially when the insights are from those unable to present an offer at that time.

# Epilogue

Whether for academic or professional development, a portfolio is the critical component to advancement in architectural praxis. The strategies outlined in this book go beyond the superficial tactics of production and delve into the methods and mindset that must be adopted to effectively create a successful portfolio that emphasizes a candidate's alignment with their audience. As portfolios are unique documents that exhibit personal characteristics, the approach to this book's guidelines may be adjusted to suit an individual author's work and personality while simultaneously catering to an equally diverse audience of potential employers and admissions officers. Throughout each chapter, strategies and insights drawn from a range of interviews facilitate not only a portfolio author's introspective assessment of their work but also a greater appreciation of their audience's perspective and needs.

Although the focus of the book is on a sustainable approach to portfolio preparation and creation, it also extends beyond portfolio production and into its use and applications. The ability to demonstrate the appropriate alignment of skills, experience, capability, and attitude in a single document is a challenge regardless of experience. This book is prefaced with a candid outline of *why* one would need it and emphasizes the necessity of focusing upon the audience as central to developing a successful portfolio. To apply solely to one organization is dangerous. With the strategies developed in this book, readers should be confident in creating different portfolios when applying to a multiplicity of employers, clients, and institutions. Target and tailor portfolios to specific audiences, but always look to alternatives as a contingency.

In the increasingly competitive architectural landscape, portfolios are currency for success and an architect's key differentiator for acceptance by employers, clients, and educational institutions.

EPILOGUE

Acceptance cannot be marred by ignorance, laziness, or arrogance. This book provides insights that prevent errors and poor decisions that often compromise an applicant's success. Starting with outlining how to filter work in order to align with audience needs through to describing what is necessary for clear visual communication, the book establishes methods to reduce gaffes that undermine an applicant's acceptance. Similarly, this book establishes methods that eliminate vestiges of laziness that erode at the potency of presentation and positive impressions. From creating new layouts to suit the medium and redoing project elements to properly taking the time to research potential audiences, this book emphasizes the measures required to create a portfolio. While this book also describes strategies for gaining and integrating feedback, it is important that all readers understand that a portfolio is an ever-evolving document. A portfolio mirrors the growth of an architect. Pride cannot stifle its development. Even the most experienced architect must continue to assemble their portfolio with the needs of their audience in mind and refine it with feedback from their contemporaries.

# Appendix

### A.1 THE ELEVATION

An elevation is an orthographic drawing used to demonstrate the façades of buildings to explore form and materiality from the exterior. In Figure A1, the elevation focuses upon the line work and tectonic qualities of the façade, both of which are crucial to their sustainable community center design. An elevation drawing can be used to draw the viewer's attention to the formal qualities of building, as depicted in Figure A2 by stripping the image of line work and allowing the complex interlocking forms of the design show through. This is a drawing that can also be useful in displaying a building in its greater context, allowing the viewer to understand its relationship to its site. This is the intention in Figure A3, where a simple use of tone is applied to emphasize the building's strong connection to its industrial context.

**A0**
*Oxalis* by [R]ed[U] x Lab.

Source: [R]ed[U]x Lab, *Oxalis*, 2011, Digital Image, 2100 x 1275, Toronto, Canada.

**A1**
A line work focused elevation drawing. *Adult Center* by Kevin Pu.

Source: Kevin Pu, *Adult Center*, 2011, Digital Image, 3834 x 1165, Toronto, Canada.

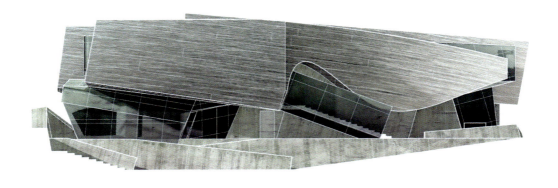

**A2**
An elevation with a focus on rendering and materiality. *Interfaith Chapel* by Han Dong.
Source: Han Dong, *Interfaith Chapel*, 2011, Physical Model, 2467 x 1468, Cambridge, Canada.

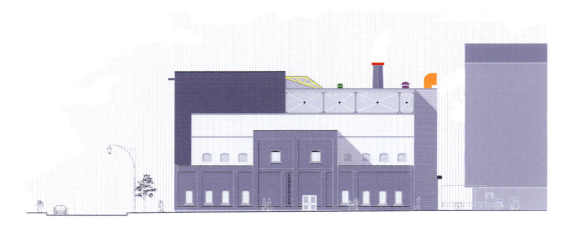

**A3**
An elevation with a strong emphasis on contextual relationships. *Condenser Distillery* by Jessica Gu.
Source: Jessica Gu, *Condenser Distillery*, 2017, Digital Image, 7859 x 3366, Toronto, Canada.

APPENDIX

## A.2 THE SECTION

A section is an orthographic drawing that cuts through a design to showcase interior spatial relationships. Such drawings can be used to illustrate the functionality and experience of spaces through light, materiality, proportions, and detail. Rendering a section with materials, as shown in Figure A4, showcases the unique interior finishes and structure's effect on the spatial experience in the design. In the case of Figure A5, the decision to color the drawing with a consistent color tone allows the line work to emphasize the details, structure, and systems integration.

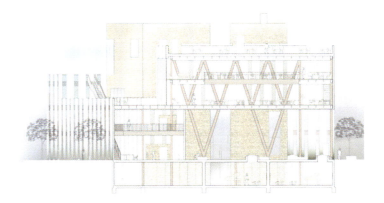

**A4**
A rendered section that shows materiality and structure. *Idea ++* by Ruslan Ivanytskyy.

Source: Ruslan Ivanytskyy, *Idea ++*, 2015, Digital Image, 1162 x 662, Toronto, Canada.

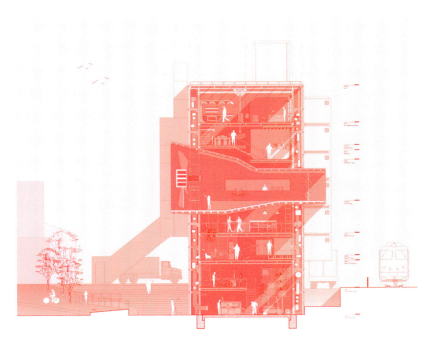

**A5**
A section that places more of an emphasis on the line work and details. *Office Dexterous* by Leon Lai.

Source: Leon Lai, *Office Dexterous*, 2015, Digital Image, 12600 x 10800, Toronto Canada.

APPENDIX

## A.3 THE PERSPECTIVE SECTION

A perspective section is a sectional drawing taken with perspectival convergence as opposed to adherence to orthographic convention. It combines both the 2D drawing of a section and the 3D aspect that showcases interior spaces. Figure A6 adds a rendered texture to the drawing, showcasing an exploration of the relationship between what

**A6**
A rendered perspective section showing interior qualities. *Toronto Architecture Center* by Destiny Megan Mendoza.

Source: Destiny Megan Mendoza, *Toronto Architecture Center*, 2017, Digital Image, 12600 x 8400, Toronto, Canada.

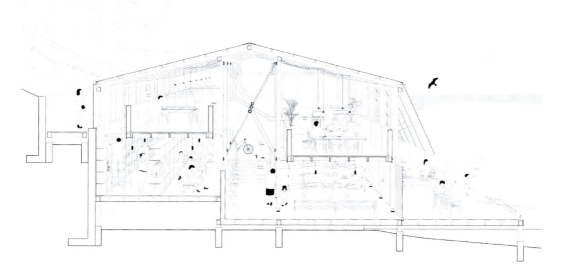

**A7**
A perspective section highlighting details using purely line work. *Non-Motorized Water Sports Centre* by Timothy Lai.
Source: Timothy Lai, *Non-Motorized Water Sports Centre*, 2018, Digital Image, 10175 x 5441, Toronto, Canada.

APPENDIX

**A8**
A rendered and line work based perspective section. *OCAD U Satellite Campus* by Lena Ma and Tatiana Estrina.

Source: Lena Ma et al., *OCAD U Satellite Campus*, 2019, Digital Image, 4724 x 7086, Toronto, Canada.

occurs within the spaces and the way light enters them, which is crucial as the building is located underground. Because it focuses mainly on details, Figure A7 allows pure line work to express a designer's understanding of wood assemblage and structure. Figure A8 combines a stylized rendering technique with technical details to create a stylized version of a perspective section to convey experience, structure, and materiality.

APPENDIX

### A.4 THE WALL SECTION

Wall sections, generally shown as partial sections at a larger scale, illustrate a greater knowledge of construction and systems than full building sections. Such a section type is frequently used to illustrate tectonic relationships and assemblies, such as in Figure A9, but can

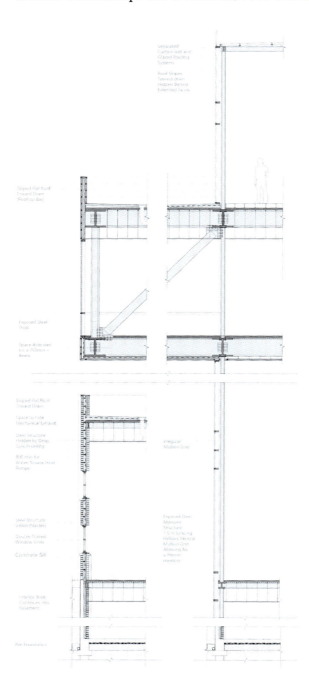

**A9**
A wall section illustrating construction detailing and relationships. *Distillery* by Michael Evola.

Source: Michael Evola, *Distillery*, 2017, Digital Image, 2485 x 2603, Toronto, Canada.

APPENDIX

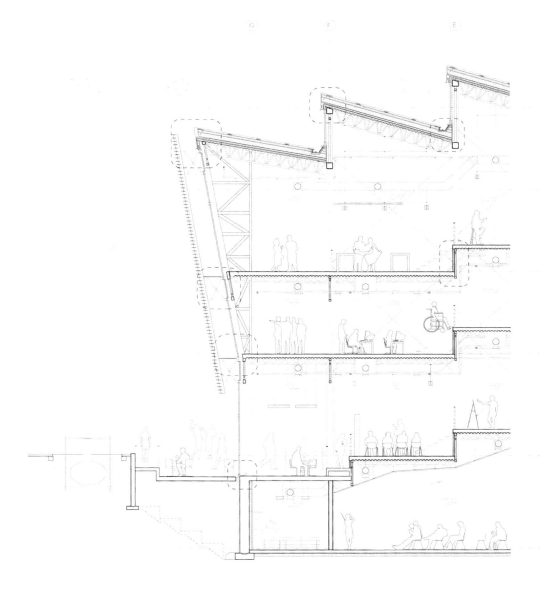

also serve to show the detailing and construction decisions made in the greater context of the program. Figure A10 is able to present exterior envelope design decisions by representing its relationship to the programming and arrangement of the interior spaces. The amount of thought put into the sustainable design elements and air circulation shown in Figure A11 is only possible through a sectional perspective.

A10
A wall section that allows for the relationship between envelope and interior spaces to be examined. *OCAD U Satellite Campus* by Lena Ma and Tatiana Estrina.

Source: Lena Ma et al., *OCAD U Satellite Campus*, 2019, Digital Image, 5819 x 6490, Toronto, Canada.

APPENDIX

**A11**
An annotated, perspective wall section showing sustainability concepts. *Adult Center* by Kevin Pu.

Source: Kevin Pu *Adult Center*, 2011, Digital Image, 4519 x 3919, Toronto, Canada.

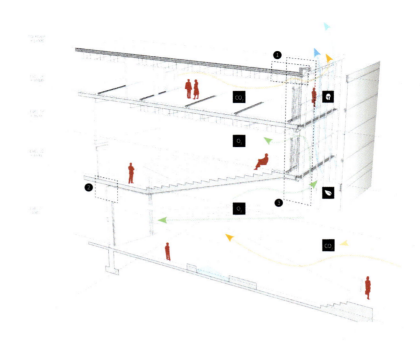

## A.5 THE SITE PLAN

A site plan illustrates the relationship between a design and its surrounding context. Frequently, such as in Figure A12, such a drawing is used to provide some contextual information, facts, and statistics that are crucial to the understanding of the project. In Figure A13, the design itself is at a very large scale, so a site plan is used to easily showcase the circulatory and programmatic relationships within the design. Site plans can also be much more abstract, such as in Figure A14, which conveys the environmental context of the project.

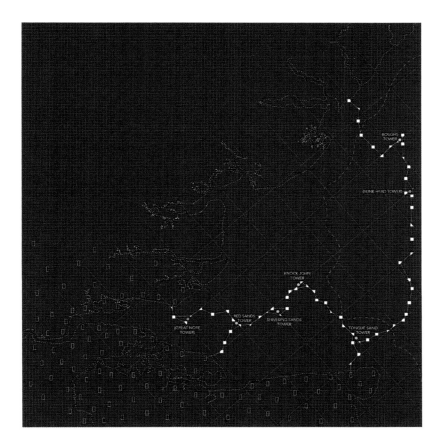

**A12**
A site plan providing a site's major surrounding context. *MSc. ARCH GRADUATION THESIS* by Ailsa Craigen.

Source: Ailsa Craigen, *MSc. ARCH GRADUATION THESIS*, 2018, Digital Image, 3354 x 3508, Delft, Netherlands.

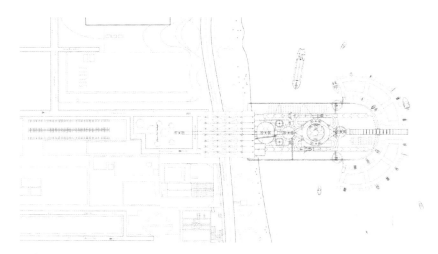

**A13**
A site plan that includes the design, along with its nearby surroundings. *Trans-Pier* by Tatiana Estrina.

Source: Tatiana Estrina, *Trans-Pier*, 2019, Digital Image, 7164 x 3675, Toronto, Canada.

APPENDIX

A14
An abstract, diagrammatic site plan showcasing concept. *Bodies of Water* by Yekaterina Korotayeva.

Source: Yekaterina Korotayeva, *Bodies of Water*, 2019, Digital Image, 6000 x 4050, Toronto, Canada.

## A.6 THE PLAN

A floor plan is a drawing that is a section cut parallel to the ground plane that is used primarily to show the circulation though and layout of spaces. Figure A15 uses pure line work to convey details ranging from what flooring is used to where landscaping is located. In certain instances, dimensions offer a better understanding of scale in rooms in relation to one another. Figure A16 showcases an isometric plan in which one is able to see the walls of the space. As a result, it demonstrates not only programmatic but also spatial relationships. Rendering a plan can result in a drawing such as Figure A17, although more abstract, still conveys the conceptual nature of the project.

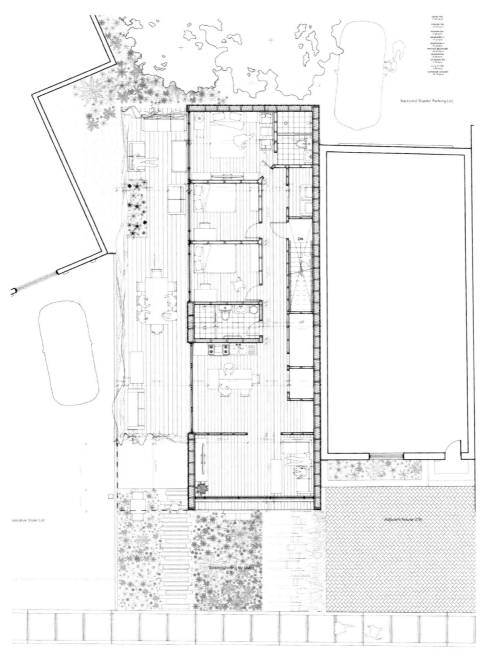

Sumach St

THIRD FLOOR
Tenant Unit Plan (+9800.0mm)

**A15**
A floor plan that includes materiality and surrounding context using pure line work.
*Duplex* by Andrew Lee.

Source: Andrew Lee, *Duplex*, 2015, Digital Image, 2345 x 3080, Toronto, Canada.

**A16**
An isometric drawing that demonstrates the spaces differently by showing the walls. *Writer's Cabin* by Ernest Wong.

Source: Ernest Wong, *Writer's Cabin*, 2015, Digital Image, 4032 x 3282, Toronto, Canada.

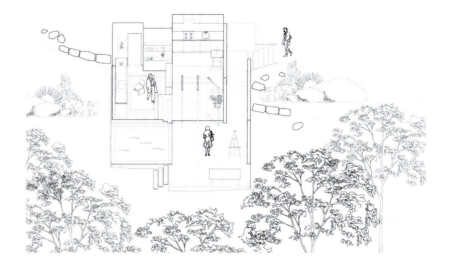

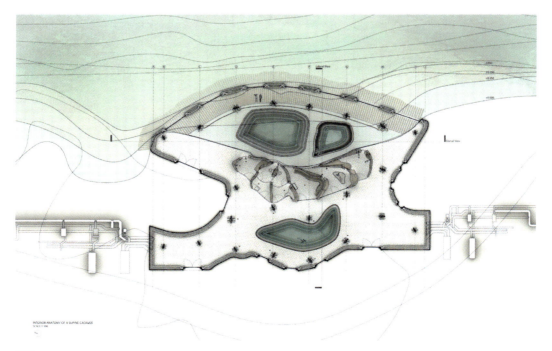

**A17**
Yekaterina Korotayeva, *Bodies of Water*, 2019, digital image, Toronto, Canada.

APPENDIX

A.7 THE PHYSICAL MODEL

Smaller scale models, such as the massing model shown in Figure A18, help designers convey a building's general form and concept with simple and clean geometries and materials. In Figure A19, the massing model includes site massing, showing how the design relates to the surrounding topography, landscape, and vegetation. For projects in an urban context, including models of the buildings surrounding the design is useful to understand how the proposal fits into the urban framework. Such a condition is explored in Figure A20, where the building is surrounded by existing context to help explain the design decisions. Physical models can also help

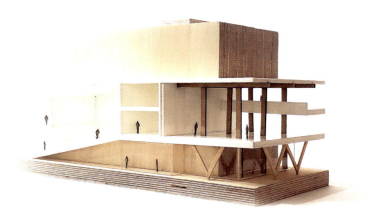

**A18**
A site plan mainly focusing on concept as opposed to technical conventions. *Bodies of Water* by Yekaterina Korotayeva.

Source: Yekaterina Korotayeva, *Bodies of Water*, 2019, Digital Image, 11770 x 7570, Toronto, Canada.

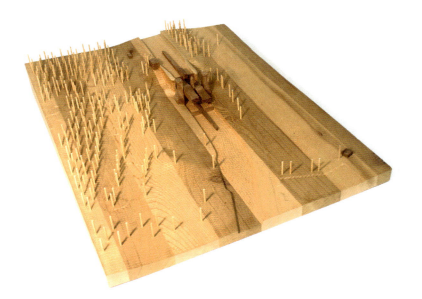

**A19**
A massing model conveying concept through massing. *OCAD U Satellite Campus* by Vivian Kinuthia and Sahrzad Soltanieh.

Source: Vivian Kinuthia et al., *OCAD University Satellite Campus*, 2019, Physical Model, 11016 x 6538, Toronto, Canada.

APPENDIX

**A20**
Site context accompanying a detailed model offers a visual on how a proposal fits in the current conditions. *Arch Sci Extension* by Andrew Lee.

Source: Andrew Lee, *Arch Sci Building Extension*, 2019, Physical Model, 7952 x 5304, Toronto, Canada.

**A21**
Models of a detail give one a better understanding of how components come together. *OCAD U Satellite Campus* by Shengnan Gao and Liane Werdina.

Source: Liane Werdina et al., *OCAD U Satellite Campus*, 2019, Physical Model, 3886 x 2550, Toronto, Canada.

students understand how the building components come together during construction. Models such as Figure A21 show audiences that the author can both fabricate a model with great care and precision – a trait that can also carry over into other tasks – and have a strong grasp of how a building would be constructed and assembled.

APPENDIX

A.8 **THE ISOMETRIC**

Isometric drawings are paraline drawings used to showcase a design at a consistent angle without the skew that comes with converging lines. Figure A22, represents the design from a bird's-eye view, representing its relationship to its site. An isometric also proves useful in showcasing interior spaces and programming, such as in Figure A23, in which some structure is removed to reveal the inner workings of the space. Figure A24 isolates individual living units to reveal the activities inside. The hand rendered technique adds a more stylized feel to the space, making it seem more playful. Isometrics are also useful in explaining complex building program, as shown in Figure A25.

**A22**
An isometric drawing that shows a design at an angle within its surrounding context. *MSc. ARCH GRADUATION THESIS* by Ailsa Craigen.

Source: Ailsa Craigen, *MSc. ARCH GRADUATION THESIS*, 2018, Digital Image, 4961 x 3508, Delft, Netherlands.

**A23**

This isometric of a detail breaks down the relation of structure and interior spaces. *MSc. ARCH GRADUATION THESIS* by Ailsa Craigen.

Source: Ailsa Craigen, *MSc. ARCH GRADUATION THESIS*, 2018, Digital Image, 3764 x 6888, Deflt, Netherlands.

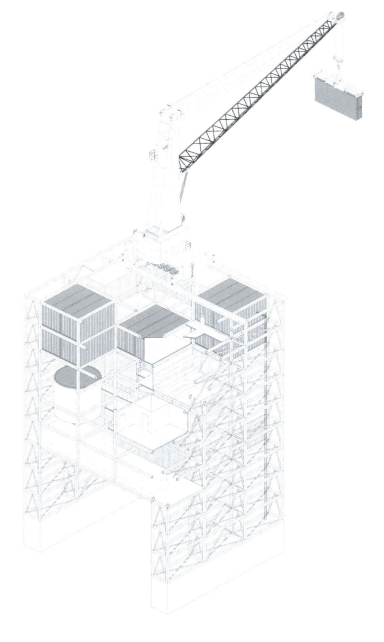

**A24**

An isometric drawing of individual components proves useful when showcasing what occurs within a design. *Youth Homeless Shelter* by Lena Ma.

Source: Lena Ma, *Youth Homeless Shelter*, 2018, Digital Image, 9328 x 3611, Toronto, Canada.

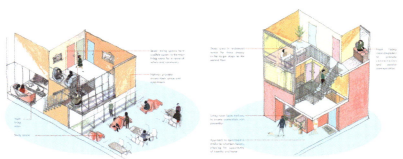

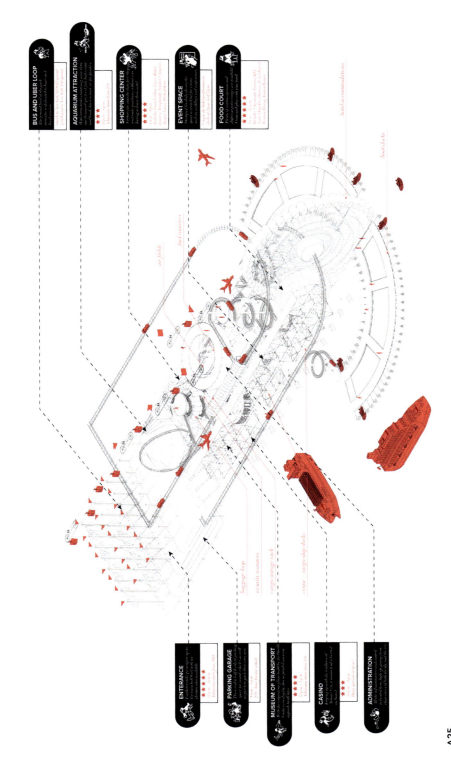

**A25**

Using an isometric provides a clear and concise way of diagramming program. *Trans-Pier* by Tatiana Estrina.

Source: Tatiana Estrina, *Trans-Pier*, 2019, Digital Image, 6226 × 3372, Toronto, Canada.

APPENDIX

## A.9 THE EXPLODED AXONOMETRIC

An exploded axonometric is similar to an isometric in it provides a 3D paraline drawing using two parallel angles, but allows authors to visually break down a project into its elements. Whether it is structural, such as in Figure A26, or detail composition, as shown in Figure A27, it allows the relationship between components to be examined to determine how they come together. Figure A28 is used to show the programming that occurs on various levels of a building, allowing one to understand the relationships between spaces.

**A26**
An exploded axonometric allows one to distinguish various components in a design. *Interfaith Chapel* by Han Dong.

Source: Han Dong, *Interfaith Chapel*, 2011, Digital Image, 5000 x 4905, Cambridge, Canada.

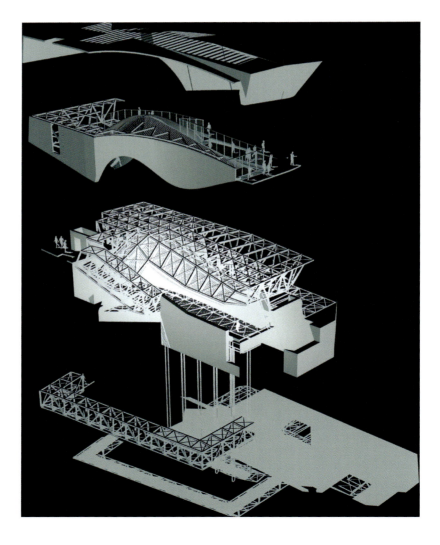

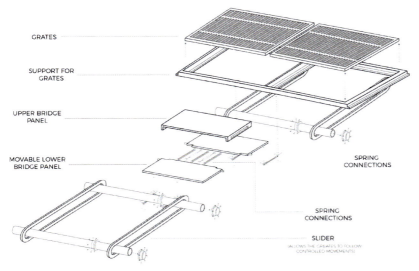

**A27**
Exploded axonometric details allow one to analyze how a design comes together. *Pier 365* by Tatiana Estrina and Martina Cepic.

Source: Martina Cepic et al., *Pier 365*, 2017, Digital Image, 2376 x 1559, Toronto, Canada.

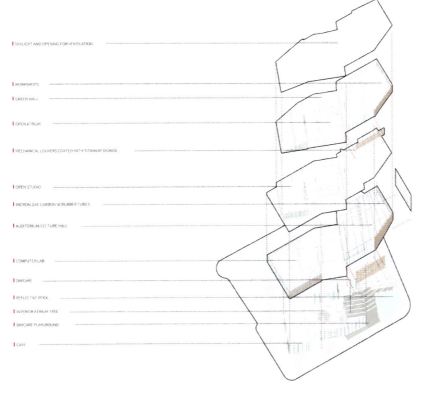

**A28**
One may use an exploded axonometric to show programming variations across floors in a building. *Adult Center* by Kevin Pu.

Source: Kevin Pu, *Adult Center*, 2011, Digital Image, 4767 x 4496, Toronto, Canada.

APPENDIX

### A.10 THE PERSPECTIVE

Perspectives are used frequently in the AEC industry to help describe the experience within unbuilt projects to clients and the general public. When one thinks of a render, one immediately imagines the feeling of a space and how it is being used, such as in Figure A29. However, renders can also represent spaces in a more abstract way, allowing the central concept to overpower the realism of the spaces, as shown in Figure A30. In Figure A31, more stylized techniques were used, straying away from the traditional photorealism, which gives the project more individuality and allows it to come across as a more conceptual proposal. Renderings help the designer break from tropes of an object in a site, and instead present the context and experiences within and around it. Figure A32 fades towards the background and darkens in the foreground to emphasize the building and its potential impact, while still hinting to its urban site conditions. In Figures A33 and A34, imagery draws attention to how the design changes over time, while also highlighting the design's ambient and functional shifts over time.

**A29**
Interior renders allow one to imagine how one would occupy a space. *Half Moon House* by Fontane Ma.
Source: Fontane Ma, *Half Moon Townhouse*, 2014, Digital Image, 4250 x 2397, Toronto, Canada.

**A30**
Abstract renders allow for a concept to be emphasized. *Community Center* by Ivan Efremov and Andrea Bickley.
Source: Andrea Bickley et al., *Community Center*, 2016, Digital Image, 4200 x 2450, Toronto, Canada.

**A31**
Renders can take on their own style and they do not have to constantly be photorealistic. *Office Dexterous* by Leon Lai.
Source: Leon Lai, *Office Dexterous*, 2015, Digital Image, 5000 x 2500, Toronto Canada.

**A32**
Fading the context towards the back allows for an emphasis to be placed on the building and its immediate surroundings. *Boading Future Vehicle R&D Complex* by Stanley Lung.

Source: Stanley Lung, *Boading Future Vehicle R&D Complex*, 2016, Digital Image, 5000 x 3000, China.

**A33**
Creating multiple renders of a design in its context at different times of the day provides one with a greater understanding of the design's functionality. *A Place to Meditate* by John Benner, Andrew Lee, Abhishek Wagle, Stephan Jones and Erik Aquino.

Source: John Benner et al., *A Place to Meditate*, 2019, Digital Image, 6583 x 2097, Toronto, Canada.

**A34**
Showcasing a design at different seasons allow one to comprehend how feasible a design is in its climate. *Futuristic Award Competition* by Stanley Lung.

Source: Stanley Lung, *Futuristic Award Competition*, 2016, Digital Image, 15749 x 10497, China.

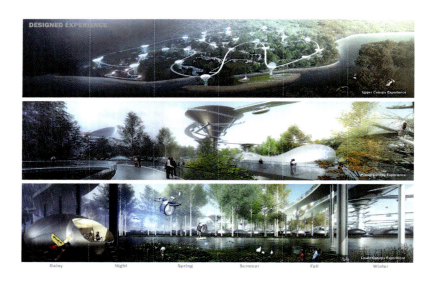

## A.11 CONCEPTUAL REPRESENTATION

Conceptual representation can be a quick way to visually communicate the main concept of a design. When abstract sketches are included alongside other imagery, drawings, such as Figure A35, are able to not only communicate the main inspiration for the overall design but also provides insights on the creativity behind one's presentation. Figure A36 shows various levels of parti development leading to a final design – a simple drawing that single-handedly captures a design concept and the design process, whereas Figure A37 focuses on explaining the sequential evolution of a design. Experiential drawings, as the unfolded section in Figures A38 and A39, are used to represent how one envisions an individual's experiences as they go through a space.

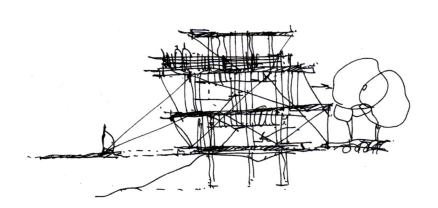

**A35**
Sketches are useful in showcasing concept and inspiration behind a design. *Cabin* by Shengyu Cai.

Source: Shengyu Cai, *Cabin*, 2015, Hand Sketch, 3676 x 2417, Toronto, Canada.

**A36**
Process parti diagrams can be used when illustrating a design process. *Cabin* by Shengyu Cai.

Source: Han Dong, *Interfaith Chapel*, 2011, Digital Image, 3888 x 2592, Cambridge, Canada.

**A37**
Conceptual diagrams demonstrate an author's thinking throughout their design. *Bodies of Water* by Yekaterina Korotayeva.

Source: Yekaterina Korotayeva, *Bodies of Water*, 2019, Digital Image, 11532 x 7697, Toronto, Canada.

**A38**
An unfolded section showcases how an author imagines one to navigate through a space. *Stargazing Observatory* by Kristen Sarmiento.

Source: Kristen Sarmiento, *Stargazing Observatory*, 2018, Digital Image, 12544 x 4050, Toronto, Canada.

**A39**
An experiential section allows the designer to convey how they believe one would experience the space. *Toronto Architecture Center* by Tatiana Estrina.

Source: Tatiana Estrina, *Toronto Architecture Center*, 2017, Digital Image, 9898 x 2473, Toronto, Canada.

# List of Illustrations

**1.0**   *Chlorophytum* by [R]ed[U]x Lab. Source: [R]ed[U]
x Lab, *Chlorophytum*, 2014, Digital Image, 4912 x
7360, Toronto, Canada.                                          7

**1.1.1**   Comparison of digital and print formatting of portfolios.   9

**1.2.1**   Religious project showcasing both technical skills
and the representation of concept. *Church of
Transition* by Timothy Lai. Source: Timothy Lai,
*Church of Transition*, 2016, Digital Drawing, 6250 x
3258, Toronto, Canada.                                          12

**1.3.1**   Image generated using digital software. *Curating
Complexity* by Antonio Cunha. Source: Antonio
Cunha, *Curating Complexity*, 2016, Digital Image,
3000 x 2000, Toronto, Canada.                                   13

**1.3.2**   Physical model created using traditional
architectural media. *Condenser Distillery* by Jessica
Gu. Source: Jessica Gu, *Condenser Distillery*, 2017,
Physical Model, 4899 x 3214 , Toronto, Canada.                  13

**1.4.1**   Comparison of poor and proper digital archiving
techniques.                                                     15

**1.4.2**   The various iterations of a design process using
sketches. *Non-Motorized Water Sports Centre* by
Timothy Lai. Source: Timothy Lai, *Non-Motorized
Water Sports Centre*, 2018, Hand Sketches, 3315 x
2648, Toronto, Canada.                                          16

**1.4.3**   The various iterations of a design process using
sketch models. *Physical Model Iterations* by Andrew
Lee. Source: Andrew Lee, *Physical Model Iterations*,
2016, Physical Models, 3883 x 2838, Toronto, Canada.            18

**1.4.4**   Transposing a project directly into a portfolio vs.
reformatting. *Weaving Waves* by Shengyu Cai and
Ruotao Wang. Source: Shengyu Cai et al., *Weaving*

| | | |
|---|---|---|
| | *Waves*, 2018, Digital Image, 7686 x 3987, Toronto, Canada. | 20 |
| 1.5.1 | Sample Portfolio Covers: Portfolio Cover by Sam Ghantous; Portfolio Cover by Ruslan Ivanytskyy; Portfolio Cover by Julianne Guevara; Portfolio Cover by Leon Lai; Portfolio Cover by Lena Ma; Portfolio Cover by John Benner. Source: Sam Ghantous, Portfolio Cover, 2012, Digital Image, 7454 x 15108, Toronto, Canada. Ruslan Ivanytskyy, Portfolio Cover, 2015, Digital Image, 7454 x 15108, Toronto, Canada. Julianne Guevara, Portfolio Cover, 2016, Digital Image, 7454 x 15108, Toronto, Canada. Leon Lai, Portfolio Cover, 2018, Digital Image, 7454 x 15108, Toronto, Canada. Lena Ma, Portfolio Cover, 2019, Digital Image, 7454 x 15108, Toronto, Canada. John Benner, Portfolio Cover, 2016, Digital Image, 7454 x 15108, Toronto, Canada. | 26 |
| 1.5.1.1 | Portfolio Cover by Rachel Law; Portfolio Cover by Fontane Ma; Portfolio Cover by Ernest Wong; Portfolio Cover by Tatiana Estrina; Portfolio Cover by Shengyu Cai; Portfolio Cover by Ariel Cooke. Source: Rachel Law, Portfolio Cover, 2019, Digital Image, 7127 x 15167, Toronto, Canada. Fontane Ma, Portfolio Cover, 2018, Digital Image, 7127 x 15167, Toronto, Canada. Ernest Wong, Portfolio Cover, 2016, Digital Image, 7127 x 15167, Toronto, Canada. Tatiana Estrina, Portfolio Cover, 2019, Digital Image, 7127 x 15167, Toronto, Canada. Shengyu Cai, Portfolio Cover, 2017, Digital Image, 7127 x 15167, Toronto, Canada. Ariel Cooke, Portfolio Cover, 2019, Digital Image, 7127 x 15167, Philadelphia, USA. | 27 |
| 1.5.2 | Binding Types and Benefits. | 28 |
| 2.0 | *Photokerytitis* by [R]ed[U]x Lab. Source: [R]ed[U]x Lab, *Photokerytitis*, 2016, Digital Image, 2550 x 3300, Toronto, Canada. | 35 |
| 2.1.1 | A modest design-build project. *Camp Winston* by [R]ed[U]x Lab. Source: Arash Ghafoori, *Camp Winston Pavillion*, 2019, Digital Image, 5184 x 3456, Kilworthy, Canada. | 36 |

## LIST OF ILLUSTRATIONS

| | | |
|---|---|---|
| **2.1.2** | Positioning statement that helps an applicant frame their portfolio and application materials. | 37 |
| **2.1.3** | An extracurricular design build in a portfolio could allow you to stand out within a group of other applicants. Nest by [R]ed[U]x Lab. Source: [R]ed[U]x Lab, Nest, 2018, Digital Image, 4407 x 2938, Toronto, Canada. | 39 |
| **2.1.4** | Design build project for a local food charity. *Night Market Cart* 2014 by [R]ed[U]x Lab. Source: [R]ed[U]x Lab, *Night Market Cart 2014*, 2014, Digital Image, 1300 x 731, Toronto, Canada. | 39 |
| **2.1.5** | Implementing cultural design elements onto a project. *Yu Village* by Fontane Ma. Source: Fontane Ma, *Yu Village*, 2016, Digital Image, 3400 x 2246, Toronto, Canada. | 40 |
| **2.1.6** | The photo looks photorealistic and it is a commodity, but it does not speak to an architectural design. *Half Moon House* by Fontane Ma. Source: Fontane Ma, *Half Moon House*, 2016, Digital Image, 5000 x 3468, Toronto, Canada. | 42 |
| **2.2.1** | Photograph of a portfolio review in session. | 44 |
| **2.3.1** | Sun study variations based on differentiating facades. Curating Complexity by AnA:Ctonio Cunha. Source: Antonio Cunha, *Curating Complexity*, 2016, Digital Image, 4724 x 1205, Toronto, Canada. | 46 |
| **2.3.2** | A sample of an architectonic exploration. *A-Voidance* by Rachel Law. Source: Rachel Law, *A-Voidance*, 2016, Digital Image, 1920 x 1080, Toronto, Canada. | 47 |
| **2.3.3** | A well-developed and researched timber construction project. *Timber Competition* by Julianne Guevara, Jimmy Hung, Ernest Wong. Source: Ernest Wong et al., *Timber Competition*, 2019, Digital Image, 5363 x 2015, Toronto, Canada. | 48 |
| **2.4.1** | A physical model epitomizing and conveying a complex design. *Interfaith Chapel* by Han Dong. Source: Han Dong, *Interfaith Chapel*, 2011, Physical Model, 3888 x 2592, Cambridge, Canada. | 49 |
| **2.4.2** | Technical knowledge goes beyond construction into other components such as sustainable design. | |

*Aspiro* by Kevin Pu. Source: Kevin Pu, *Aspiro*, 2011, Digital Image, 3320 x 5427, Toronto, Canada. 50

2.4.3 Good design work is not defined by imagery alone but its resolution in the details. *Cocoon* by Erik Aquino. Source: Erik Aquino, *Cocoon*, 2016, Digital Image, 5016 x 2276, Toronto, Canada. 51

2.5.1 A stylistic, representational render. *Non-Motorized Water Sports Centre* by Timothy Lai. Source: Timothy Lai, *Non-Motorized Water Sports Centre*, 2018, Digital Image, 6128 x 2829, Toronto, Canada. 53

2.5.2 A utopian representation of the revitalization of a riverbed. *Futuristic Award Competition* by Stanley Lung. Source: Stanley Lung, *Futuristic Award Competition*, 2016, Digital Image, 13007 x 9979, Toronto, Canada. 55

2.5.3 An extracurricular project coordinated, financed, and managed by students. *Aqueous* by [R]ed[U]x Lab. Source: [R]ed[U]x Lab, *Aqueous*, 2016, Digital Image, 4207 x 2364, Toronto, Canada. 56

2.6.1 A student design competition for micro apartment design. *In-Between* by Ryerson's CCA Team. Source: Shengnan Gao et al., *In-Between*, 2018, Digital Image, 3151 x 2607, Toronto, Canada. 59

2.6.2 A design competition entry for rooftop micro housing in Hong Kong. A Small Building by Andrew Lee. Source: Andrew Lee, *Small Building*, 2018, Digital Image, 3000 x 911, Toronto, Canada. 60

2.7.1 A design build project designed, built, and managed by students. *Tripix* by [R]ed[U]x Lab. Source: [R]ed[U]x Lab, *Tripix*, 2019, Digital Image, 6000 x 4000, Toronto, Canada. 63

2.7.2 An example of an architecture student expanding their design skills in lighting design. *Absorb* by Brant York. Source: Brant York, *Absorb*, 2016, Digital Image, 9767 x 4209, Toronto Canada. 64

2.7.3 Clothing and costume design using digital fabrication by architecture students. *Cosplay Design* by Alyssa Carere; *Jacket Design* by Connor Gagnon; *Dress 708* by Jessica Feng and Zeenah Mohammed Ali. Source: Alyssa Carere, *Cosplay Design*, 2019, Costume

LIST OF ILLUSTRATIONS

|        | Design, 4488 x 6171, Toronto, Canada. Connor Gagnon, *Jacket Design*, 2018, Clothing Design, 4488 x 6171, Toronto, Canada. Jessica Feng et al., *Dress 078*, 2018, Clothing Design, 4488 x 6171, Toronto, Canada. | 65 |
|--------|---|---|
| 2.7.4  | Sketches done while traveling exploring the tectonics of the architecture. *Travel Sketches* by Shengyu Cai. Source: Shengyu Cai, *Travel Sketches*, 2015, Hand Sketch, 4976 x 2984, Toronto, Canada. | 66 |
| 3.0    | *Stomata* by [R]ed[U]x Lab. Source: [R]ed[U]x Lab, *Stomata*, 2019, Digital Image, 2500 x 1667, Toronto, Canada. | 73 |
| 3.1.1  | Undergraduate students gaining experience constructing an extracurricular design piece. *Tripix* by [R]ed[U]x Lab. Source: [R]ed[U]x Lab, *Tripix*, 2019, Digital Image, 7163 x 4547, Toronto, Canada. | 77 |
| 3.1.2  | Student competition entry demonstrating innovation in heavy timber construction. Source: Ernest Wong et al., *Timber Competition*, 2019, Digital Image, 21154 x 10629, Toronto, Canada. | 77 |
| 3.1.3  | Parametric modelling tools used in the production of a design build. *Parklet TO* by John Benner and [R]ed[U]x Lab. Source: John Benner et al., *Parklet TO*, 2016, Digital Image, 3334 x 2389, Toronto, Canada. | 78 |
| 3.2.1  | A first year cabin design focused on engagement with views to landscape. *Cabin* by Shengyu Cai. Source: Shengyu Cai, *Cabin*, 2015, Digital Image, 3000 x 1487, Toronto, Canada. | 82 |
| 3.3.1  | A project that uses the changing water levels in different seasons to create a floating platform. *Pier 365* by Tatiana Estrina and Martina Cepic. Source: Martina Cepic et al., *Pier 365*, 2017, Digital Image, 4600 x 2869, Toronto, Canada. | 86 |
| 3.3.2  | Early student work tends to require additional revisions and development. *Unfolded Ribbon* by Jeff Jang. Source: Jeff Jang, *Unfolded Ribbon*, 2016, Digital Image, 2505 x 2144, Toronto, Canada. | 87 |
| 3.3.3  | First year work may have good intentions and ideas, but often require revisiting. *Cabin* by Gloria Zhou. Source: Gloria Zhou, *Cabin*, 2017, Digital Image, 5031 x 4850, Toronto, Canada. | 88 |

| | | |
|---|---|---|
| **3.3.4** | Portfolios should aspire to have at least a few projects that demonstrate an adequate breadth and depth of knowledge. Duplex by Andrew Lee. Source: Andrew Lee, *Duplex*, 2015, Digital Image, 1888 x 1873, Toronto, Canada. | 89 |
| **3.3.5** | Rearrangement of boards to adapt to portfolio spreads. *Uproot* by Tatiana Estrina. Source: Tatiana Estrina, *Uproot*, 2018, Digital Image, 8003 x 3537, Toronto, Canada. | 91 |
| **3.3.6** | Various physical model iterations. *Axial Housing* by Jeff Jang. Source: Jeff Jang, *Axial Housing*, 2014, Physical Model, 3543 x 987, Toronto, Canada. | 92 |
| **4.0** | *Tripix* by [R]ed[U]x Lab. Source: [R]ed[U]x Lab, *Tripix*, 2019, Digital Image, 3903 x 5854, Toronto, Canada. | 101 |
| **4.1.1** | Mistakes and effective techniques for layouts in a portfolio. | 102 |
| **4.1.2** | A juxtaposition between a dense layout and one that allows the images to be more easily read. *Cabin* by Destiny Megan Mendoza. Source: Destiny Megan Mendoza, *Cabin*, 2017, Digital Image, 7082 x 4514, Toronto, Canada. | 104 |
| **4.1.3** | Axonometric view which does not immediately emphasize the design of the project. *King Street Art Cafe and Residence* by Kristen Sarmiento. Source: Kristen Sarmiento, *King Street Art Cafe and Residence*, 2018, Digital Image, 1650 x 1183, Toronto, Canada. | 104 |
| **4.1.4** | A layout which allows for flexibility in various sizes of imagery. *Parallel Divergence* by Ariel Cooke. Source: Ariel Cooke, *Parallel Divergence*, 2016, Digital Image, 4846 x 2798, Philadelphia, USA. | 105 |
| **4.1.5** | An over emphasis on the detailing in a portfolio spread without any design context. *Distillery* by Ernest Wong. Source: Ernest Wong, *Distillery*, 2018, Digital Image, 4748 x 2865, Toronto, Canada. | 106 |
| **4.1.6** | Complex geometry and intricate design work mandates some technical resolution to go beyond simple, fantastic imagery. *Parallel Divergence* by Ariel Cooke. Source: Ariel Cooke, *Parallel Divergence*, 2016, Digital Image, 5100 x 6600, Philadelphia, USA. | 107 |

| | | |
|---|---|---|
| **4.1.7** | Sample Layout Configurations: *Precarious Medellin* by Han Dong; A-Voidance by Rachel Law; Terrera Fabricata by Sam Ghantous. Source: Han Dong, *Precarious Medellin*, 2013, Digital Image, 4016 x 6142, Cambridge, Canada. Rachel Law, *A-Voidance*, 2016, Digital Image, 4016 x 6142, Toronto, Canada. Sam Ghantous, *Terrera Fabricata*, 2013, Digital Image, 4016 x 6142, Toronto, Canada. | 108 |
| **4.1.7.1** | *TCA* by Shengnan Gao. *Unfolded Ribbon* by Jeff Jang. *Idea ++* by Ruslan Ivanytskyy. Source: Shengnan Gao, TCA, 2017, Digital Image, 4016 x 6142, Toronto, Canada. Jeff Jang, *Unfolded Ribbon*, 2016, Digital Image, 4016 x 6142, Toronto, Canada. Ruslan Ivanytskyy, *Idea ++*, 2015, Digital Image, 4016 x 6142, Toronto, Canada. | 109 |
| **4.1.8** | Illustration of how a master volume of projects can be used to create different portfolios that cater towards different firms and schools. | 111 |
| **4.1.9** | Sample figure sheet for test printing. *Homeless Shelter* by Destiny Megan Mendoza. Source: Destiny Megan Mendoza, *Homeless Shelter*, 2018, Digital Image, 1962 x 2331, Toronto, Canada. | 112 |
| **4.1.10** | Unnecessary representation of simplistic evolution of the massing. *Toronto Architecture Center* by Monika Mitic. Source: Monika Mitic, *Toronto Architecture Center*, 2017, Digital Image, 4657 x 1664, Toronto, Canada. | 113 |
| **4.1.11** | Photorealistic imagery is not needed for potent design conveyance. *MSc. ARCH GRADUATION THESIS* by Ailsa Craigen. Source: Ailsa Craigen, *MSc. ARCH GRADUATION THESIS*, 2018, 9449 x 6125, Digital Image, Delft, Netherlands. | 114 |
| **4.1.12** | Effective diagram displaying the design evolution. *Bodies of Water* by Yekaterina Korotayeva. Source: Yekaterina Korotayeva, *Bodies of Water*, 2019, Digital Image, 12000 x 8100, Toronto, Canada. | 115 |

| | | |
|---|---|---|
| **4.1.13** | A diagram of structure in a heavy timber construction project. *Timber Competition* by Julianne Guevara, Jimmy Hung and Ernest Wong. Source: Ernest Wong et al., *Timber Competition*, 2019, Digital Image, 1367 x 1772, Toronto, Canada. | 116 |
| **4.2.1** | Samples of font types and uses. | 119 |
| **4.2.2** | Comparison of different trackings of text. | 120 |
| **4.2.3** | Illustration of various text justification mistakes. | 121 |
| **4.2.4** | Comparison of font legibility on different backgrounds. *A-Voidance* by Rachel Law. Source: Rachel Law, *A-Voidance*, 2016, Digital Image, 2225 x 528, Toronto, Canada. | 121 |
| **4.2.5** | Comparison of text size. | 122 |
| **4.2.6** | Sample of text hierarchy. | 122 |
| **4.2.7** | Image showcasing the air circulation within a design. *Adult Center* by Kevin Pu. Source: Kevin Pu, *Adult Center*, 2011, Digital Image, 6128 x 2916, Toronto, Canada. | 123 |
| **4.3.1** | An applicant must keep in mind that the legibility of a portfolio depends on the medium of presentation and the device on which the content is viewed. | 125 |
| **5.0** | *Terra Fabricata* by [R]ed[U]x Lab. Source: [R]ed[U]x Lab, *Terra Fabricata*, 2010, Digital Image, 3000 x 4000, Toronto, Canada. | 135 |
| **5.1.1** | Portfolio project ordering and pacing methods. | 136 |
| **5.1.2** | A developmental process from concept to reality. *Tripix* by [R]ed[U]x Lab. Source: [R]ed[U]x Lab, *Tripix*, 2019, Digital Image, 10092 x 2407, Toronto, Canada. | 138 |
| **5.1.3** | Sample of independent student research merging the computer science field with architecture. *Digital Sketchbook* by Sam Ghantous. Source: Sam Ghantous, *Digital Sketchbook*, 2013, Digital Image, 5013 x 2907, Toronto, Canada. | 139 |
| **5.1.4** | Self-initiated research on two-way kerfing of wood. *Wood 3.0* by Filip Tisler. Source: Filip Tisler, *Wood 3.0*, 2016, Physical Model, 1024 x 768, Toronto, Canada. | 140 |
| **5.2.1** | Breakdown of the flip test process. | 141 |

| | | |
|---|---|---|
| **5.2.2** | The presentation of this project emphasizes the technical considerations beyond the final product. *Parklet TO* by John Benner and [R]ed[U]x Lab. Source: John Benner et al., *Parklet TO*, 2016, Digital Drawing, 4714 x 3156, Toronto, Canada. | 144 |
| **5.2.3** | A project that exhibits an understanding of detailing and program. *Condenser Distillery* by Jessica Gu. Source: Jessica Gu, *Condenser Distillery*, 2017, Digital Drawing, 9518 x 7313, Toronto, Canada. | 147 |
| **5.3.1** | An example of how showcasing too much process can distract from the main purpose of the project. *Parallel Divergence* by Ariel Cooke. Source: Ariel Cooke, *Parallel Divergence*, 2016, Digital Image, 4784 x 2962, Philadelphia, USA. | 150 |
| **5.3.2** | Spread before feedback was provided. *Cabin* by Shengyu Cai before feedback. Source: Shengyu Cai, *Cabin*, 2015, Digital Image, 4775 x 3017, Toronto, Canada. | 151 |
| **5.3.3** | Spread after feedback was provided. Smaller images were removed and a feature render was added to complement the line work. *Cabin* by Shengyu Cai after feedback. Source: Shengyu Cai, *Cabin*, 2015, Digital Image, 4820 x 3050, Toronto, Canada. | 152 |
| **6.0** | *Fraktur* by [R]ed[U]x Lab. Source: [R]ed[U]x Lab, *Fraktur*, 2018, Digital Image, 2000 x 950, Toronto, Canada. | 163 |
| **6.2.1** | Juxtaposition of the headings emphasized in a resume for professional applications and academic admissions. | 171 |
| **6.4.1** | Sample of a university application reference form that many masters programs require during their admission process. | 184 |
| **6.4.2** | Sample of a poor letter of reference. | 185 |
| **7.0** | *Flummox* by [R]ed[U]x Lab. Source: [R]ed[U]x Lab, *Flummox*, 2016, Digital Image, 5184 x 3456, Toronto, Canada. | 193 |
| **7.1.1** | This website displays images that allow one to quickly view the range of projects at once. *Website* by [R]ed[U]x Lab. Source: [R]ed[U]x Lab, *Website*, 2018, Digital Image, 3500 x 3531, Toronto, Canada. | 196 |

| | | |
|---|---|---|
| **7.1.2** | How one would navigate through this particular architectural portfolio website. Personal Website by Liam Hall. Source: Liam Hall, *Personal Website*, 2019, Digital Image, 4517 x 7500, Toronto, Canada. | 197 |
| **A0** | *Oxalis* by [R]ed[U]x Lab. Source: [R]ed[U]x Lab, *Oxalis*, 2011, Digital Image, 2100 x 1275, Toronto, Canada. | 217 |
| **A1** | A line work focused elevation drawing. Adult Center by Kevin Pu. Source: Kevin Pu, *Adult Center*, 2011, Digital Image, 3834 x 1165, Toronto, Canada. | 217 |
| **A2** | An elevation with a focus on rendering and materiality. *Interfaith Chapel* by Han Dong. Source: Han Dong, *Interfaith Chapel*, 2011, Physical Model, 2467 x 1468, Cambridge, Canada. | 218 |
| **A3** | An elevation with a strong emphasis on contextual relationships. *Condenser Distillery* by Jessica Gu. Source: Jessica Gu, *Condenser Distillery*, 2017, Digital Image, 7859 x 3366, Toronto, Canada. | 218 |
| **A4** | A rendered section that shows materiality and structure. *Idea ++* by Ruslan Ivanytskyy. Source: Ruslan Ivanytskyy, *Idea ++*, 2015, Digital Image, 1162 x 662, Toronto, Canada. | 219 |
| **A5** | A section that places more of an emphasis on the line work and details. *Office Dexterous* by Leon Lai. Source: Leon Lai, *Office Dexterous*, 2015, Digital Image, 12600 x 10800, Toronto Canada. | 219 |
| **A6** | A rendered perspective section showing interior qualities. *Toronto Architecture Center* by Destiny Megan Mendoza. Source: Destiny Megan Mendoza, *Toronto Architecture Center*, 2017, Digital Image, 12600 x 8400, Toronto, Canada. | 220 |
| **A7** | A perspective section highlighting details using purely line work. *Non-Motorized Water Sports Centre* by Timothy Lai. Source: Timothy Lai, *Non-Motorized Water* Sports Centre, 2018, Digital Image, 10175 x 5441, Toronto, Canada. | 220 |
| **A8** | A rendered and line work based perspective section. *OCAD U Satellite Campus* by Lena Ma and Tatiana Estrina. Source: Lena Ma et al., *OCAD U Satellite Campus*, 2019, Digital Image, 4724 x 7086, Toronto, Canada. | 221 |

## LIST OF ILLUSTRATIONS

**A9** A wall section illustrating construction detailing and relationships. *Distillery* by Michael Evola. Source: Michael Evola, *Distillery*, 2017, Digital Image, 2485 x 2603, Toronto, Canada.   222

**A10** A wall section that allows for the relationship between envelope and interior spaces to be examined. *OCAD U Satellite Campus* by Lena Ma and Tatiana Estrina. Source: Lena Ma et al., *OCAD U Satellite Campus*, 2019, Digital Image, 5819 x 6490, Toronto, Canada.   223

**A11** An annotated, perspective wall section showing sustainability concepts. *Adult Center* by Kevin Pu. Source: Kevin Pu *Adult Center*, 2011, Digital Image, 4519 x 3919, Toronto, Canada.   224

**A12** A site plan providing a site's major surrounding context. *MSc. ARCH GRADUATION THESIS* by Ailsa Craigen. Source: Ailsa Craigen, *MSc. ARCH GRADUATION THESIS*, 2018, Digital Image, 3354 x 3508, Delft, Netherlands.   225

**A13** A site plan that includes the design, along with its nearby surroundings. *Trans-Pier* by Tatiana Estrina. Source: Tatiana Estrina, *Trans-Pier*, 2019, Digital Image, 7164 x 3675, Toronto, Canada.   225

**A14** An abstract, diagrammatic site plan showcasing concept. *Bodies of Water* by Yekaterina Korotayeva. Source: Yekaterina Korotayeva, *Bodies of Water*, 2019, Digital Image, 6000 x 4050, Toronto, Canada.   226

**A15** A floor plan that includes materiality and surrounding context using pure line work. *Duplex* by Andrew Lee. Source: Andrew Lee, *Duplex*, 2015, Digital Image, 2345 x 3080, Toronto, Canada.   227

**A16** An isometric drawing that demonstrates the spaces differently by showing the walls. *Writer's Cabin* by Ernest Wong. Source: Ernest Wong, *Writer's Cabin*, 2015, Digital Image, 4032 x 3282, Toronto, Canada.   228

**A17** A site plan mainly focusing on concept as opposed to technical conventions. *Bodies of Water* by Yekaterina Korotayeva. Source: Yekaterina Korotayeva, *Bodies of Water*, 2019, Digital Image, 11770 x 7570, Toronto, Canada.   228

**A18** A massing model conveying concept through massing. *OCAD U Satellite Campus* by Vivian Kinuthia and Sahrzad Soltanieh. Source: Vivian Kinuthia et al., *OCAD University Satellite Campus*, 2019, Physical Model, 11016 x 6538, Toronto, Canada. 229

**A19** A massing model showing surrounding context allows one to explain their design intentions that were influenced by the site. *Wood 3.0* by Filip Tisler. Source: Filip Tisler, *Wood 3.0*, 2016, Physical Model, 6000 x 4000, Toronto, Canada. 229

**A20** Site context accompanying a detailed model offers a visual on how a proposal fits in the current conditions. *Arch Sci Extension* by Andrew Lee. Source: Andrew Lee, Arch Sci Building Extension, 2019, Physical Model, 7952 x 5304, Toronto, Canada. 230

**A21** Models of a detail give one a better understanding of how components come together. *OCAD U Satellite Campus* by Shengnan Gao and Liane Werdina. Source: Liane Werdina et al., *OCAD U Satellite Campus*, 2019, Physical Model, 3886 x 2550, Toronto, Canada. 230

**A22** An isometric drawing that shows a design at an angle within its surrounding context. *MSc. ARCH GRADUATION THESIS* by Ailsa Craigen. Source: Ailsa Craigen, *MSc. ARCH GRADUATION THESIS*, 2018, Digital Image, 4961 x 3508, Delft, Netherlands. 231

**A23** This isometric of a detail breaks down the relation of structure and interior spaces. *MSc. ARCH GRADUATION THESIS* by Ailsa Craigen. Source: Ailsa Craigen, *MSc. ARCH GRADUATION THESIS*, 2018, Digital Image, 3764 x 6888, Deflt, Netherlands. 232

**A24** An isometric drawing of individual components proves useful when showcasing what occurs within a design. *Youth Homeless Shelter* by Lena Ma. Source: Lena Ma, *Youth Homeless Shelter*, 2018, Digital Image, 9328 x 3611, Toronto, Canada. 232

**A25** Using an isometric provides a clear and concise way of diagramming program. *Trans-Pier* by Tatiana Estrina. Source: Tatiana Estrina, *Trans-Pier*, 2019, Digital Image, 6226 x 3372, Toronto, Canada. 233

**A26** An exploded axonometric allows one to distinguish various components in a design. *Interfaith Chapel* by Han Dong. Source: Han Dong, *Interfaith Chapel*, 2011, Digital Image, 5000 x 4905, Cambridge, Canada. 234

**A27** Exploded axonometric details allow one to analyze how a design comes together. *Pier 365* by Tatiana Estrina and Martina Cepic. Source: Martina Cepic et al., *Pier 365*, 2017, Digital Image, 2376 x 1559, Toronto, Canada. 235

**A28** One may use an exploded axonometric to show programming variations across floors in a building. *Adult Center* by Kevin Pu. Source: Kevin Pu, *Adult Center*, 2011, Digital Image, 4767 x 4496, Toronto, Canada. 235

**A29** Interior renders allow one to imagine how one would occupy a space. *Half Moon House* by Fontane Ma. Source: Fontane Ma, *Half Moon Townhouse*, 2014, Digital Image, 4250 x 2397, Toronto, Canada. 236

**A30** Abstract renders allow for a concept to be emphasized. *Community Center* by Ivan Efremov and Andrea Bickley. Source: Andrea Bickley et al., *Community Center*, 2016, Digital Image, 4200 x 2450, Toronto, Canada. 237

**A31** Renders can take on their own style and they do not have to constantly be photorealistic. *Office Dexterous* by Leon Lai. Source: Leon Lai, *Office Dexterous*, 2015, Digital Image, 5000 x 2500, Toronto Canada. 237

**A32** Fading the context towards the back allows for an emphasis to be placed on the building and its immediate surroundings. *Boading Future Vehicle R&D Complex* by Stanley Lung. Source: Stanley Lung, *Boading Future Vehicle R&D Complex*, 2016, Digital Image, 5000 x 3000, China. 238

**A33** Creating multiple renders of a design in its context at different times of the day provides one with a greater understanding of the design's functionality. *A Place to Meditate* by John Benner, Andrew Lee, Abhishek Wagle, Stephan Jones and Erik Aquino.

Source: John Benner et al., *A Place to Meditate*, 2019, Digital Image, 6583 x 2097, Toronto, Canada. 238

**A34** Showcasing a design at different seasons allow one to comprehend how feasible a design is in its climate. *Futuristic Award Competition* by Stanley Lung. Source: Stanley Lung, *Futuristic Award Competition*, 2016, Digital Image, 15749 x 10497, China. 238

**A35** Sketches are useful in showcasing concept and inspiration behind a design. *Cabin* by Shengyu Cai. Source: Shengyu Cai, *Cabin*, 2015, Hand Sketch, 3676 x 2417, Toronto, Canada. 239

**A36** Process parti diagrams can be used when illustrating a design process. *Cabin* by Shengyu Cai. Source: Han Dong, *Interfaith Chapel*, 2011, Digital Image, 3888 x 2592, Cambridge, Canada. 240

**A37** Conceptual diagrams demonstrate an author's thinking throughout their design. *Bodies of Water* by Yekaterina Korotayeva. Source: Yekaterina Korotayeva, *Bodies of Water*, 2019, Digital Image, 11532 x 7697, Toronto, Canada. 240

**A38** An unfolded section showcases how an author imagines one to navigate through a space. *Stargazing Observatory* by Kristen Sarmiento. Source: Kristen Sarmiento, *Stargazing Observatory*, 2018, Digital Image, 12544 x 4050, Toronto, Canada. 241

**A39** An experiential section allows the designer to convey how they believe one would experience the space. *Toronto Architecture Center* by Tatiana Estrina. Source: Tatiana Estrina, *Toronto Architecture Center*, 2017, Digital Image, 9898 x 2473, Toronto, Canada. 241

**B1** Henry Mai, *Photo of Vincent Hui*, 2018, photograph, Toronto, Canada. Source: Henry Mai, Photo of Vincent Hui, 2018, Photograph, 2679 x 3433. 256

# About the Author

**Vincent Hui** holds several degrees including a Master of Architecture (Waterloo) and Master of Business Administration (Schulich at York). As a faculty member in Ryerson's Department of Architectural Science, he teaches a variety of courses, from design studios to advanced architectural computing and digital fabrication. He has been awarded several teaching distinctions across different universities, including the 2015 Ontario Confederation of University Faculty Associations' Teaching Award and most recently, Ryerson University's 2018 President's Award for Teaching Excellence. He has cultivated an extensive record of publications and research on design pedagogy, advanced simulation and rapid prototyping, and technological convergence in design praxis. A proponent of increasing connections to industry and the greater community, he has developed the Architectural Science Co-op program, as well as multiple programs for aspiring young designers. He currently serves as a co-director of Ryerson University's Design Fabrication Zone where he has mentored several award-winning projects and innovative startups.

**B1**
Henry Mai, *Photo of Vincent Hui*, 2018, photograph, Toronto, Canada.

# Index

academic admissions letters 165–6
accomplishments 57–61, 175–6
alignment 8–9, 24–5, 52–3, 73–80, 110, 166–7; alignment chart 74–6
annotations 124
archiving 17
arrogance 92–3
art projects 66–7
assets 38, 40–1
attention 23–4
audience demands 8, 88–9; *see also* alignment
awards *see* accomplishments

background *see* experience
Baktash, P. xvi, 2–4, 31, 97, 131, 159–60, 189; *see also* construction drawing
BIM documentation 41, 80–1, 106–7, 149, 203
binding 25–8
Brooks, A. xiii–xiv, 2–4, 30, 32, 97, 131, 160, 189

career center 177–8
cliché 175
collaborative work 160–1, 174–5
collaborators 160–1, 174–5
colleague feedback 153
commodity skills 41, 173
competency questions 208
competition 42–5
complementary fit 168–9
complementary materials 200–4

conceptual representation 239–42
consistency 46
construction drawing: conceptual representation 239–42; elevation 217–18; exploded axonometric 234–5; isometrics 231–3; perspective section 220–1, 236–8; plan 226–8; section 219; site plan 224–6; wall section 222–4; *see also* BIM documentation
cover 23–5
cover letter 163–9
creativity 12–14, 45–9
critical thinking *see* creativity
Cumulative Grade Point Average (CGPA) 179–80
curating 17–18, 135, 175–6, 205–6
curiosity 70–1
CV/curriculum vitae 158–60, 169–70, 175; *see also* résumé

demand fulfillment 168
design competitions 54–5, 59–60, 62–3, 138–9
design objective 45–6, 115
design skill 30–1, 80–4
design-build projects 56–7, 62–3
detailing 12–13, 32, 41, 49, 52, 82, 86–7, 223
Deutsch, R. xvii, 2–5, 31, 33, 71, 96–8, 130–2, 159, 161, 188, 190
developmental work 149–50
diagrams 117

differentiation 36–8;
accomplishments 57–61; assets
38, 40–1; competition 42–5;
creativity and critical thinking
45–9; experience 52–7;
passion 61–7; technical
skill 49–52
digital fabrication 40–1, 74–5, 81,
148, 201
digital modeling 40, 49–50, 81,
92, 138
digital portfolios 9–10, 125–8
documentation 158–60; cover
letter 163–9; hardcopy
documents 200; letter of
intent 163–9; letters of
reference 182–6; résumé 169–78;
transcripts 178–81

editing 19–20, 149; *see also*
feedback
education 36–7, 43–4, 106, 169–71,
176, 178–81
elevation 217–18
errors 86–8, 91–3
experience 52–7, 79;
résumé 169–78
explanations 174–5
exploded axonometric 234–5
external assessment 178–81
external perspectives: application
documents 158–60; collaborators
160–1; creation advice 4–5;
curiosity 70–1; design strengths/
technical skills/passion 30–1;
group work 160–1; interviews 189;
networking 189–90; page
length 3–4; presentation 96–8;
reference letters 189–90; social
media 188–9; style 96; technical
knowledge 31–2; time spent
reviewing 2–3; traits 190–1
extracurricular projects 54–5,
62–3, 138–9

feedback 16–17, 22, 43, 92,
149–56, 210–11; colleague 153;
industry 151–3; portfolio
review 153–6; professorial 151–2;
*see also* flip test
file structures 15, 17
flip test 140–9
follow-up 209–11
fonts 118–20

gathering 16–17
group work 160–1, 174–5

hardcopy documents 200
hardcopy portfolios 9
hobbies 173–4

ignorance 85–90
imagery 24–5, 111–17;
alignment 110; conveyance
103, 105; diversity 106–10,
113; hierarchy 96, 113;
legibility 103, 114;
prioritization 105–6, 114;
unconventional 117
impression 140–1, 145–8
improving content 90–1
industry feedback 151–3
infographics 177
interactive media 124–8
interviews 189, 204–9
interview questions 207–9
introductory declaration 164–6
isometric(s) 231–3

job descriptions 78–9

Kolavrevic, B. xiv, 3–4, 30–1, 130,
158, 189

languages 173–4
layout 101–3, 110–11
laziness 90–2
leadership roles 60–1

legibility 103, 124
letter of intent 158–60, 163–9
letters of reference/letters of
    recommendation 158–60,
    182–6, 189–90
line weights 113

media 9–10
memorability 146–8
messaging 7–8, 11
models *see* digital modeling;
    physical models
multimedia content 9–10

Nakhaei, O. *xvi*, 2, 30, 70, 159, 190
networking 189–90
nomenclature 15

online content 193–200
online portfolios 43, 125–8
onscreen content 201

pacing 135–40
page numbering 125
parti drawings 93, 103, 114,
    124, 239
parametric modeling 31, 35, 78, 97,
    106, 138, 154–6
passion 14, 30–1, 61–7
PDF portfolios 126–7
personal projects 63–7, 138–9
personalization 167–8
perspective imagery 113–14, 236–8;
    *see also* renderings
perspective section 220–1
photorealism 106, 113–14, 145
photos 41, 53–4, 60, 91–2
physical artifacts 200, 203
physical models 203–4, 229–30
plan 226–8
portrait photo 176–7
positioning statement 36–8
preparation: feedback 149–56; flip
    test 140–9; pacing 135–40

presentation 91–2, 96–8;
    layout 101–3; online
    portfolios 125–8; page
    numbering 125; text 117–25;
    *see also* imagery
pride 92–3
printing 113
process imagery 138
professorial feedback 151–2
project diversity 137–8
prototypes 203–4

references 158–60, 182–6, 189–90
rendering 50–1, 75, 81–2,
    89–90, 93, 105, 106, 113–14,
    219–21, 236
research 20–1
résumé 158–60, 169–78, 205
retention 140–1
review 153–6; *see also* flip test;
    feedback
revising content 90–1

sample sheet 206
scheduling 21–2
screenshots 138
section 219
site plan 224–6
sketching 12–13, 16–17, 49–50,
    60, 66–7, 131–2; parti drawings
    93, 103, 114, 124, 239
skill *see* commodity skills; design
    skill; technical skill
social media 188–9, 194–200
software 50–1, 79–80, 84
supplemental materials 62
supplemental technologies 202–3
Suzuki, G. xv, 2, 4, 30, 33, 70, 96,
    130, 132, 158, 190–1

Tayona, N. xv, 2–3, 5, 32, 70, 96,
    131, 158, 160, 188–9
technical knowledge 31–2,
    51–2, 89–90

INDEX

technical skill 12–14, 30–3, 49–52,
79–82, 84–5, 173
test exercise 84
test sample sheet 113, 206
text 117–25; fonts 118–20; image
annotations, 124; measure 120;
orphans 120–22; page
numbering 125; widows 120–22
thesis intention 165–6
thesis project 47–9
tools *see* technical skill
traits 190–1
transcripts 158–60, 178–81
typography *see* text

uncompensated initiatives 56
unfolded section 239,
241–2
unique value proposition
35–8

validation 182–6

wall section 222–4
websites 193–208
wording 174–5
work experience 52–7, 79,
171–6
workflow 79–80